Middle Eastern Cooking

LIFE WORLD LIBRARY
LIFE NATURE LIBRARY
TIME READING PROGRAM
THE LIFE HISTORY OF THE UNITED STATES
LIFE SCIENCE LIBRARY
INTERNATIONAL BOOK SOCIETY
GREAT AGES OF MAN
TIME-LIFE LIBRARY OF ART
TIME-LIFE LIBRARY OF AMERICA
FOODS OF THE WORLD
THIS FABULOUS CENTURY

Foods of the World

Middle Eastern Cooking

by

Harry G. Nickles

and the Editors of

TIME-LIFE BOOKS

photographed by

David Lees and Richard Jeffery

TIME-LIFE BOOKS, NEW YORK

THE AUTHOR: A former senior editor of *Holiday* magazine, Harry G. Nickles *(far left)* retired in 1968 to devote full time to writing, and now lives in Bucks County, Pennsylvania, his native state. The son of Greek immigrants, he has had a lifelong interest in the Middle East. He speaks fluent Greek and holds a Ph.D. in Byzantine history from the University of Pennsylvania. With his wife Muriel, Mr. Nickles made a 6,000-mile tour of the Middle East to get material for this book.

THE FIELD PHOTOGRAPHER: David Lees *(left)* was born in Italy to English parents and now lives in Rome with his wife and twin sons. He took up photography at 15 and got his first assignment from LIFE magazine at the end of World War II. From his base in Italy, Mr. Lees has made frequent trips to the Middle East to photograph scenes and stories, from Biblical subjects to modern irrigation projects.

THE TEST KITCHEN PHOTOGRAPHER: Richard Jeffery *(far left)* is a free-lance photographic illustrator and still-life photographer. He lives in Manhattan with his wife and son and does much of his work in his studio there. His hobbies are gardening and sailing. (The still-life materials for Mr. Jeffery's photographs were selected by Yvonne McHarg.)

THE CONSULTING EDITOR: Michael Field *(left)*, consulting editor and one of America's leading culinary experts, supervised the adapting and writing of the recipes for this book. His books include *Michael Field's Cooking School* and *Michael Field's Culinary Classics and Improvisations.*

The names of a group of special consultants who contributed and tested recipes used in this book are listed on page 206.

THE COVER: Coffee and a pomegranate, two Middle Eastern staples, provide a rich texture contrast to the intricately shaped, ornamented tableware characteristic of the region.

TIME-LIFE BOOKS

EDITOR: Maitland A. Edey
Executive Editor: Jerry Korn
Text Director: Martin Mann
Art Director: Sheldon Cotler
Chief of Research: Beatrice T. Dobie
Picture Editor: Robert G. Mason
Assistant Text Directors: Harold C. Field, Ogden Tanner
Assistant Art Director: Arnold C. Holeywell
Assistant Chief of Research: Martha T. Goolrick

PUBLISHER: Rhett Austell
Associate Publisher: Walter C. Rohrer
Assistant Publisher: Carter Smith
General Manager: Joseph C. Hazen Jr.
Business Manager: John D. McSweeney
Production Manager: Louis Bronzo

Sales Director: Joan D. Manley
Promotion Director: Beatrice K. Tolleris
Managing Director, International: John A. Millington

FOODS OF THE WORLD

SERIES EDITOR: Richard L. Williams
Series Chief Researcher: Helen Fennell
EDITORIAL STAFF FOR MIDDLE EASTERN COOKING:
Associate Editor: William Frankel
Picture Editor: Kaye Neil
Designer: Albert Sherman
Assistant to Designer: Elise Hilpert
Staff Writers: Gerry Schremp, Ethel Strainchamps, Carolyn Tasker
Chief Researcher: Sarah B. Brash
Researchers: Joan Chambers, Marjorie Chester, Evelyn Constable, Myra Mangan, Ruth Silva, Carolyn Stallworth
Test Kitchen Chef: John W. Clancy
Test Kitchen Staff: Fifi Bergman, Sally Darr, Leola Spencer

EDITORIAL PRODUCTION
Color Director: Robert L. Young
Assistant: James J. Cox
Copy Staff: Rosalind Stubenberg, Grace Hawthorne, Florence Keith
Picture Department: Dolores A. Littles, Joan Lynch
Traffic: Arthur A. Goldberger

Published simultaneously in Canada.
Library of Congress catalogue card number 70-85530.

The text for this book was written by Harry G. Nickles, recipe instructions by Michael Field, picture essays and appendix material by members of the staff. Valuable assistance was provided by the following individuals and departments of Time Inc.: Editorial Production, Robert W. Boyd Jr.; Editorial Reference, Peter Draz; Picture Collection, Doris O'Neil; Photographic Laboratory, George Karas; TIME-LIFE News Service, Murray J. Gart; Correspondents Helga Kohl (Athens), Charles Lanius (Istanbul), Marlin Levin (Jerusalem), Ann Natanson (Rome), Parviz Raein (Teheran), and Mohamed Wagdi (Cairo).

Contents

The Recipe Booklet that accompanies this volume has been designed for use in the kitchen. It contains all of the 60 recipes printed here plus 61 more. It also has a wipe-clean cover and a spiral binding so that it can either stand up or lie flat when open.

New Discoveries in an Ancient Heritage

More and more American tourists are visiting the Middle East to marvel at the monuments of the past. The churches, synagogues and mosques of the Holy Land, the Pyramids of Egypt, the Parthenon of Greece—these are some of the more obvious destinations, but the whole area is dotted with magnificent relics of past ages and beautiful houses of worship (the mosques of Damascus, Baghdad and Isfahan are particularly breathtaking). A time comes, however, when the most assiduous traveler must eat, and for such occasions the Middle East spreads a marvelously appetizing table.

My own preoccupation with the Middle East and its cooking began as a birthright rather than as a tourist's discovery. My parents were Greeks before they became Americans—or rather, in the idiom of their generation, Greek-Americans. During my childhood we lived in a small New Jersey town, and one of my earliest memories is of the aromas in my mother's kitchen—aromas spicier and much more pungent than those in the homes of my nonhyphenated American schoolmates. When I invited one of them to have dinner with us, the main course of my mother's company meal might be a hearty platter of lamb stewed with okra or string beans and further distinguished by a fragrant tomato-onion sauce. The sight always startled my young guests (who were probably prepared for fried pork chops and succotash), but more often than not they finished every last bite on their plates.

Some years of my later boyhood were spent living in Greece, but it was not until World War II, when I saw military duty in several parts of the Middle East, that I really came to appreciate the genius and greatness of the region's cuisine. In one billet, in Cairo, our cook was a tall, ebony-skinned Sudanese wizard who turned out hot, full-course meals, exquisitely spiced, on a one-burner stove: for example, a spinach-and-lentil soup flavored with cloves and allspice, followed by grilled fish rubbed lightly with powdered coriander and served in a nest of feathery dill. At private homes we basked in the full glow of Arab hospitality, with a huge welcome and twice the amount of food we could consume, and first heard the saying, "The food equals the affection"—which apparently means that you don't truly love your host unless you overeat. In Greece, just after the war, someone doomed my unit to a diet of Army C rations, all canned and tasting drearily alike—but we were saved by the motherly Greek women in the kitchen, who civilized the military fodder with oregano and basil, olive oil and fresh tomatoes. Thus Hellenized, even Spam could become a minor banquet.

Memories of such experiences have drawn me back to the Middle East more than once, most recently with my wife Muriel as a helpmeet in an agreeable task of gastronomic research. It was a long, constantly exciting journey, reaching 2,200 miles from Greece in Europe eastward to Iran and the Caspian Sea in Asia, and 1,300 miles from Turkey southward to Egypt in Africa. We zigzagged hungrily and happily through the Arab nations, feeling at times like pioneers as we ventured into lands that few Americans have seen, and learned to follow unaccustomed table manners—in an Arab sheikh's tent, for instance, where we sat on a richly figured carpet and scooped up rice and meat with our hands. And of course we stopped in Israel, which belongs on every Middle Eastern itinerary, and came away enthusiastic over the fare served there, both traditional dishes and newly created ones.

Everywhere we went, in fact, our palates were supremely gratified. The ancient monuments, sights, sounds and smells of old civilizations still alive and vigorous in the 20th Century—these formed background pleasures to our eating, but the meals themselves rank with the best we have ever had. Naturally, an inept cook can ruin the most delectable delicacy, but this must occur very seldom in the Middle East; it did not happen to us, except for a few meals in hotel restaurants with pretentious Western menus.

What follows is largely an account of our findings in one extensive culinary jaunt. The subject encompasses the cookery of several proud and independent nations, each inventive in its own kitchens—yet an underlying unity prevails throughout the several national cuisines. The very names of certain vegetables are recognizable in several languages. Our okra is called *bamya* in Turkey and *bamia* in Syria; eggplant is *bademjan* in Persia, *badinjan* in Lebanon and oddly transformed to *melitzana* (still a kindred word) in Greece; and easiest of all for the connoisseur of foreign food names, spinach is *esfanaj* in Persian, *ispanak* in Turkish and *spanaki* in Greek. Because of such widespread similarities, it is not clear just which peoples developed what foods or recipes. Ancient records are so meager and marching armies and peaceful ships and caravans have crisscrossed the area so long that no one can search out definite origins of ingredients and cooking methods. Only the scholar in me minds that so little is known about the early history of Middle Eastern cookery; the rest of me rejoices in its survival.

One less pleasant note must be added. Modern jets and international business enterprise are breaking down the age-old gastronomic heritage of the Middle East, enfeebling it or shouldering it aside to pander to Western tastes in food. This book may be one of the last to bite into the subject in its pristine, mouth-watering state. So here, while time and the demons of progress still spare it, is one of the world's great cuisines. —*Harry G. Nickles*

I

Nine Nations–One Cuisine

The five foodstuffs assembled for a group portrait on the opposite page became parts of the Middle Eastern cuisine at widely separated points in history, but all are now important in cooking throughout the region. Garlic was enjoyed by the ancient Egyptians; eggplant and lemon, though not indigenous to the Middle East, have been used there for many centuries; the most recent arrivals, tomatoes and green peppers, were brought from the New World.

When my wife and I set out to report on the cuisine of the Middle East, I knew we were embarking on a varied, enjoyable—and unusual—assignment. I was already personally acquainted with part of the region, my parents' homeland of Greece and the regions in which I saw military service during World War II, but others among its diverse countries promised the mystery of the *Arabian Nights*. We were not disappointed. Every stop on our long odyssey from New York to the eastern Mediterranean lived up to our expectations of pleasurable surprise and challenge, for the cooking of the Middle East is like no other in the whole world. Its exotic dishes, often vivid with spices, make up a cuisine that has been evolving for thousands of years, perfected by generations of artful cooks. Some traditions reach back into prehistory; it was in the Middle East—specifically in Mesopotamia, which corresponded roughly to present-day Iraq—that man first learned to raise livestock and to farm the soil. In all the 9,000 or so years since that time, the region has explored and developed its native foods. The rulers of ancient Sumeria, Babylonia and Egypt presided at magnificent banquets when the people of Western Europe still gnawed half-cooked bear bones. Later empires—Persian, Greek, Arab, Byzantine and Turkish—added sophistications and refinements, adopting one another's recipes like friendly neighbors even in the ebb and flow of conquest. The result is the food we sampled, a Middle Eastern cuisine that is at once homogeneous and diverse, lavish and thrifty, plain and imaginatively seasoned.

The cuisine is easier to define than the region that produced it. Geographers, historians and politicians—let alone cooks—have never agreed on

where the Middle East begins and ends; military men draw its boundaries to suit their own logic and logistics. Even the name is something of an innovation. Before World War II, "Near East" meant a region including the Balkan nations of Europe, the countries of Southwest Asia, and sometimes Egypt, which is almost entirely in Africa. Beyond lay the "Middle East," centered on India; and farther still, the "Far East," on the Pacific rim of Asia. To a European, the names marked a sensible eastward progression across the map. But at the outbreak of war the British moved their Middle East Command from India to Egypt and a process of renaming began—initiated, one might say, by military accident. Today, the term "Middle East" has largely displaced "Near East"; there is still no consensus, however, on the exact extent of this elusive piece of geography, although unquestionably it includes the countries at the eastern end of the Mediterranean Sea.

The cooking of the region is distinctive, however, and in this book the Middle East is defined in terms of its culinary style. There are ripples and overlaps, cultural and culinary, extending beyond the area we cover, but the nine nations I describe in the following chapters—Greece, Turkey, Lebanon, Syria, Jordan, Iraq, Israel, Iran (Persia) and Egypt—make up the ancient heart of the Middle East. They are contiguous, tracing a great ragged arc that runs through parts of Europe, Asia and Africa from Greece to Egypt, and in them the Middle Eastern cuisine was born and developed.

In so large an area, disparate tastes and preferences in food inevitably appear: there are subcuisines within the whole. Greek and Turkish cooking makes one unit; Arabic cooking another. Iran stands out for ingenuity and brilliance. Israel teems with recipes brought in by dozens of immigrant nationalities, and now, I discovered, it is producing original dishes never cooked anywhere before. For all these divergences, however, the nine separate countries of the culinary Middle East are bound together by certain foods and by certain attitudes toward food.

The most widespread of these attitudes is the religious taboo against the eating of any meat from a pig. Except in Greece, a Christian country, you are unlikely to be served bacon with your eggs. Most people know that this is true of Israel, whose dietary laws are discussed in Chapter 6. Yet it is also true of the Muslim nations. A divine prohibition against pork was announced in the 7th Century A.D. through the Arabian Prophet Muhammad, founder of the faith, who set down this revelation in the Koran:

> *Forbidden to you are*
> *carrion, blood, the flesh of swine,*
> *what has been hallowed to other than God,*
> *the beast strangled. . . .*

Like all religious commandments, this one is sometimes broken; the infidel visiting the Muslim lands and Israel too will occasionally find pork on expensive menus. But its quality is not what a Westerner is used to, and anyone who has savored the sweet meat of Virginia's peanut-fed pigs will be put off by the flat taste and toughness of their eastern cousins.

The very opposite is true of lamb, the staple meat of the Middle East. Though it is never served pink, as Western connoisseurs prefer, my wife and

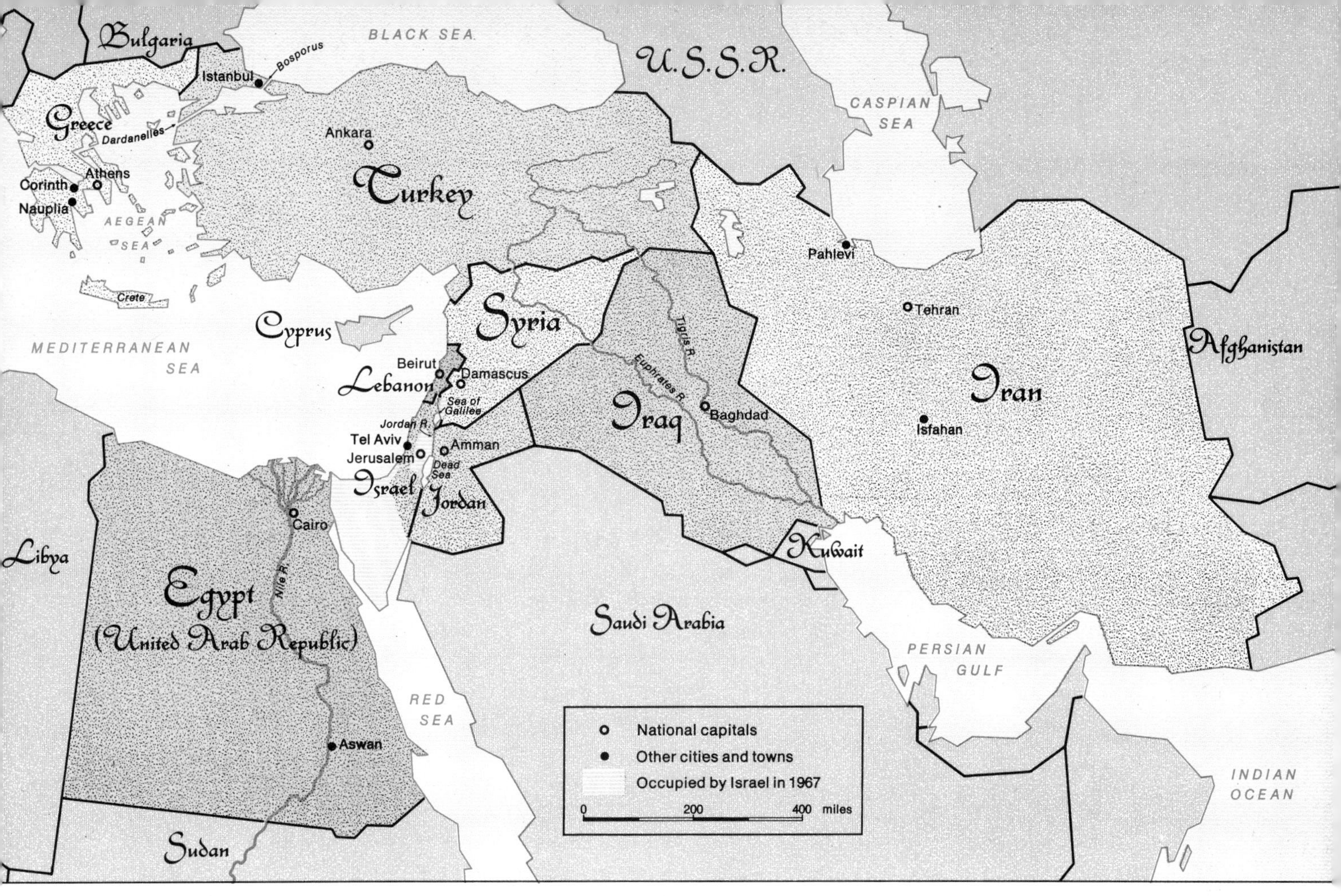

For all their diversity, the nine Middle Eastern nations shown in color on this map above make a unified culinary world of their own. In all of them, lamb is the basic meat and wheat bread a basic source of carbohydrates; eggplant is a favorite vegetable, and yoghurt the preferred form of milk. These similarities of cuisine have persisted for centuries despite vast geographical, cultural and political differences that otherwise set the countries apart.

I found it flavorful and tender even when boiled in plain salted water. Middle Eastern lamb is almost never more than a day old; when a caravan takes to the desert, a slaughter may precede every meal. Frequently the lamb is spitted whole and turned to succulence over an outdoor fire, or the body cavity is stuffed with unexpected mixtures of rice, pine nuts, almonds and currants. When smaller cuts are used, they may enter into an enormous repertoire of stews; more characteristically, they are cubed and cooked on skewers. This is shish kabob (a name derived from the Turkish word *şiş,* which means "sword or skewer," and *kebab,* "lamb or mutton"), one of the few Middle Eastern dishes known to Americans—though few of us have tried some of the variations I came across: pieces of the heart, liver and other innards cooked in the same fragrant way, or kabobs made with ground lamb into which was mixed some veal for a blend of flavors.

Beef is not favored in the Middle East, which has neither pasturage nor climate suited to the best stock; in the windows of butcher shops, sides of beef are outnumbered about seven to one by carcasses of lamb and mutton. Kid has its admirers, and so does camel; I was informed that the hump is the choicest portion to roast. (It may be unlikely that Western supermarkets will ever stock camel meat, but it may also be significant that one notable encyclopedia for gourmets, *Larousse Gastronomique,* lists nine ways to prepare it, including camel feet *à la vinaigrette.)*

Of all the Middle East's ingenious ways with meat, the one I enjoyed most was the kind of dish made of ground meat mixed with rice, herbs and spices, and wrapped in leaves or stuffed into vegetables. One version we encountered in many places is *dolma,* in which such a mixture, often enhanced with fresh mint or dill, is encased in tender vine leaves to be simmered in a little water and lemon juice, perhaps with cracked lamb bones tossed in the pot for a richer flavor. Sometimes the wrapper was cabbage, or the spinachlike portion of Swiss chard, or a long, narrow vegetable like zucchini or carrot hollowed out so deftly it looked intact when stuffed. The stuffing simply depended on the mood and habit of the cook, who can vary flavors and textures with cheese, tomatoes, chick-peas or even yoghurt.

Everywhere we went we ate eggplant; the Turks alone claim to have 40 methods of cooking it, and one expert puts the figure for the whole Middle East at more than 120! Despite this profusion of recipes, we learned that only a few cooking methods are fundamental. The first step is to salt the flesh of the eggplant and let it stand as long as half an hour to sweat out its bitter juice. If it is to be mashed, the skin is first loosened by searing—preferably over a wood or charcoal fire for smokiness of flavor, though a gas flame or electric broiler will do.

In one down-to-earth approach, the eggplant is then stuffed like any other vegetable—hollowed out if it is cylindrical, cut in half and scooped out if it is one of the plump bulbous varieties common in the United States. The finest recipes in this category turn the eggplant into a melt-in-the-mouth sort of stew, redolent with the wildly mixed aromas of onions, tomatoes, olive oil, parsley and garlic. Sliced and fried, the pliant eggplant may be dressed with tangy yoghurt or sour pomegranate juice—and always with garlic as well. A mashed version may be flavored with lemon juice, garlic and nutty sesame oil, or it may become the rich purée known in Israel as "mock liver," which includes onions, eggs and chicken stock (both make appetizing dips). But the unquestioned king of Middle Eastern eggplant dishes is the one called, in its Arabic form, *musakka'a* (*see Recipe Index,* which also includes a recipe listed under the Greek spelling, *moussaka*), in which fried eggplant slices and well-seasoned ground lamb or mutton are arranged in layers and baked to a complex and irresistible compound of tastes.

Aside from shish kabob, the only Middle Eastern food popular in the West is yoghurt, the tangy curdled milk that provides good food value with few calories. Actually, American yoghurt is no more than an imitation of the Middle Eastern variety. In America it is not made from whole milk; it lacks the refreshing tartness of the original; and it is often turned into a sort of sour-cream sundae by the addition of fruit.

The yoghurt I had in the Middle East was generally made at home, fermented by a culture—the starter—saved from the previous batch. It was served to me at all hours of the day in many different forms. In its snow-white natural state, with a buttery film on top, it is a common side dish for almost any meal as well as a favorite between-meals snack. Sprinkled with sugar, it makes a simple dessert or it can go into a splendid cake along with farina, sugar, chopped almonds and grated orange rind. In summer it is made into a tart, cold soup adorned by thin, crisp slices of cucumber; in winter it enhances several hot, thick ones. Diluted with water and lightly salted, it quenches thirst better than a carbonated soft drink. Hung in a bag until the whey drains out, it thickens into a creamy cheese for spreading on bread, particularly good at breakfast.

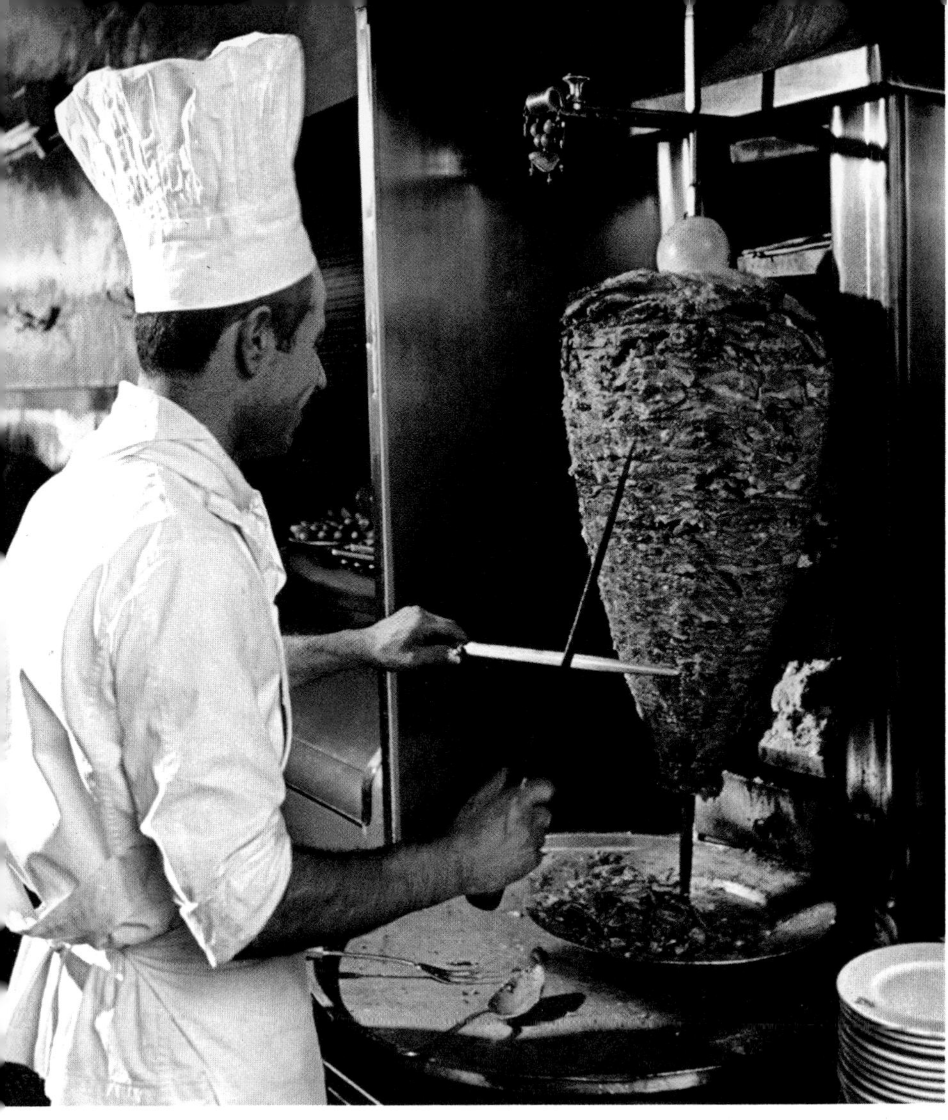

Sharpening his knife so that he can cut paper-thin slices, a Beirut chef prepares to serve pieces of crisp roast lamb from a giant kabob. This construction of marinated lamb slices, called a *chawarma,* will rotate before burning charcoal until the cooking and slicing process reaches the center. Slices from it are eaten either in a sandwich of Arab bread or as a main course with an accompaniment of tart purée called *hummus bi tahina* (*Recipe Index*).

Like some Americans, Middle Easterners feel that yoghurt is the health food supreme. I was assured that it confers long life and good looks, prolongs youth and fortifies the soul. Several people also insisted it can cure ulcers, relieve sunburn and forestall a hangover. In Iran, girls use it as a facial, and in Iranian villages it is mixed with chopped garlic and swallowed as a remedy for malaria. So great is this attachment to yoghurt in the Middle East that many a housewife, preparing to emigrate to a foreign land, spreads a cloth with her home-grown culture, waits until it dries, and packs it among her indispensable possessions as a starter for use in her new home.

The other foodstuff I came across everywhere we went was olives and their oil. Like butter, olive oil conveys to food its own special flavor; a good olive oil, extracted from the first pressing of fresh ripe olives, can even give a humble bean soup an illusory but welcome taste of meat. A whole family of vegetable dishes, known in much of the Middle East by various forms of the word *yakhni,* calls for at least a half cup of olive oil (along with onions, tomatoes and some water) to make no more than six or eight servings. The okra or string beans absorb the other liquids but not the oil, which appears at the bottom of one's plate as a small, savory pool.

The olive, a standby of daily existence, grows in dozens of shapes and colors. There are small black ones that seemed to be mostly pit (but were well

Roasting an eggplant gives it a smoky flavor, whether the job is done in Middle Eastern style over a fire, as shown in the picture above, or at the kitchen stove. Either method takes about 15 or 20 minutes. When the skin chars and begins to blister, the eggplant is ready to be peeled. In puréed form, it then becomes the base for such dishes as *baba ghannooj* (a hotly seasoned dip) or *hünkâr begendi* (a cheese and eggplant mixture). Both recipes are listed in the Recipe Index.

Eggplant: A Middle Eastern Favorite

The plump, purple eggplant is not only ornamental but also—as Americans have been discovering in this century—good eating. The Arabs found that out more than 1,500 years ago, when they brought the eggplant from India to the Mediterranean and immediately began to devise an armamentarium of recipes for it. Just as a Frenchman is likely to claim that he knows 1,000 ways to cook an egg, so a Syrian or Turk will boast of having 1,000 eggplant recipes. In many of them the first step is roasting the eggplant over an open fire *(above)*. But the eggplant may also be peeled and cut up, then sprinkled with salt or soaked in brine to draw off its slightly bitter moisture and prevent it from absorbing too much oil when it is fried. Unlike most American eggplants which are generally large and somewhat pear-shaped, the ones preferred in the Middle East are slim and small; many resemble the tiny egg-shaped vegetables only two or three inches long, from which the plant probably got its name, and these are cooked whole. When buying an eggplant, whatever its size or shape, look for uniform color and a firm fruit with unshriveled skin. Heft it, too; the heavier the eggplant in relation to its size, the fewer useless seeds it will have inside.

worth the trouble of nibbling for the meat), others that are blue-black and oblong, and still other purplish-yellow giants the size of walnuts, their flesh pulpy and bland but as hard to stop eating as peanuts. Methods of pickling are even more various—sometimes the olives are simply stored in water with a little olive oil and vinegar added. Often they are slit to increase the absorption of flavors and marinated in a variety of seasonings, lavish or simple: ginger, garlic, nutmeg, turmeric and crushed coriander seeds make up one style of marinade, celery stalks and lemon slices another. Shops display really profuse assortments of olives, including one incendiary kind flecked with bits of hot red chili.

As old as the olive in the Middle East are basic grains and legumes—chiefly wheat and rice, beans, lentils and chick-peas. Wheat bread is more than the staff of life there; it is so holy that a piece of it dropped on the floor must be picked up and kissed in atonement—and I saw this happen more than once. A meal without bread is unthinkable, and if the bread is not homemade, it is bought fresh and warm, sometimes twice a day. But the noblest form achieved by wheat, to my mind, is the food called *bulgur* or *burghul*, made by boiling the grains and drying them. The process brings out the cereal flavor of the wheat, and *burghul* adds a different note to soups, to stuffings and even (after soaking) to summer salads. It also goes well with ground lamb, either raw or cooked, and is used as a substitute for rice in a pilaf.

That last fact may be the highest compliment I could pay to *burghul*, because the rice I ate in the Middle East is absolutely the best I ever tasted. In its plain boiled form, it comes to the table with a perfection of texture seldom found anywhere else. But the Middle East likes its rice tricked up, too. It is often fried lightly in butter before the boiling, and rich meat or fish stock, depending on the main dish to be complemented, may take the place of water for boiling. Sometimes Middle Eastern rice may gleam buttercup yellow from saffron, or pink from fresh tomato juice.

Beans and lentils rank just behind bread and rice in popularity and longevity of use (the red pottage for which the Biblical Esau gave up his birthright was made of lentils). The American recipes for these protein-rich legumes usually call for the addition of salt pork, bacon or frankfurters—all of them meats with similar tastes. In the Middle East there is no such restraint. Boiled beans are served cold at breakfast with a dressing of olive oil and lemon juice—and perhaps a bit of garlic for extra taste. Lentils can be cooked with *burghul*, rice, potatoes or homemade noodles, or with such vegetables as tomatoes and green peppers; almost always, they gain additional flavor from onions fried in olive oil.

Chick-peas, a legume less familiar in the United States (except in the Southwest, where they are known by their Spanish name of *garbanzos)* are worth discovering. Toasted and salted, they make fine cocktail nibbles, crunchier than peanuts. Puréed and beaten with sesame oil and seasonings, they become a piquant dip. They can add unexpected nuggets of flavor to a salad, or an attractive topping to a rice dish. Street vendors sell them in the form of *felafel*—ground, mixed with a little *burghul* and spices, and deep fried. In Israel (where *felafel* is sometimes called the "Israeli hot dog") I bought it at a kiosk as an outdoor snack, tucked inside half a dish of Arab bread and sharing the hollow with salad and a dab of vigorous hot sauce. American host-

Continued on page 18

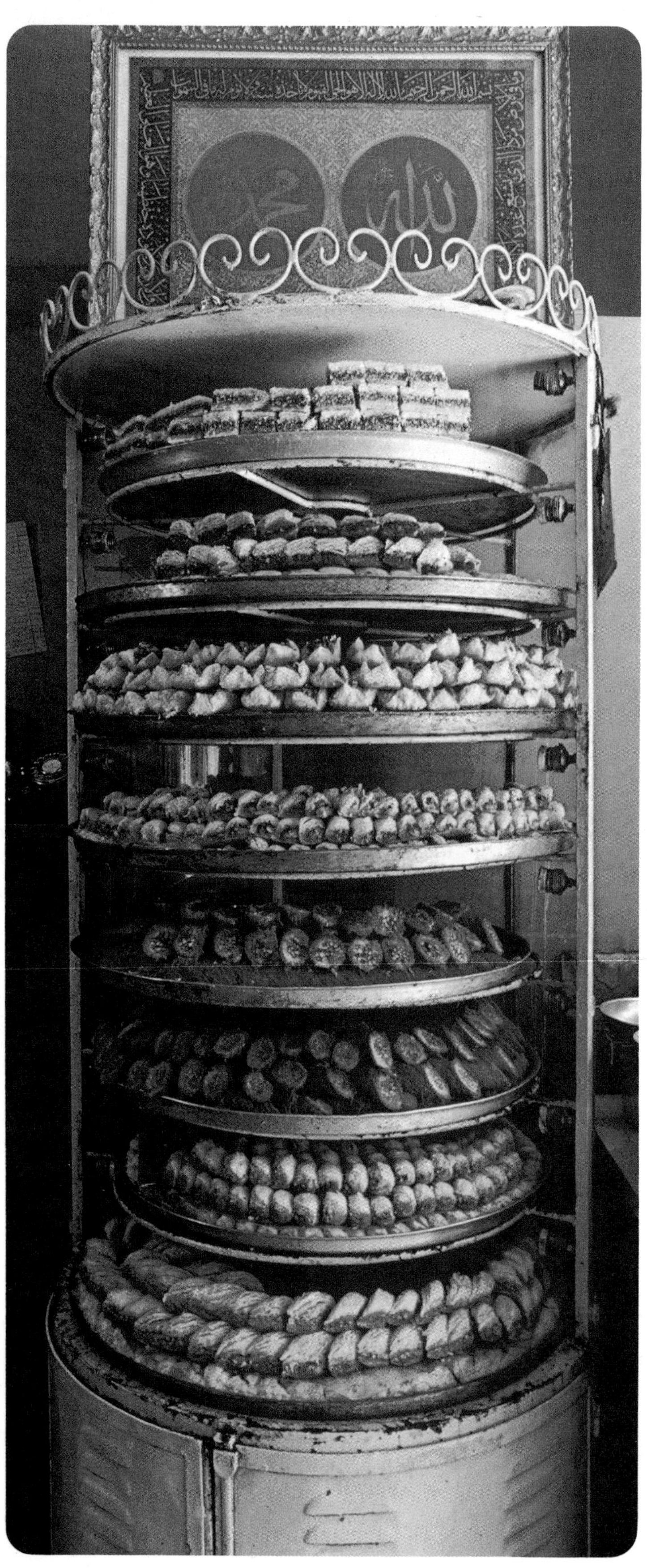

A Treasury of Sweets in an Eastern Tradition

Sweetmeat shops dispensing nut-filled pastries and glazed fruits are to the Middle East what candy stores and ice-cream parlors are to America. This part of the world, always a treasure house of nuts, became the sweetmeat kitchen of the ancient world. Techniques for drying and glazing the fruits indigenous to the region—particularly dates, figs and apricots—probably originated in ancient Persia, and the nuts that grew there—walnuts and pistachios—were natural complements to the glazed fruit. Nobody knows where or when the practice of baking fruits and nuts between paper-thin layers of dough began, but it is known that the finely milled flour required for such confections was first produced in the Middle East. Today such pastries, often drenched in honey, are favorites among all the people living around the eastern rim of the Mediterranean, from the Greeks to the Iranians.

Eight kinds of pastry are displayed at the Patisserie Scheherazade in Amman, Jordan, under a plaque bearing the names of Muhammad *(left)* and Allah. The shape of each sweet, from a layered rectangle to a stuffed roll, indicates its ingredients.

A GALAXY OF GOODIES IN A LEBANESE SHOP

The couple enjoying an afternoon coffee behind sweet-laden trays at Ahmad Arayssi's Patisserie Orientale—a shop that has served the people of Beirut, Lebanon, for a century and a quarter—have chosen their pastry from some 20 varieties. Their table also contains a plate of *kaik*, a semi-sweet bread. The bakers of the *patisserie* work throughout the day to replenish the trays in the foreground. In the pictures at the left, one of these bakers is shown preparing *baklava*. Steps include *(top to bottom)* trimming the thinly rolled dough around a hoop the size of the baking tray; spreading a sheet of dough from the rolling pin onto a layer of ground nuts; marking the pastry into individual diamond-shaped servings; and sprinkling finely chopped pistachios over the baked *baklava*. Versions of *baklava* differ mainly in the kind of filling; a recipe for a walnut *baklava* appears on page 40.

esses would find little balls of *felafel* delightful as a hot hors d'oeuvre.

It must be obvious by now that I am saying Middle Eastern cooking gains much from herbs and spices. For many centuries this region was a sort of funnel through which spices moved to Europe from the Orient—the Indies that Columbus set out to discover—and Middle Eastern spice traders became expert on the subject and thereby became rich. Today the Middle East has available just about all the spices that are common in the United States, along with a number of exotic ones that are unknown or hard to come by anywhere else. There is *mahlab,* for instance, derived from black-cherry kernels, which adds a fruit flavor to breads and sweet buns. *Sumak* lends a sourish, woodsy taste to meats, and *sumak* and thyme together, in a blend called *zaatar,* do wonders for the cream cheese produced from yoghurt. For tartness, especially where sweet, ripe fruits are incorporated in stews, the Middle Eastern cook is not limited to vinegar or lemon juice. She also has two ingredients little known in the West: verjuice (a sour liquid pressed from unripe grapes) and dried whole limes, which can be cooked and served with the other ingredients to deliver a sharp surprise to the Western palate.

Floral and herbal essences form another exotic part of the repertory. Tea is now popular in Turkey and Iran, but throughout the Middle East a number of *tisanes* or herb teas survive from older times, when herbs were the only medicines men knew. Jasmine, saffron, rose, camomile, hollyhock, violet, anise, ginger and pussy willow: each yields an aromatic infusion used as a specific cure but I assure you that each is a delightful beverage in its own right. Finally there are the concentrated, perfumelike "waters" that are distilled from rose or orange petals—particularly the petals of the pink damask rose and the blossoms of the bitter-orange tree, prized above all others for the strength of their scent. A few drops of these Middle Eastern elixirs transform a commonplace rice pudding into a subtle delicacy, and an innocent Iranian "ice cream"—actually a sort of sherbet—consisting of sugar, water and rose water is a delight to be remembered.

The sweets of the Middle East will linger in my memory for years to come. The region has a vast collective sweet tooth, indulged by an equally vast collection of pastries and confections. There are *halva,* the candy based on various kinds of flour, shortening, sweetening and nuts, as well as preserved fruits and fruit syrup drinks. But the Middle Eastern sweet best known in the West, I suppose, is *baklava*—a marvelously rich pastry of chopped nuts baked between layers of thin dough and steeped in honey or simple syrup that has been flavored with cinnamon and lemon juice. I could not possibly taste all the variations of these enticing pastries, but the endearing Arabic names of two versions stuck in my mind: *zind es sit* (the lady's wrist) and *kul wa-shkur* (eat and praise).

Surprisingly, this treasure hoard of sweets is served mostly on holidays or social calls, seldom as dessert. That course, I found, is represented simply by a bowl of fresh fruit, which may include such unexpected ingredients as tender young cucumbers. Two fruits often served to me remain too neglected in the West: the acid-fleshed quince, which can be cooked into a fine preserve, and the pomegranate, whose scores of seedlets yield a rich red juice that makes a first-rate breakfast drink—or adds a refreshing briskness to fried eggs. The famous figs of this part of the world, particularly those

Opposite: Among the nomadic Arabs of the desert, a centuries-old ritual for the making and serving of coffee is faithfully observed, and every Bedouin tent contains the equipment it requires. The implements, shown from bottom to top, include a long-handled iron ladle for roasting coffee beans; a wooden shaker in which the roasted beans are cooled; a brass mortar and pestle for grinding the roasted beans; a set of coffee cups in a brass case; a large pot for boiling water; a vessel in which frankincense is burned during the coffee ritual; and two smaller pots in which the coffee is brewed and served. The greenish cardamom seeds in the foreground are pulverized and added to the coffee after it is brewed.

Strong stone fences enclose fields and pastures on the outskirts of the Greek island village of Kastro, which gleams in innumerable coats of whitewash. In the evening, the farmers or fishermen of such a village gather in their *tavernas* to drink *retsina* or *ouzo* and pass the time in games, dancing and small talk. On special occasions, such as the celebration of a wedding *(opposite)*, wives and children join them. This group dancing to the music of a fiddle and a *bouzouki* is doing the *syrtos*—one of the few Greek folk dances in which village women participate.

from the area of Izmir, in Turkey, earn their reputation, and so do the melons of Iran, whose sweet and fragrant flesh has yet to be duplicated in the so-called "Persian" melons grown in America.

No meal eaten in the Middle East ended without coffee or tea, but coffee takes precedence most of the time. Coffee is a social beverage, offered to guests by housewives and to customers by merchants; to refuse it borders upon insult. There are two distinct but similar ways of preparing it, Turkish and Arabic. Both are served black, in cups the size of a demitasse or smaller. And both are brewed by starting with green beans, roasting them to a chocolate brown color, pulverizing them at once, either with mortar and pestle or in a handsome cylindrical coffee mill of chased brass, and quickly steeping them in boiling water.

The Turkish version is made in a coffeepot that has a long handle to protect the fingers from the fire and a shape narrowing from the bottom to the open neck to intensify the foaming action as the coffee boils up. Water, sugar and coffee are stirred together to your taste; then, at the first bubbling surge, the pot is whisked from the fire. It is returned briefly one or two more times to build up the foamy head, which is poured into each cup in equal amounts, to be followed by the rest of the brew, grounds and all. The dregs soon settle to the bottom, and the rich, brown coffee that covers them is ready to be enjoyed, with more sugar if you like. The Arabs prepare coffee in a single boil; they almost never use sugar; they pour the liquid into a second pot, leaving the sediment in the first, and then add such heady spices as cloves or cardamom seeds.

For those who prefer a stronger drink, the Middle East has a distinctive anise-flavored apéritif distilled from various fruits, chiefly grapes or dates, and variously called *arak, raki* and, in Greece, *ouzo.* Like the French Pernod, it turns milky white when diluted with water, which may account for its nickname of "lion's milk." But the nickname surely refers, too, to the potency

of the drink. *Arak's* strength is held in respect, and appetizers always come with it—which in turn may help to explain the abundance of appetizers served throughout the Middle East.

Clearly, the various national styles of cooking in the Middle East bear strong points of family resemblance. Give or take a peppercorn or coffee bean, an uninquisitive traveler can cover the entire region eating nothing but variations of half a dozen dishes. No such simplified menu will be set forth in this book, for we are dealing with the cuisines of some 120,000,000 people, scattered across more than 1,600,000 square miles, speaking 5 major languages, writing in 4 alphabets and professing 3 of the world's great religions. This scope and diversity produce a limitless variety of foods as well as people. Come and see: taken one by one, each of the nine nations of the Middle East has its own character and cuisine.

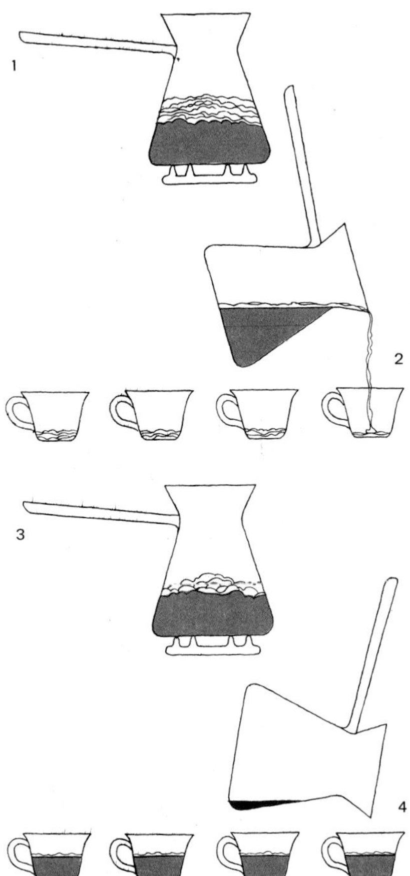

COFFEE, TURKISH STYLE

The technique for brewing Turkish coffee, illustrated above, is as unusual as the vessel in which it is made—a small, narrow-necked, long-handled pot called a *jezve*. *Jezves* can be bought from Middle Eastern stores in the United States *(see Mail-order Sources)*; the brewing method is easily managed in American kitchens. To serve four in the demitasse-sized cups always used in Turkey, measure 4 tablespoons of pulverized Turkish coffee and 2 of sugar into an 8-ounce *jezve*. Add 3/4 cup of cold water, stir well and bring to a boil over moderate heat (1). Pour the surface froth into 4 cups (2), add 2 tablespoons of cold water to the pot and bring to a boil again (3). Pour the coffee into the cups (4) and serve it hot.

Greece, land of my forebears and the first stop along our ragged arc, displays two characteristics not shared with the other nations—her Christian religion and her special heritage from the Golden Age of Athens in the Fifth Century B.C., when art and thought first flowered in Europe. The old Greek language, though greatly changed, is still spoken today, and there are other reminders of ancient times as well. One is the gesture that signifies "no." The modern Greek makes that gesture with a sharp upthrust of his chin, often raising his eyebrows to accentuate the refusal; Homer describes the god Zeus doing exactly the same thing.

From the thickly forested north to the dry south, where the air sparkles almost every day and people turn gloomy when it rains, Greece is a nation of talkers, unstoppable conversationalists. And nowhere is the art of conversation practiced more intensely than in provincial *tavernas,* which, taken collectively, form an institution similar to the Englishman's pub. A *taverna* is not only a drinking spot but a social center where, for hours on end, men play cards or backgammon and declare opinions and counter-opinions, while their women cook, wash, clean and work in the fields.

The basic drink is wine, a local product stored in huge casks lining the *taverna* walls. Most of the customers prefer white *retsina,* a resin-flavored wine imbued with the fresh smell of evergreen trees. (Its rosé cousin, *kokkineli,* is less strongly resinated, as a rule, and I recommend it to the first-time taster.) But the *taverna* also doubles as a sort of provincial cocktail lounge. A workingman or shopkeeper stops in after working hours for an *ouzo* or two, then goes home in a glow to relish his one-dish dinner, which may be a simple, fragrant *psarosoupa,* a soup of fish, rice, tomatoes and vegetables. If the *taverna* itself serves food, the patrons do not call for a menu, for there is none. Instead, they walk into the kitchen and lift the lid off every bubbling copper cauldron, inspect the meat turning on a spit in the big fireplace—a suckling pig, perhaps—and make their selections. Often they split portions with one another so that all can enjoy a bit of each dish.

Just across the narrow strip of water called the Bosporus that separates Europe from Asia is Turkish Istanbul, once the Greek city of Constantinople, the glittering and gluttonous capital of the medieval Byzantine Empire. Upper-class Byzantines ate a huge variety of meat, game, fowl and seafood, seasoned from an arsenal of spices and herbs, and this lavish cuisine was taken over by the Turks when they captured Constantinople in 1453. Hap-

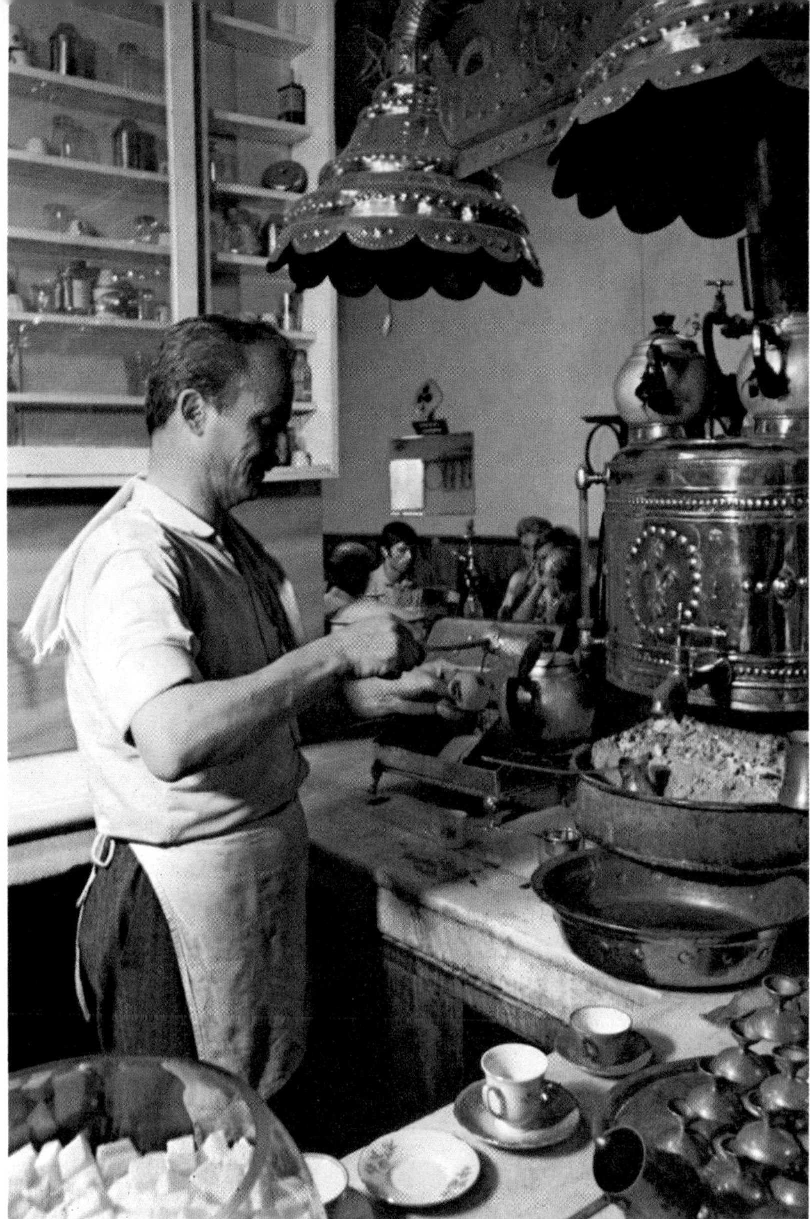

Coffee brewed to the customer's own specifications is poured from a copper *jezve* by Hulusi Harmanci, who prepares each pot to order in an Istanbul coffeehouse. Custom brewing is the rule in a country like Turkey, where every man has fiercely held opinions on the strength and sweetness of the drink and its preparation is viewed as a sensitive art. Tea gets almost as much loving attention and its preparation often involves elaborate vessels like the brass samovar at right.

pily for them, they already knew how to make the most of it. When they swept into the Byzantine Empire from their Asiatic homeland, the Turks were no longer simple milk-and-meat-eating nomads. They had overcome sophisticated Persia as early as 1055, and from that time had picked up all sorts of fine cooking on their westward drive to Constantinople.

In large part, the land they conquered was a primitive one. Today, Istanbul is Westernized, and inland Ankara, the capital, has modern buildings and tree-lined boulevards. But a few miles south of Ankara, in the Anatolian steppe that extends down to provincial Konya, life has changed little in the last 3,000 years. I saw a woman hoeing the earth with a transistor radio at her side, but I'm sure she still hauls water on a yoke slung over her shoulders, burns animal dung for fuel and uses an oil lamp for light. In Konya itself, which trades in grain and horses, a man sought the best native restaurant for lunch by standing in each doorway and shouting to the proprietor, inquiring about the day's meat. With his meal he probably drank sheep's milk. And his food was undoubtedly cooked in a copper vessel lined with a protective coat of tin; when reddish marks show through inside the pot, the local *kalayci*—the Turkish word for tinker—is summoned to renew the coating.

Some travelers consider these inland reaches the real Turkey, but the coastal centers certainly offer a richer and more interesting life. Bursa, which lies south of Istanbul across the Sea of Marmara, draws the produce of the lush green countryside around it to a lively open-air bazaar. There, the traditional woman's veil and baggy pants survive a few steps from the main streets, where Western fashions flounce. Marmaris, a little port at the southwest tip of Turkey, still offers the pine honey that connoisseurs have admired for centuries. Orchards and stands of pine climb the hills behind the village, and in its center the sights are few but intriguing: someone walks past you holding a big fish just taken from the water; a butchered lamb is delivered to a shop, followed by some hopeful dogs; at the beach, a trained bear sits patiently in the shallows while its mistress gives it a scrubbing. East of Marmaris, along the southern coast, I found a brave new "riviera" taking form, offering to the gourmet superlative—and still inexpensive—seafood, vegetables and fruits, especially melons and grapes.

Far more cosmopolitan is Izmir, on Turkey's Aegean coast. It is famous for the sweet, chewy, yellow Smyrna figs, which it exports dried, flattened and strung in loops on rushes. The city is Turkey's largest export center, with wharves piled high with olives, grapes, tobacco and cotton. Between the green hills and the splendid harbor, the streets of Izmir are clean underfoot and the parks give off the sweet smells of jasmine and roses. And on the outskirts of the city, cars and camel caravans compete for road space, and you can still see a ship of the desert plod disdainfully past a shiny late-model automobile without giving it a glance.

In Lebanon, Syria, Jordan and Iraq, the camels somehow seem more at home. It was there that I enjoyed one of the high spots of my trip: a genuine Arab feast presided over by a genuine sheikh in a Bedouin tent. To be sure, these Arab nations have their modern factories, dams, irrigation pro-

A string of camels rocks over the barren earth near the Jordan River, as they have for thousands of years. Peculiarly adapted to life in a hot, arid land, camels not only subsist on sparse vegetation but possess a unique ability to go for a long time without drinking; they store water not in their humps but in their red blood cells, which expand greatly in size to hold moisture for future use.

jects, new roads for new trucks (and for some aged ones, emitting noxious smells). Yet old crafts, such as the making of wooden boxes inlaid with mother-of-pearl in intricate patterns, are still practiced in tiny shops; camel trains still carry bales and sacks of goods along centuries-old desert routes, and the fine old-fashioned cooking persists.

The ancient ways are least visible in Lebanon, whose capital of Beirut is called the Paris of the Middle East. Facing the Mediterranean in a 120-mile-long strip of land, Lebanon is one of the world's smallest states—and to me, one of the liveliest. In Beirut and elsewhere, I found excellent restaurants, bars, nightclubs with belly dancers and floor shows from Europe. Beirut's Casino du Liban is the biggest and busiest gambling spot in the Middle East.

Here we saw the Arab taste for multiple appetizers carried to a high point. In Lebanon, people spend at least three hours at table, drinking *arak* and nibbling at tiny servings of pickled vegetables, broiled meats and fish, roasted chicken, boiled shrimp, various cheeses and eggplant in a variety of complex forms. Yet even in this business-minded nation, the most highly Westernized in the Middle East, the farmer in the uplands of the interior still sets out for his apple orchard, wheatfield or vineyard at dawn and comes home at sunset to his village with its church or mosque. I say church or mosque, because the population is roughly half Christian and half Muslim, though the Lebanese consider themselves Arabs.

Syria, like Jordan and Iraq, is nearly all Muslim. A form of Aramaic, the language of Jesus, is spoken in places, but the universal language is Arabic. Perhaps the purest Arab stock—the lineal descendants of the troops who swept up from the Arabian Peninsula in the 7th Century A.D. to spread the word of the Prophet—survives in the nomadic Bedouins who now wander the bleak Syrian desert. Much of the country is scorched plateau, but there are several fertile regions: the strip of about 100 miles of Mediterranean coast on the west, the northeastern area where the Euphrates River rolls down from

Overleaf: Refreshing cool fruits like this glimmering crescent of melon or a bunch of dewy grapes are a special delight in the arid Middle East. Both melon and grapes thrive in sandy areas where there are long periods of dry weather, and the glaring sun and heat of a Mideastern summer bring out their sweetness to the fullest. They have been raised here since ancient days. What seems to be a muskmelon appears in an Egyptian picture dating from around 2400 B.C., and this fruit presumably originated in and around Persia. It is not known when or where grapes were first cultivated; but the Sumerians who ruled southern Mesopotamia 5,000 years ago, had a word for them—*gestin*.

Turkey on its way to Iraq, and the country around Damascus, the capital, watered by the Barada River. Give a Syrian water and he will grow some of the lushest fruits on earth (apricots, peaches, apples and pears are only a few) and raise the plumpest flocks of sheep. From the sheep comes *kibbi,* made of lamb and wheat pounded together; it is prepared in neighboring countries as well, but in northern Syria, in Aleppo, it takes a delightful form: seven concentric balls of *kibbi,* a big one outside and progressively smaller ones within, with a pistachio nut nestling at the core.

Jordan is old land, Biblical land; and according to Deuteronomy, the capital of the Ammonites—the present-day city of Amman, Jordan's capital—had in its possession the iron bed, nine cubits long, of Bashan's gigantic ruler, Og. But despite this long history Jordan was established as an independent state only in modern times. Its boundaries were drawn after World War I by Western statesmen, who gave it an odd hatchet shape and marked its limits with arbitrary straight lines that have no relevance to natural frontiers. Lines like these, ruled across a uniform desert landscape, do not separate cultures or culinary habits; it is not surprising that Jordanians eat foods similar to those of their Arab neighbors.

Iraq has its share of these foods; it also bears the greatest weight of history on its shoulders. It has known Ur, where Abraham was born; Babylon, the Baghdad of the caliphs—storybook cities that were great in their day. Today Iraq is famous for growing dates—about three fourths of the world's supply, and the mainstay of the Bedouin's daily fare. It deserves to be equally famous for *masgoof,* the delightful custom of eating broiled river fish outdoors. In this land of the Tigris and Euphrates Rivers, a tourist enjoying *masgoof* beside one of the rivers' banks cannot avoid thoughts of the enormity of human time in the Middle East.

In nearby Israel, where Jesus and the Hebrew prophets preached, the impression we gained was one of newness rather than antiquity. To be sure, Jerusalem still crowns the Judean hills, golden-toned in the sunshine, and other Biblical sites survive along this narrow foothold of land on the Mediterranean. But in coastal Tel Aviv, the nation's largest city, we found ourselves surrounded with up-to-date bustle and animation. Along the Dizengoff, Tel Aviv's Fifth Avenue and Champs Élysées, people crowd the outdoor cafés, drinking tea or coffee—or perhaps a *gazoz,* a fruit-flavored pop—eating sweets, chatting in groups. A child strolls by licking an ice-cream cone; another bites into a huge ear of corn. Adults try the latest thing in street food, a slice of well-seasoned grilled beefsteak nestled inside a half portion of Arab bread. The feeling on the Dizengoff is festive—a mood quite proper to the city that has become the heart of Israel's night life, theater, press, industry and commerce.

Equally modern is Israel's attention to food. New agricultural techniques have made the old description of Palestine in Deuteronomy apply to Israel today: "A land of wheat and barley, and vines and fig trees, and pomegranates; a land of oil olive, and honey." To these have been added others: on the cool hills, a variety of fruit trees; in the hot Jordan Valley, guavas, mangos, citrus fruits, dates, bananas and avocados. Israel now exports Jaffa oranges, melons and flowers. It is the world's third largest exporter of avocados, after California and South Africa (though not all are meant for eating;

part of the surplus domestic crop goes into shampoo and soap). In the Negev Desert to the south, thousands of barren acres have been transformed by irrigation into gleaming green fields.

All this impresses every tourist and I was no exception, but I was not really prepared for one surprise: the multiplicity of cuisines based on these foodstuffs. People of at least 80 nationalities have swarmed into the country and all of them like to eat as they did in the lands they left. Tel Aviv must have one of the greatest medleys of cooking on earth, ranging from the Russo-Polish, which leans toward such dishes as blintzes and borsht, to the great variety of styles that the Israelis lump under the category called Oriental, which covers all non-European dishes—Arabic, North African, Indian and the Far East. (It may sound odd to hear Israelis speak of their fellow citizens from North Africa—which lies west of Israel—as Orientals, yet North African cooking does in fact resemble that of the Middle East because of the historic influence of Arabic culture in the area.)

This mélange is leading to a culinary revolution. Young people of European ancestry are acquiring a taste for Middle Eastern flavors. At the same time, in a development that is perhaps more significant for the future, Israeli culinary experts are devising original dishes, neither European nor Oriental, using the domestic ingredients that are in plentiful supply—particularly cit-

Lively sidewalk cafés line Dizengoff Street in Tel Aviv, the largest city in Israel. The attractions of the cafés and the smart shops scattered among them keep Dizengoff Street—like its older and bigger counterparts in Paris and Rome—alive at all hours with fashionable young coffee-drinkers, strollers and girl-watchers.

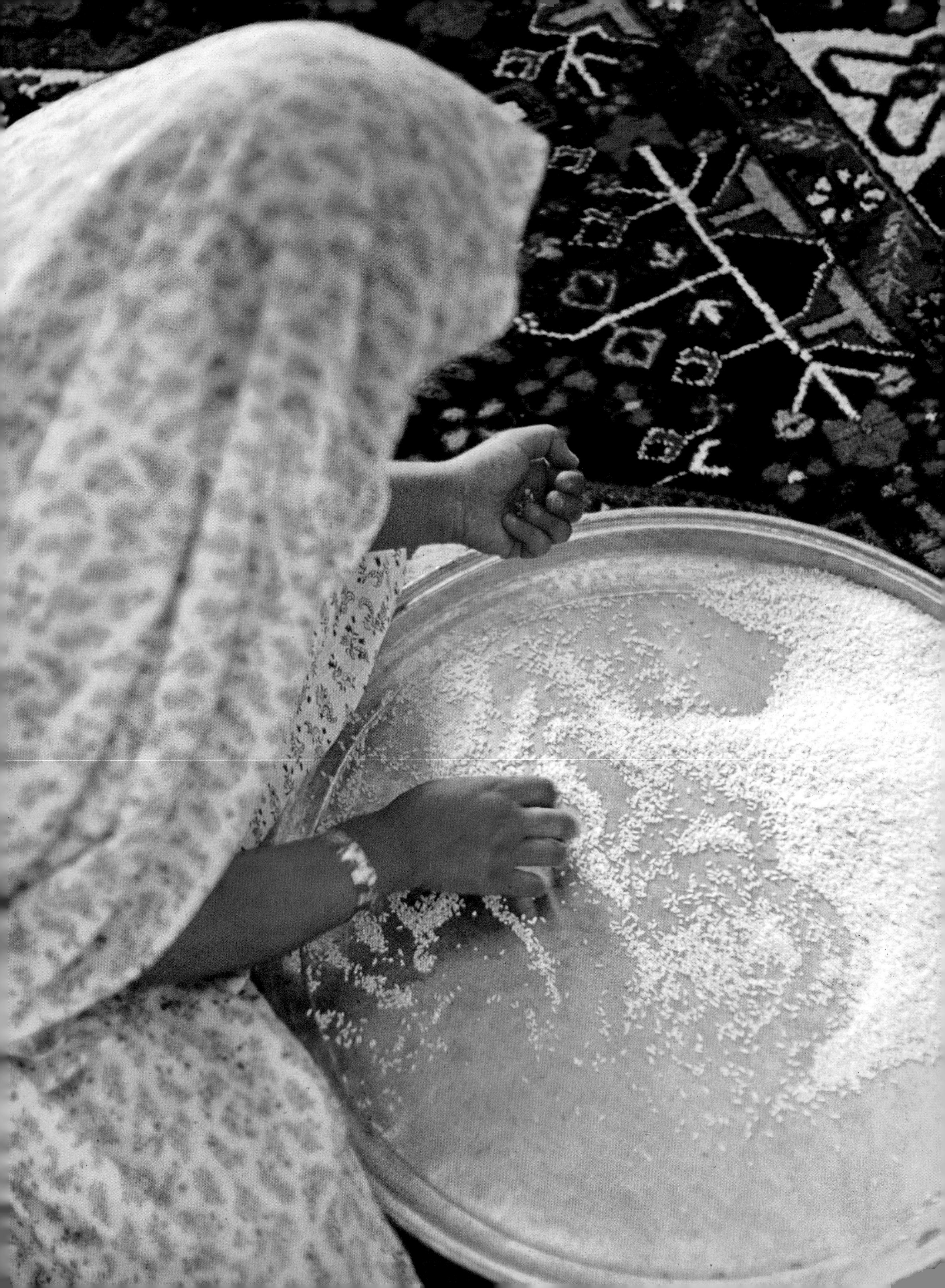

rus fruits combined with the excellent local poultry. National competitions encourage this kind of cooking; a male winner earns the title of Wizard of the Kitchen, a woman is honored as Queen of the Kitchen. But the culinary revolution is far from over; it will be years before the Israeli melting pot produces a single, unified cuisine.

Iran has its own splendid variety in food, but the variety has not been imported or recently created, as in Israel. In this land the Persians began to develop a rice-based cuisine 10 centuries ago and worked out sophisticated ways of serving the basic grain. It is now the main dish of the Persians' descendants in Iran, and all meats, vegetables and fruits are satellites, used as toppings or served as side dishes. Not that these other foods are second-rate. The Iranians are masters at cooking fruits with meat, and once you see their fruits you understand why—I gorged on an orange nine inches in diameter, and was told about 100-pound melons.

The national dish, though, is *chelo kebab,* a combination of rice, well-marinated lamb, yoghurt, raw egg and *sumak,* so popular that many restaurants serve nothing else. It is honored as a part of national tradition, and Westernized families, who ordinarily eat European food, go out occasionally for a meal of *chelo* to teach the children how good it is—and because they miss it the way a Texan away from home misses chili. One story I was told indicates how Iranians feel about their *chelo.* The proprietor of a famous *chelo* house was once jailed for political reasons; in a few months he was released and doing business again because his patrons, who included high government officials, complained that the quality had fallen off at his restaurant.

If *chelo* is the national dish, tea, hot and sweet, is the national drink. The smallest village has its beloved teahouse, the *ghavakhane.* (Mysteriously, the word means "coffeehouse," though coffee is never served there.) Like the Greek *taverna,* the Iranian teahouse is a kind of all-male club, and a center of local entertainment. The men listen to the radio, but give equal time to a professional storyteller recounting the glories of ancient Persia. Their favorite is invariably the *Shah-Nama* or "Book of Kings," a long epic poem that traces Persia's history back to the earliest legendary rulers, the first of whom is credited with the invention of cooking. Its author, Firdausi, who lived about 1000 A.D., is considered Persia's greatest poet; Omar Khayyam, who came along later and is admired in the West for the sweet melancholy of his *Rubáiyát,* has a lower rating in his homeland.

With this respect for the past goes a commitment to progress. A vigorous literacy drive has taught more than a million people to read and write. Serfs are now landowners, women have equal rights with men (though they do not yet throng to the teahouses), and a network of dams is being thrown up to improve the farmer's lot through electricity and irrigation. Sometimes such innovations meet an unexpected reception. The first time a movie was shown in one village, the audience broke through the screen in pursuit of the fleeing villain; in another, the elder wanted to prepare a banquet of *chelo kebab* for the two-dimensional actors.

Traditional ways are not easily forgotten in Iran. Walking down a village *kuche,* or lane, the traveler scents aromatic cooking—subtle blends of dill, cinnamon, nutmeg, turmeric, but seldom garlic, which is considered vulgar —under way in the walled-in houses. The walls lend privacy to a tiled

Opposite: An Iranian housewife scans and sifts a tray of the rice that will be part of her family's main dish, removing small pebbles, chaff and discolored grains. The cultivation of rice, which originated in India, was introduced into Persia in very early times, and Iranian rice is now ranked among the best in the world. With the exception of Iran and Iraq, which grow most of the rice they consume, the other countries of the Middle East are heavy rice importers.

Brought to Egypt from the New World by way of Europe, corn grows straight and tall along the Lower Nile in the shadow of the pyramids at Giza. Out of place though it may look to Americans, corn, called *zura,* has long been a major crop. It is used chiefly for making bread, but it also serves as poultry feed, while the cobs and stalks are dried for fuel.

courtyard in which young cherry and apricot trees grow, and to a little pool in which goldfish flit and a fountain makes liquid music. The Persian garden that inspires the nation's poets is not romance but reality—and it is worth mentioning that the English word "paradise" derives from the Persian word for "garden."

Egypt, across the Suez in Africa, surges with change as turbulent as Iran's. In less than two decades its economy, once wholly agricultural, has developed industries that provide 25 per cent of the national income. There are canning and freezing plants for vegetables, fruits, chicken, shrimp and sardines. Household appliances are manufactured, including a sewing machine that goes by the charmingly historic brand name of Nefertiti—and this in a nation that not long ago had to import its needles.

Egyptian women now have the vote, and study in coeducational classes that we visited at Cairo's al-Azhar, an ancient mosque-university where the traditional study of Muslim theology has been expanded to include engineering and science. By Egyptian law, primary education is compulsory for all children, and the bright ones can go on to secondary school, college and graduate school—all free of charge. In rural areas without domestic electricity, eager students do their homework under street lamps.

The most significant transformation in modern Egypt is based upon the reclamation of desert lands. Until recent years only the banks of the Nile River, its broad delta and a few oases could be cultivated. Now the High Dam at Aswan, south of Cairo, brings the river's gift of water into what used to be a wasteland. West of the Nile in the Western Desert, tawny acres are turning green, thanks to the discovery and successful tapping of an enormous lake 3,000 feet underground. In the Nile Delta itself, in Tahrir Province, another irrigation scheme enables as many as 10 crops of alfalfa to be reaped from a single field in a year. To cultivate these new farmlands, the government resettles families of fellaheen, the poverty-stricken peasants who

have lived in hovels along the Nile; it gives them long-term loans at no interest, sells them livestock at cost, and provides them with housing that boasts such amenities as indoor plumbing.

Not all fellaheen, who make up three fourths of Egypt's 32,000,000 people, will know the luxury of resettlement—nor would all of them want it. Through their millennia of attachment to the land, they have acquired living habits that resist change. Many of them think of farming machines as monsters, threatening unemployment. Their traditional fare is based on bread; an adult's daily ration of it comes to three pounds or more. He usually eats three meals a day—the *futoor* at dawn, a midday *ghada* in the fields, and the *asha,* a hot meal, at home after his day's work. He eats raw vegetables, such as tomatoes, cucumbers and turnips, and cooked ones, such as beans and lentils, or zucchini or okra stewed in butter. Fish is an occasional treat for him, and meat of any kind is a rarity.

These must have been the foods of the peasants and slaves who toiled for the Pharaohs; today's farmer, spare of figure and seldom tall, closely resembles the drawings of his ancestors on the walls of ancient Egyptian tombs and temples. In these pictures my wife and I saw the lavish range of the tables set so long ago for the ruler and his court. One series shows, stage by stage, how men sowed wheat, harvested it, threshed it, and finally gauged it for entry into the royal accounts. Another series shows in detail the preparation of some of the 30-odd kinds of bread developed by the royal bakers. Slaves are seen at work in a flourishing onion patch, a beekeeper attends his hive and trained baboons pick figs. And in one picture, a squatting man force-feeds a goose.

The Pharaohs may or may not have known the taste of *pâté de foie gras,* but it is clear that they ate supremely well. And I am glad to report that a good part of their *gourmandise* has come down to this day, not only in Egypt, but in all of the Middle East.

Although the following recipes are given specific names in Greek, Turkish, or Arabic, some variation of nearly all these dishes can be found in any of the Middle Eastern countries discussed in this book.

Şiş Kebabi (*Turkey*)

BROILED SKEWERED LAMB

To serve 4

- 1 large onion, peeled and cut into 1/8-inch-thick slices and separated into rings
- 2 tablespoons olive oil
- 4 tablespoons fresh lemon juice
- 2 tablespoons salt
- 1/2 teaspoon freshly ground black pepper
- 2 pounds lean boneless lamb, preferably from the leg, trimmed of excess fat and cut into 2-inch cubes
- 1 large, firm, ripe tomato, cut crosswise into four slices
- 1 large green pepper, cut into quarters, seeded and deribbed
- 2 tablespoons heavy cream

Drop the onion rings into a deep bowl and sprinkle them with the olive oil, lemon juice, salt and pepper. Add the lamb and turn the pieces about with a spoon to coat them well. Marinate at room temperature for at least 2 hours, or in the refrigerator for 4 hours, turning the lamb occasionally.

Light a layer of coals in a charcoal broiler and let them burn until a white ash appears on the surface, or preheat a stove broiler to its highest point.

Remove the lamb from the marinade and string the cubes tightly on 3 or 4 long skewers, pressing them firmly together. Thread the tomato slices and green pepper quarters alternately on a separate skewer. If you are broiling the lamb in a stove, suspend the skewers side by side across the length of a roasting pan deep enough to allow a 1-inch space below the meat.

Brush the meat evenly on all sides with the cream. Broil 4 inches from the heat, turning the skewers occasionally, until the vegetables brown richly and the lamb is done to your taste. For pink lamb, allow about 10 minutes; for well-done lamb, which is more typical of Middle Eastern cooking, allow about 15 minutes. Watch the vegetables carefully; they will take less time to cook than the lamb and should be removed when done.

Slide the lamb off the skewers onto heated individual plates. Serve with *pilav* (*Recipe Index*) and the broiled tomato and green pepper.

Kiliç Şiş (*Turkey*)

BROILED SKEWERED SWORDFISH

To serve 4

- 1 small onion, cut into 1/4-inch-thick slices and separated into rings
- 4 tablespoons fresh lemon juice
- 4 teaspoons olive oil
- 2 teaspoons salt
- 1/2 teaspoon freshly ground black pepper
- 1 1/2 pounds swordfish sliced 1 inch thick, skinned, boned and cut into 1-inch cubes
- 20 large bay leaves

In a deep bowl combine the onions, 2 tablespoons of lemon juice, 2 teaspoons of oil, the salt and pepper. Add the fish, tossing it about with a spoon to coat it well. Marinate at room temperature for 2 hours, or in the refrigerator for 4 hours, turning the fish occasionally. Place the bay leaves in a bowl, pour in 2 cups of boiling water and let them soak for 1 hour.

Light a layer of coals in a charcoal broiler and let them burn until a white ash appears on the surface, or preheat a stove broiler to its highest point.

Drain the bay leaves and remove the fish from the marinade. String the cubes of fish and the bay leaves alternately on 3 or 4 skewers, pressing them firmly together. Combine the remaining 2 tablespoons of lemon juice and 2 teaspoons of oil and brush the mixture evenly over the fish. If you are broiling the fish in a stove, suspend the skewers side by side across the length of a roasting pan deep enough to allow a 1-inch space below the fish. Broil 3 inches from the heat, turning the skewers occasionally, for 8 to 10 minutes, or until the fish is golden brown and feels firm when pressed lightly with a finger. Slide the fish off the skewers onto heated individual plates, and serve with *pilav* (*Recipe Index*).

Turkey's famous swordfish and lamb *kebabs* bedeck a bowl of rice.

To make 30

6 tablespoons olive oil
1 cup finely chopped onions
⅓ cup uncooked long- or medium-grain white rice
¾ cup water
½ teaspoon salt
Freshly ground black pepper
2 tablespoons pine nuts (pignolia)
2 tablespoons dried currants
40 preserved grape leaves
2 tablespoons cold water
Lemon wedges

Yalantzi Dolmathes (*Greece*)

STEAMED GRAPE LEAVES WITH RICE, PINE NUT AND CURRANT STUFFING

In a heavy 10- to 12-inch skillet, heat 3 tablespoons of the olive oil over moderate heat until a light haze forms above it. Add the onions and, stirring frequently, cook for 5 minutes, or until they are soft and transparent but not brown. Add the rice and stir constantly for 2 to 3 minutes, or until the grains are coated with oil. Do not let them brown. Pour in the water, add the salt and a few grindings of pepper and bring to a boil over high heat. Reduce the heat to low, cover tightly, and simmer for about 15 minutes, or until the rice is tender and has absorbed all the liquid. In a small skillet, heat 1 tablespoon of the remaining olive oil and in it cook the pine nuts until they are a delicate brown. Add them to the rice, then stir in the currants.

In a large pot, bring 2 quarts of water to a boil over high heat. Drop in the grape leaves and immediately turn off the heat. Let the leaves soak for 1 minute, then drain them in a sieve and plunge them into a bowl or pan of cold water to cool them quickly. Gently separate the leaves and spread them, dull sides up, on paper towels to drain.

Layer the bottom of a heavy 2- to 3-quart casserole with 10 of the leaves. Following the directions above, stuff each of the remaining 30 grape leaves with about 1 tablespoon of the rice mixture. Stack the stuffed leaves, side by side and seam sides down, in layers in the casserole and sprinkle them with the remaining 2 tablespoons of oil and the cold water. Place the casserole over high heat for 3 minutes, reduce the heat to low and simmer, tightly covered, for 50 minutes. Then uncover and cool to room temperature.

To serve, arrange the stuffed grape leaves attractively on a platter or individual plates and garnish with lemon wedges.

To serve 4

1 cup uncooked long- or medium-grain white rice
4 tablespoons butter
½ cup finely chopped onions
The giblets (liver, heart and gizzard) of the chicken, coarsely chopped
2 tablespoons pine nuts (pignolia)
2 cups water
1 tablespoon dried currants
2 tablespoons salt
Freshly ground black pepper
4 tablespoons butter, melted
A 3- to 3½-pound chicken
3 tablespoons yoghurt

Dajaj Mahshy (*Arab States*)

ROAST CHICKEN WITH RICE AND PINE NUT STUFFING

Place the rice in a sieve or colander and wash under hot running water until the water runs clear. Drain, and set aside.

In a heavy 3- to 4-quart saucepan, melt the 4 tablespoons of butter over moderate heat. When the foam begins to subside, add the onions and, stirring frequently, cook for 5 minutes, or until they are soft and transparent but not brown. Add the giblets and pine nuts and cook for 2 or 3 minutes. When the giblets show no trace of pink and the pine nuts are a delicate brown, stir in the rice and continue cooking until the grains glisten with butter. Add the water, currants, 1 tablespoon of the salt, and a few grindings of pepper. Bring to a boil, reduce the heat to low, cover and simmer for 25 to 30 minutes until the rice has absorbed all the liquid in the pan. Remove from the heat and with a fork stir in the melted butter.

Preheat the oven to 400°. Pat the chicken thoroughly dry inside and out with paper towels, and spoon about 1 cup of the rice mixture into the cavity. (Set the remaining rice aside.) Lace the opening closed with skewers or by sewing it with a large needle and heavy white thread. Fasten the neck skin to the back with a skewer and truss the bird securely.

Combine the yoghurt with the remaining 1 tablespoon of salt and a few grindings of pepper and brush about half of the mixture over the chicken. Place the chicken, breast side up, on a rack in a shallow roasting pan. Roast

To shape a stuffed vine leaf or *dolma (recipe opposite),* spread a grape leaf, dull side up, flat on a plate and place a tablespoon of the stuffing on the center of the leaf. Turn up the stem end of the leaf (1) and then, one at a time, fold over each of the sides to enclose the stuffing completely (2 and 3). Starting again at the stem end, roll the grape leaf gently but firmly into a compact cylinder (4 and 5). The surfaces of the leaf will cling together sufficiently to hold the grape leaf *dolma* in shape.

in the middle of the oven for 15 minutes, then reduce the heat to 350°. Baste the chicken with the remaining yoghurt mixture and roast for 1 hour more. To test the chicken for doneness, pierce the thigh with the point of a small, sharp knife. The juice that runs out should be pale yellow; if it is tinged with pink, roast the chicken another 5 to 10 minutes.

Transfer the bird to a heated platter, remove the trussing strings, and let the chicken rest for 5 minutes or so for easier carving. Fluff the reserved rice mixture with a fork, warm it over low heat, and serve it in a separate bowl.

Pilav (Turkey)

STEAMED SAUTÉED RICE

To serve 4 to 6

2 tablespoons butter plus 4 tablespoons melted butter
1 cup uncooked long- or medium-grain white rice
2 cups chicken stock, fresh or canned
½ teaspoon salt
Freshly ground black pepper

In a heavy 2- to 3-quart saucepan, melt the 2 tablespoons of butter over moderate heat. When the foam begins to subside, add the rice and stir for 2 or 3 minutes until all the grains are evenly coated. Do not let the rice brown. Pour in the stock, add the salt and a few grindings of pepper, and bring to a boil, stirring constantly. Cover the pan and reduce the heat to its lowest point. Simmer for 20 minutes, or until all the liquid has been absorbed and the rice is tender but still slightly resistant to the bite.

Pour in the 4 tablespoons of melted butter and toss the rice with a fork until the grains glisten. Drape a towel over the rice and let it stand at room temperature for about 20 minutes before serving.

Three Middle Eastern staples—eggplant, chick-peas, and tomatoes—are blended in the savory meatless *musakka'a* above.

Musakka'a (*Arab States*)

BAKED EGGPLANT, TOMATO AND CHICK-PEA CASSEROLE

To serve 6

1½ cups dried chick-peas (garbanzos), or substitute drained, canned chick-peas, thoroughly drained and rinsed under cold water
Olive oil
2 medium-sized eggplants, about 1 pound each, washed but not peeled, and cut into 2-inch cubes
3 medium-sized onions, peeled and cut into ¼-inch-thick slices
3 teaspoons salt
Freshly ground black pepper
12 medium-sized fresh, ripe tomatoes, peeled, seeded and finely chopped (*see garides me saltsa, page 61*), or substitute 4 cups chopped, drained, canned tomatoes
1½ cups water

NOTE: Starting a day ahead, wash the dried chick-peas in a sieve under cold running water, then place them in a large bowl or pan and add enough cold water to cover them by 2 inches. Soak at room temperature for at least 12 hours. Drain the peas and place them in a heavy 2- to 3-quart saucepan.

Add enough fresh water to the chick-peas to cover them completely and bring to a boil over high heat. Reduce the heat to low and simmer partially covered for about 2 to 2½ hours until the peas are tender but still intact. Replenish with more boiling water from time to time if necessary. Drain the peas in a sieve or colander. (Canned chick-peas require no cooking and need only to be drained and rinsed thoroughly under cold running water.)

Preheat the oven to 400°. In a heavy 12-inch skillet, heat about 1 inch of oil over high heat almost to the smoking point. Drop in the eggplant cubes and, stirring frequently, cook for about 5 minutes, or until they are lightly browned on all sides. With a slotted spoon, transfer them to a 9-by-14-by-2½-inch baking-serving dish and spread them out evenly.

Add the onions to the oil remaining in the skillet and, stirring frequently, cook over moderate heat for 8 to 10 minutes, or until they are soft and delicately browned. Watch carefully for any signs of burning and regulate the heat accordingly.

Spread the onions and all of their cooking oil on top of the eggplant and pour over them an additional ½ cup of olive oil. Sprinkle the onions with 1 teaspoon of the salt and a few grindings of pepper. Scatter the chick-peas on top, and cover them with the tomatoes. Sprinkle with the remaining 2 teaspoons of salt and a few grindings of pepper and pour in the water.

Bring the *musakka'a* to a boil on top of the stove, then bake in the lower third of the oven for 40 minutes, or until the vegetables are very tender. Cool the *musakka'a* to room temperature and serve directly from the baking dish, accompanied by Arab bread (*Recipe Index*).

Domatorizo Pilafi (*Greece*)

TOMATO PILAF

To serve 4

2 medium-sized fresh, ripe tomatoes, coarsely chopped
4 tablespoons butter, plus 4 tablespoons melted butter
1 teaspoon salt
Freshly ground black pepper
2 cups beef stock, fresh or canned
1 teaspoon tomato paste
1 cup uncooked long- or medium-grain white rice

In a heavy 2- to 3-quart saucepan, combine the tomatoes, 4 tablespoons of butter, the salt and a few grindings of pepper. Stirring and mashing the tomatoes with a spoon, cook over moderate heat for 5 minutes until the mixture is thick and fairly smooth. Add the stock and the tomato paste, bring to a boil and cook briskly for 5 minutes. Purée the mixture through a fine sieve set over a bowl, pressing down hard on the tomatoes with the back of a spoon before discarding the seeds and coarse pulp.

Measure the purée and return it to the saucepan. There should be 2 cups. If there is more, boil it briskly over high heat until reduced to the required amount; if there is less, add more stock. Bring to a boil over high heat, then pour in the rice. Stir once or twice, reduce the heat to low, cover tightly and simmer for about 20 minutes, or until all the liquid has been absorbed and the rice is tender but still slightly resistant to the bite.

Add the 4 tablespoons of melted butter and toss the rice with a fork until the grains glisten. Drape a towel over the rice and let it stand at room temperature for 20 minutes or so before serving.

To make one 9- by 13-inch pastry

- 3/4 pound butter (3 quarter-pound sticks), cut into 1/4-inch bits
- 1/2 cup vegetable oil
- 40 sheets *filo* pastry, each about 16 inches long and 12 inches wide, thoroughly defrosted if frozen
- 4 cups shelled walnuts pulverized in a blender or with a nut grinder or mortar and pestle

SYRUP

- 1 1/2 cups sugar
- 3/4 cup water
- 1 tablespoon fresh lemon juice
- 1 tablespoon honey

Baklava (*Greece*)

LAYERED PASTRY WITH WALNUTS AND HONEY SYRUP

Clarify the butter in a heavy saucepan or skillet in the following fashion: Melt the butter slowly over low heat without letting it brown, skimming off the foam as it rises to the surface. Remove the pan from the heat, let it rest for 2 or 3 minutes, then spoon off the clear butter and discard the milky solids at the bottom of the pan.

Preheat the oven to 350° and stir the vegetable oil into the clarified butter. Using a pastry brush coat the bottom and sides of a 13-by-9-by-2 1/2-inch baking dish with about 1 tablespoon of the mixture.

Fold a sheet of *filo* in half crosswise, lift it up gently and unfold it into the prepared dish. Press the pastry flat, fold down the excess around the sides and flatten it against the bottom. Brush the entire surface of the pastry lightly with the butter and oil mixture, and lay another sheet of *filo* on top, folding it down and buttering it in similar fashion. Sprinkle the pastry evenly with about 3 tablespoons of walnuts.

Repeat the same procedure using two sheets of buttered *filo* and 3 tablespoons of the pulverized walnuts each time to make 19 layers in all. Spread the 2 remaining sheets of *filo* on top and brush the *baklava* with all of the remaining butter and oil mixture.

With a small, sharp knife score the top of the pastry with parallel diagonal lines about 1/2 inch deep and 2 inches apart, then cross them diagonally to form diamond shapes. Bake in the middle of the oven for 30 minutes. Reduce the heat to 300° and bake for 45 minutes longer, or until the top is crisp and golden brown.

Meanwhile, make the syrup. Combine the sugar, water and lemon juice in a small saucepan and, stirring constantly, cook over moderate heat until the sugar dissolves. Increase the heat to high and, timing it from the moment the syrup boils, cook briskly, uncovered, for about 5 minutes, or until the syrup reaches a temperature of 220° on a candy thermometer. Remove the pan from the heat and stir in the honey. Pour the syrup into a bowl or pitcher and set it aside.

When the *baklava* is done, remove it from the oven and pour the syrup over it. Cool to room temperature, and just before serving, cut the *baklava* into diamond-shaped serving pieces.

To serve 2 to 4

- 1 medium-sized cucumber (about 1/2 pound)
- 2 cups yoghurt
- 2 teaspoons distilled white vinegar
- 1 teaspoon olive oil
- 2 teaspoons finely cut fresh mint leaves or 1 teaspoon dried mint
- 1/2 teaspoon finely cut fresh dill leaves or 1/4 teaspoon dried dill weed
- 1 teaspoon salt

Cacik (*Turkey*)

COLD YOGHURT AND CUCUMBER SOUP

With a small, sharp knife, peel the cucumber and slice it lengthwise into halves. Scoop out the seeds by running the tip of a teaspoon down the center of each half. Discard the seeds, and grate the cucumber coarsely. There should be about 1 cup.

In a deep bowl, stir the yoghurt with a whisk or large spoon until it is completely smooth. Gently but thoroughly beat in the grated cucumber, vinegar, olive oil, mint, dill and salt. Do not overbeat. Taste for seasoning, adding more salt if necessary, and refrigerate the soup for at least 2 hours, or until it is thoroughly chilled.

Serve the *cacik* in chilled individual soup plates, and add an ice cube to each portion if you like.

A bowl of creamy yoghurt, accompanied by fresh fruit, is a cooling meal in the Middle East at any time of day. Desert nomads long ago discovered how to turn fresh milk into a long-lasting, semisolid fermented food by adding a "starter" from a previous batch of soured milk. The product came to be called *laban* in Jordan, *mast* in Iran, *yaourti* in Greece and *yoghurt* in Turkey.

Making Your Own Yoghurt

The best yoghurt is homemade yoghurt. Few Americans ever make it, possibly because like all living things, the bacterial cultures that transform milk into yoghurt are somewhat unpredictable, but you can experiment with the process, using unflavored commercial yoghurt as the culture or "starter." Pour one quart of milk into a heavy 2- to 3-quart enameled casserole with a tightly fitting lid. Stirring constantly to prevent any skin from forming on the top, heat the milk slowly until it reaches a temperature of 180° on a candy or deep-frying thermometer, or until small bubbles form around the edge. Remove from the heat and, stirring occasionally, allow the milk to cool to lukewarm (110° on the thermometer). Immediately stir in 1/4 cup of commercial yoghurt. Put the lid in place and wrap the top and sides of the casserole with towels to keep it warm. Then place the casserole in a warm draft-free spot where it can stand undisturbed. After 6 hours or so, remove the wrapping. At this stage the yoghurt should be jelled and somewhat firm. Transfer it to the refrigerator without shaking the casserole or stirring its contents, and chill the covered yoghurt for 4 hours, or until it is firm. A quarter cup of it can serve as your "starter" next time.

II

Greece: The Meeting of East and West

Sheep on their way to market pause to browse at the foot of timeless Doric columns, ruins of a marble rotunda at Delphi. Ancient as is this seat of the great pagan oracle, the Greek taste for lamb is even older; sheep much like these have been raised in Greece since prehistoric times.

It was late morning and I sat with my wife at a sidewalk café in Athens, sipping a beer as I marveled how the city had changed since my last visit ten years earlier. Muriel had something else on her mind: This was her first visit to the Middle East and she was beginning to doubt that Greece should be included in my book on Middle Eastern food.

The day before we had dined in the resplendent hotel restaurant, a place of dark wood paneling, big chandeliers and tail-coated waiters who looked like ambassadors. The menu offered raised-pinkie Continental fare—even the rolls were served in individual cellophane shrouds—and our meal was imitation *grande cuisine,* though the décor and the check were the real thing. Now at the sidewalk café where long ago I used to lunch on a spicy, sea-flavored stew of squid with fresh tomatoes and olive oil, Muriel picked up the menu and pointed to the preponderance of Western entries—including, of all things, *Wienerschnitzel.* Then she looked out at the teeming traffic of downtown Athens and wrinkled her nose at the exhaust-tainted air. "I just don't think this is the Middle East or *any* East," she said.

Muriel's doubt is understandable. We are all taught to think of Greece as Western, not Eastern—the cornerstone of Western civilization—and from our point of view it is. But the Greeks know that this Western cornerstone was built by Eastern hands and minds. From ancient times the dominant influences in Greece have been Eastern, and the Greeks have concerned themselves, in food as in all else, more with the East than the West.

The area's first known inhabitants were a pre-Greek people of the Stone Age, about 7000 B.C., who came into Greece from the east. They brought their pottery-making art with them—and also many of the foods that are Greek staples today: the succulent lamb and sheep and such vegetables as peas and beans. The Greeks themselves arrived about 2000 B.C. from the north, but soon some of them moved eastward to establish cities in Asia Minor. Greek merchantmen found most of their trade to the east, and they called at ports in Egypt, where in the Fifth Century B.C. the Greek historian Herodotus wrote an awed description of "tree wool"—cotton—and where Greek soldiers sometimes served Egyptian rulers as mercenaries.

It is true that Greek colonists ranged westward too, as far as Spain, but the known, the civilized world, lay east of Greece, and Greece remained part of that world until it was enveloped by the growing Roman Empire in the mid-Second Century B.C. For a time, under Roman rule, Greece Janus-like faced equally east and west—but not for long, as history is measured. It was fixed in an eastward attitude again by the partition of the Roman Empire in 330 A.D., and remained part of the Byzantine Empire based in Constantinople (now Istanbul) for more than 11 centuries. Eventually, in 1453, Constantinople fell to the Ottoman Turks, and Greece lived under Turkish rule for almost four centuries. It did not emerge as an independent nation again until 1830, and by that time the cuisine was thoroughly Middle Eastern.

As I came to the end of my history lecture, Muriel was more than half persuaded. The clincher would be a taste of Greece's very Middle Eastern food, some savory lamb or beef, perhaps, or a subtle baked dish rich in olive oil and spices. It was a little after 1:30 in the afternoon, and suddenly the other patrons in the café began to leave. Most of them were men, sitting in pairs or groups, talking sociably and drinking beer or *ouzo,* the anise-flavored apéritif that turns cloudy white, almost opalescent, when it is diluted with water. Since no Greek will drink without eating, they had also been nibbling on one *meze* (appetizer) or another—salty black and green olives, potato chips, tangy white cubes of the goat's-milk cheese called *feta*. Now these men were swarming home for lunch.

For our own midday meal we sought out a small, unpretentious restaurant only a couple of minutes' walk from the Westernized café—sitting under its turned-up nose, one might say. The restaurant was crowded and we had to wait briefly for a table. But the air smelled of freshly grated *kefalotiri,* spaghetti cheese—the Greek version of Parmesan, yellow and firm—and I knew at once what my main course would be. When we looked at the menu, my nostalgia was gratified and Muriel was finally oriented in the right direction, eastward. Except for a "hamburger special" the offerings were all traditionally Greek, making no concessions to that collective bulldozer, the tourist.

We began with an appetizer of *tzatziki,* a refreshing cold blend of yoghurt, chopped cucumber and minced garlic. Muriel went on to the Greek-style roast "veal," rubbed well with lemon. (It was actually yearling beef, which the Greeks prefer because it has a more robust flavor than milk-fed veal.) My spaghetti fulfilled the promise of its aroma. The sauce was ground beef cooked with the usual onions and tomatoes but rendered aromatic with a pinch of cinnamon, and in the Greek manner it was all but dry, not like the runny spaghetti sauces encountered so often in Italy. The cheese matched the hearty flavor of the sauce, and it did more. It triggered a memory of my father, who loved this same cheese cut in domino shapes, fried quickly in butter and eaten searing hot. And this memory triggered another, of my mother. She had a trick she used on any pasta. She dusted it generously with this cheese in its grated form, then poured browned butter on the pasta just before serving, so that every strand glistened and took on a nutty flavor.

After lunch we strolled through the National Gardens, a park at the very center of the city, to have our coffee outdoors. Our path took us under palm trees, past formal flower beds, into breezes scented by flowering orange, and on to the Zappeion, another mid-city park. There we lingered over coffee at the park's outdoor café, basking in the midafternoon sunshine. And in that scented air and brilliant light, the food-rich memories of my own Greek past came flooding in upon me.

My parents came to the United States about 1905 as Greek-born immigrants, and our family lived in Greece for a time after World War I. I was 11 when we got there, with a palate that could appreciate both American apple pie and my mother's Greek specialties. During our years in Greece, however, we lived in small towns and had nothing on our table that was not Greek. Few American-born youngsters can have had a similar experience.

Reminiscing in the park, I thought of a simple rural dish whose taste I have never really forgotten. The name of the dish is forbidding in transliteration—*kolokithokorfades*—but it simply means "zucchini tops" or blossoms. To enjoy it at its best one must have a vegetable garden, as we did. The bright yellow blooms of the slender, green squash are picked in spring, in a thinning-out process that improves the vine's eventual yield. Then they are simmered lightly in butter with spring scallions and a dab of tomato sauce, and served under a small flurry of grated cheese. I refused to touch *kolokithokorfades* the first time it was offered to me, saying I would not eat flowers, but the fragrance that arose from my plate quickly ended my rebellion.

Another dish I came to love was *taramosalata (Recipe Index),* a dip (or a spread or a salad dressing; it is versatile) made of carp roe. A few tablespoons of the light orange roe are beaten together with a little lemon juice, a lot of olive oil, and some slices of white bread that have been soaked in water, squeezed and torn into small pieces. Grated onion and a touch of garlic are optional additions. The result is a smooth, cream-colored mixture, a bit thicker than mayonnaise, tangy yet retaining the delicate marine flavor that marks the roe of any kind of fish, like a gustatory echo of the fish itself.

The food I had the most trouble learning to like as a boy in Greece—and one that I still am sometimes wary of, though it is eaten with delight by most Greeks—is *skordalia (Recipe Index),* a garlic-heavy sauce used with fish. A cousin of the *aïoli* of France, *skordalia* is distinguished by the addition of mashed potatoes and sometimes of walnuts or almonds, all pounded with garlic, olive oil and lemon juice. Varying the quantities of liquid ingredients makes the sauce either runny or firm; the cook can add either more potatoes or more garlic to make it blander or stronger. My family liked it strong.

Among us all, my grandmother was perhaps the most ardent lover of garlic. She lived in the village of Tzintzina, in the Parnon Mountains not far from Sparta, and we vacationed with her in summer. Today the trip can be made by car, but in those days we traveled on muleback for nine hours, led by a guide who knew the bewildering passes. I remember the pine-scented air and the sound of the icy brook that rushed through the village, providing water for irrigation and power for the local flour mill. I savored the pungent smell of wild thyme on a slope warmed by the sun—but I cannot pretend that I enjoyed everything my grandmother served at mealtimes. One typical dish was *vlita,* a mustard-flavored green that she boiled, dressed with olive oil, and assassinated with clove after clove of chopped garlic.

Yet we ate well in Tzintzina. There were homemade macaroni and noodles, the first rolled into strings by hand, the second flattened into thin sheets and cut into little diamond shapes, and both spread out in the sun to dry. Toward the end of summer we had whole baskets of ripe purple figs with honey-sweet flesh. And when the grapes were harvested, the women of the village made a curious sweetmeat from fresh, unfermented grape juice and flour. The juice was boiled to reduce its volume and intensify its sweetness. Then the ashes of burned vine twigs were put in, clarifying the liquid as they settled. This was followed by decanting and straining to remove all sediment. The liquid was again reduced by boiling, the flour was added and the mixture was turned into a shallow pan to cool. The result was a chewy pudding, faintly dusty on the tongue but with a rich flavor of grapes.

In contrast with such village fare, a substantial repertoire of more complicated dishes is prepared by Greeks in larger centers. Many of these dishes are associated with festivals, notably Easter, which is the most significant occasion of the year for both the soul and the appetite. The Easter season begins with a period of masquerading and merrymaking known as *apokria*—the equivalent of the Western carnival or "farewell to meat." Then the forty-day Lenten fast sets in, its austerity relieved by the pleasure of making a meal of such foods as grainy *halva,* the ubiquitous Middle Eastern sweet usually based on semolina or farina, oil and plain sugar.

For the Easter Sunday Resurrection service Greeks go to church on Saturday night. Everyone holds an unlighted white candle. Toward midnight the church is plunged into an expectant darkness, a reminder of Jesus in the tomb. At the moment when Saturday passes into Sunday, the priest emerges from the altar enclosure holding a lighted candle and chanting the sonorous canticle that proclaims the Resurrection. "Come ye, receive the Light," he sings, lighting the candles of his parishioners from his own. One by one, from the front of the church to the back, the candles are lit until the interior fills with a warm and cheerful glow.

With this symbolic defeat of death, the Lenten fast ends. The faithful make their way homeward shielding the flames of their candles. The women have already laid the table for a meal to stir repressed appetites. The traditional foods are ready: a bowl of eggs dyed glowing red, braided or twisted loaves of sweet bread adorned with red eggs (*Recipe Index*), and the soup called *mayeritsa,* with which the long fast is broken. At the table each member of the family selects an egg and bangs it against his neighbor's; this turns into a sort of round robin, and the one whose egg survives intact wins all the others, at least in theory. But there are no squabbles over the winnings —how many hard-boiled eggs can one person eat?

Besides, the *mayeritsa* is coming. It is a by-product of the whole lamb that almost every Greek family has selected for roasting on Easter Sunday. For this post-midnight supper some of the intestines and innards—liver, heart, lungs and tripe—are cooked in stock and seasoned with fresh dill and scallions.

Feta **cheese, olives,** tomatoes and stuffed grape leaves *(page 37)* go well with the dip called *taramosalata (page 61).*

After hours of boiling, the soup is enlivened at the last minute with *avgolemono,* the tart egg-and-lemon sauce of Greece. *Avgolemono* is at its best when made at home because the cook must work fast to turn out the true frothy product. She beats eggs rapidly with lemon juice, adds a little of the broth to warm the eggs and keep them from curdling, then turns the mixture into the soup, which is kept just below the boil, and stirs steadily for a couple of minutes until the eggs are cooked. The bowls are whisked to the table, still foamy and ready for a blessing from the pepper grinder.

Oddly, I remember little about the Easter feast of the next day, except for the succulent lamb. We were eating *meat* again!

The memory of other holidays in Greece evokes one image—sweets, especially those made for Christmas and New Year's Day. The usual Greek dessert is fruit, but during the year-end holiday season housewives top off a long session at the table by serving sweetened fritters. One of my favorites was *diples,* or "rolls," so named because the thin, small sheets of dough are usually rolled up with two forks as they are being fried. Another was *loukoumades,* also fried, but with yeast in the dough so that they puff up into feathery golden brown balls an inch or two in diameter. The chief ingredients of both these confections are eggs and flour, sometimes with olive oil worked in during the kneading, sweetened with honey syrup and flavored with a sprinkle of cinnamon and perhaps some chopped nuts.

The first of January is the Feast of Saint Basil, who was not only a holy man but also a philanthropist—which may be why Greeks exchange gifts on this day rather than at Christmas. Everyone, even the children, stays up to see the New Year in, singing *kalanda,* carols addressed to the saint. This is the time to assess one's chances for the coming year. People crack walnuts hoping not to find an unlucky hollow one, or the head of the house breaks a pomegranate, looking for a promise of abundance in the fruit's red, tightly crowded seeds. At midnight the New Year's cake—the *vasilopita,* named for Saint Basil, whose name in Greek is Vasilios—is brought out. It may be a loaf of sweet bread, an oversized flat cookie or an elaborate cake, but it invariably has a gold or silver coin imbedded in it before the baking, to hearten the one who finds it in his slice.

Festive sweets may also be produced, of course, at times that have no religious significance. For any occasion involving guests, for example, the Greek hostess unfailingly keeps on hand at least one kind of rich, fruity "spoon" sweet—a syrupy preparation meant to be eaten with a spoon. She makes them from seasonal fruits boiled with about an equal weight of sugar. I have often been made welcome in Greek homes with such supercompotes, made with fresh cherries, plums, small bitter oranges, apricots, strawberries, quinces, and even walnuts picked at the moment when the outer pulp has turned brown but the shell has not yet hardened. Most surprising was to be offered sweetened tomatoes—seedless baby plum tomatoes, each stuffed with a crunchy hazelnut. There was no trace of tartness left in them, but the fresh tomato tang was there.

The serving of spoon sweets amounts to a social ritual. It would be bad manners to hurry the visitor, and the hostess waits a decent interval before serving him. At the right moment she brings out a treasured tray, the equivalent of a formal tea service in the West. Its splendor varies with her affluence,

Continued on page 56

To Celebrate Christ's Resurrection

The solemn Lenten season and its joyous Easter climax, marked throughout the Christian world, are nowhere so faithfully observed as in Greece, where they are honored as the holiest times of the year. During the seven weeks of Lent the Greek Orthodox Church forbids its communicants to consume *any* animal product—not only meat, but fish, eggs, butter, milk and cheese. On Wednesdays and Fridays of the first six weeks and on every day of the seventh, wine and olive oil are forbidden, too. Many Greeks follow these strict prohibitions to the letter *(below)*, and Sunday becomes doubly joyous in its celebration of the Resurrection and release from abstention. Preparations for the feast of lamb, Easter eggs, Easter cakes and bread begin on Holy Saturday as the women see to the baking and the men manage the preparation of the paschal lamb. But to many in Greece even more enjoyable than Sunday's dinner is the first post-Lenten meal, served immediately following midnight Mass on Holy Saturday, when families share a nocturnal dinner that begins with red-dyed Easter eggs and goes on to *mayeritsa*, a soup made of the lamb's innards—a foretaste of the Sunday feast to come.

God's blessing on a meatless, wineless Holy Saturday supper is invoked by Christos Constantinou *(at left below)* in his house in the village of Arachova, on the slopes of Mount Parnassus. The frugal meal, which will be shared with the villager's parents, his wife and their two young daughters, consists of boiled beans and boiled potatoes, lettuce and scallions, bread, olives, *halva* and water.

Carrying a flickering candle, a priest of the town of Delphi re-enters his church with his acolytes *(left)* after the midnight mass that ushers in Easter Sunday. On the stroke of midnight the priest had walked outside at the head of his congregation—each bearing a candle lighted during the service—and proclaimed "Christos anesti" (Christ is risen), and through all of Greece church bells were rung, fireworks were set off, guns were fired and ships at sea blew their whistles. Later, parishioners carried their lights home and ate a late supper. Then the men set the fires at the communal lamb-roasting pits. By dawn on Easter, smoke from many such pits streaks the long slope of Mount Parnassus, and the villagers of Delphi look down at neighboring Chrisso *(below)* through a haze of gray.

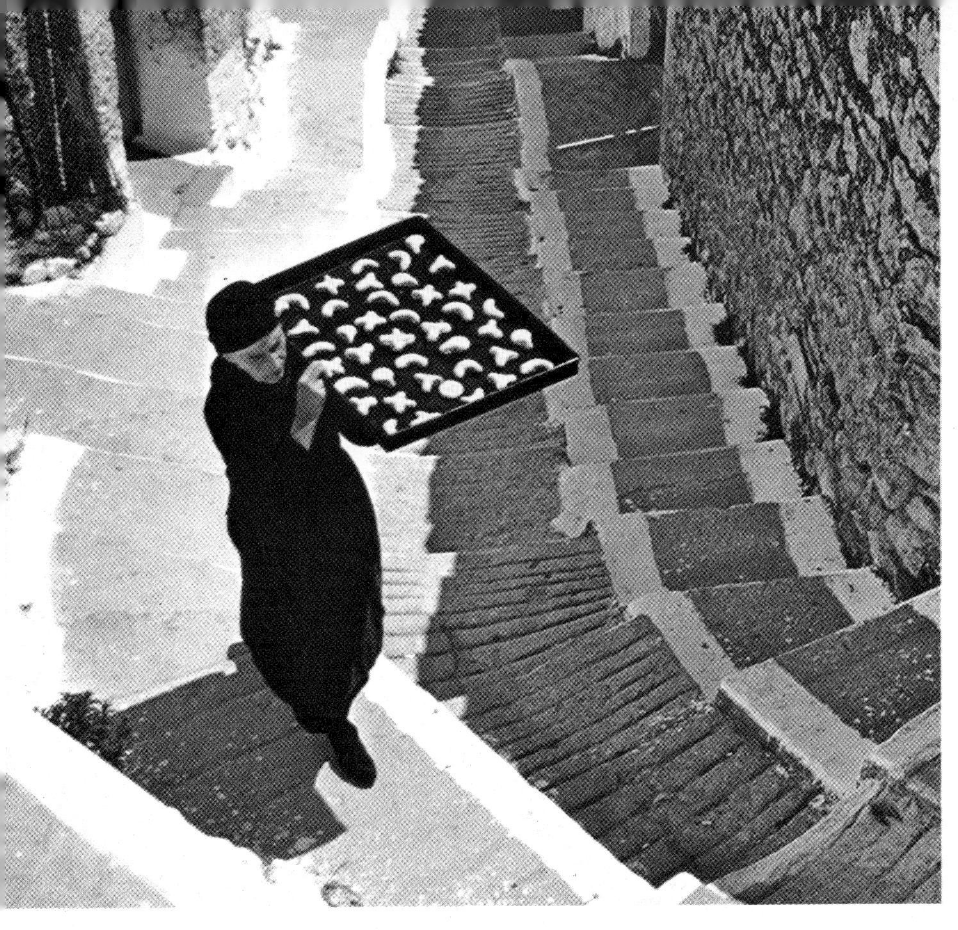

All Saturday and Sunday preparations for the feast go on. The Constantinous' Easter bread would more than fill their oven, so grandmother carries some of it through the narrow white-washed streets to the village shop for baking *(left)*. The other grandmother of the family separates the entrails of a lamb while a kid, spared from the slaughter, nuzzles her skirts *(below left)*. The entrails are used in making *kokoretsi*, an Easter sausage. But the main dish will be the lamb itself, and on Sunday morning men and boys like the two shown below carry whole lambs from all over the village to the roasting pit *(overleaf)*. There the men gather to turn the spits until the meat is done, occasionally sharpening their appetites with *retsina*. Invariably, the roasting becomes a pre-feast jamboree.

Grandfather Constantinou *(above)* opens wide for a sample of Easter lamb, his first roast meat in seven long weeks. It is a morsel of liver, one of the choice bits grilled and seasoned by the women of Arachova to be offered to anyone who passes by while the men of the village are roasting the lambs *(preceding pages)*. The women give away only a few such tidbits. Most of the innards are skewered, bound with lamb intestine and roasted as *kokoretsi*. At left, the Constantinous' own *kokoretsi* is tested for doneness by Christos, head of the house. The Constantinous always have their Easter feast in their cool courtyard. After the meal, neighbors drop in for a visit and a glass of wine; at right Magda Constantinou dances with one of them while three generations of the family look on. The meat dishes have been removed, but other foods remain: puffy Easter bread, red Easter eggs, a bowl of yoghurt, chunks of *feta* cheese, salad and a platter of fresh fruits.

but always it carries a bowl filled with the compote and set in a deep tray ringed with notches that hold spoons in an upright position. Around this centerpiece are glasses of cold water, one for each guest. The tray is first proffered to the eldest of the visitors, and he takes a spoon, dips into the bowl, eats his mouthful and drinks from his glass. Invariably the guest expresses a goodwill wish; if the occasion is purely social the wish may be the simple, all-covering Greek phrase: "Whatever you long for."

On our second night in Athens, Muriel and I dined out with a Greek couple in the Plaka, the old quarter of the city, at the foot of the Acropolis. The time was 9:30 in the evening, but we were the first patrons in the dining room. All Athens likes its dinner late. This makes for little sleep but is no disadvantage in a city where the daily siesta is so deeply rooted a habit that, just before the hot summer days arrive, the hours of siesta are officially proclaimed by the police. Only mad dogs and tourists are in the streets from about 1:30 to 5:00, and even they seem to tiptoe.

At dinner, while the pianist tinkled light Continental melodies, we enjoyed very non-Continental food—two dishes that we make at home and often serve when we entertain. One is *tiropites,* or cheese puffs; the other is *moussaka (Recipe Index),* a pie of ground meat and eggplant. Both are complicated, but nearly all the work can be done a day in advance. In fact, Muriel makes about a hundred cheese puffs at a time—roughly a two-hour task —and keeps them in the freezer for months.

To make *moussaka,* she starts with the smallest eggplants she can find, preferably no bigger than half a banana, and this for two reasons: they have tiny seeds or none at all, and their flesh, far firmer than that of the full-blown vegetable, soaks up less of the olive oil and butter in which they will be fried. Like the ingredients of bouillabaisse, those of *moussaka* can be varied in unexpected ways. Muriel sometimes includes potatoes and squash or even replaces the eggplant entirely with potatoes. For meat she might use ground beef, although as a purist she prefers lamb or mutton, cooking it with chopped onions, tomato paste, red wine, a generous flavoring of minced parsley and a dash of cinnamon. Meat and eggplant are combined in a casserole in alternate layers, each dusted with grated spaghetti cheese—and now Muriel can set the *moussaka* aside until serving time approaches, either the same day or the next. At that point she prepares the crowning touch, a custard sauce made with eggs, milk, flour, more grated cheese and a whiff of nutmeg, and pours it over the casserole. An hour in a moderate oven does the rest, blending all the flavors in a subtle unity.

The cheese puffs make an ideal hot hors d'oeuvre. Muriel uses the traditional *filo,* a pastry that comes in sheets as thin as onionskin, and cuts it into long strips about an inch and a half wide. These she brushes well with butter, then adds a dab of filling and rolls up the strip in a tricky zigzag that produces a little triangle of several layers of *filo.* The filling is a mixture of *feta* and pot cheese, with beaten eggs added to make sure it puffs up in the oven. And it does, beautifully, while the outside turns to flaky brown.

One other dish impressed me that night in the Plaka. It was a casserole of shrimp baked in a tomato sauce that contained crumbled *feta (Recipe Index).* The sauce was thin, because *feta* melts quickly when cooked, but the combination of flavors was appetizing. Such fine shrimp was a rare treat, I learned, for Greek waters no longer yield the abundant catches that fishermen used to bring in. While I savored my all-Greek dinner, our companions surprised me by ordering broiled pork tenderloin as their main course. I had not realized that the Greek appetite for pork is growing, while the traditional preference for lamb is diminishing. Today, as in my boyhood, farmers keep a hog or two for the family table, but now there is also a hog-raising establishment near Athens that turns out not only fresh pork but the smoked and cured versions and even sausages.

The four of us enjoyed another unexpected dish, listed on the menu as "rural salad." It was a heaped-up assortment of greens, radishes, cucumber slices, tomato wedges and scallions, plus black olives and chunks of *feta,* all tossed in vinaigrette sauce and sprinkled with fresh mint. In the United States, especially in New York and in such places as Tarpon Springs, Florida, where much of the population is of Greek ancestry, this marvelous jumble is known as Greek salad, but I had never seen it before in Athens.

Our restaurant filled gradually as we ate. By 11 o'clock it was crowded. When we got up, a little past 11:30, a waiting party of four began edging toward our table. We were on our way to another eating place, not for more food after the hearty *moussaka,* but to sip wine and absorb the atmosphere of that boisterous Greek institution, the *taverna.*

We had a choice of many colorful *tavernas,* which are not only taverns in the sense of tippling places but Greek-style cabarets as well. Some cherish a distinctive feature of some sort: one features a tall tree growing through its three stories; another is known for its fancy frescoes; a third keeps canaries by the dozen. Some go so far as to present floor shows and chanteuses. Less pretentious places provide a small conventional orchestra, and a fiddler or guitarist may come to your table and play a romantic tune.

In the most authentic Greek *tavernas,* you will be entertained by musicians playing the *bouzouki,* the long-necked mandolinlike instrument made famous in the film *Never on Sunday.* A woman sings to their accompaniment, often about unrequited love, and fittingly the melody is pitched in sad, Oriental minor keys. The decibel level is astonishing. Many patrons, like us, show up after dinner to nibble at the best fruit in season, drink piny *retsina,* watch the spontaneous dancing of other patrons—and join the loud, frenzied performance. With no trace of inhibition, a man may leave his party and make for the open floor, where he twirls and stamps, snaps his fingers, and puts his body at the command of the intricate rhythm and the pathos of the *bouzouki's* song. When he finishes his dance, all emotion spent, he ignores the applause that follows him to his chair.

One day of our visit we drove south from Athens to Nauplia, a town that lies in the Peloponnesus, a four-fingered peninsula dotted with relics of the legendary past. We skirted Corinth, the ancient Peloponnesian city famed for its wealth and licentious ways—and for a small seedless raisin that was the fruit originally called a "currant." The road went by fruit orchards, groves of young olive trees and vineyards in new leaf, and soon we were passing oranges and lemons piled up for sale beside the highway. But in the distance, towering some 1,900 feet above the Peloponnesian plain, was Acrocorinthus, an acropolis, or high fortified place, dating from a time when citrus fruits were unknown in Greece. And presently we came to the hoariest site along the

A Greek *salata horiatiki,* or "rural salad," contains raw vegetables in season, *feta* cheese and ripe or green olives. Anchovies or sardines are optional additions. The salad is tossed with an oil-and-vinegar dressing just before it is served.

route, the ancient city of Mycenae. There, at the time of the Trojan War, Agamemnon ruled in a gastronomic splendor suggested by two of the excavated buildings—the impressively large Houses of the Oil Merchant and the Wine Merchant, whose owners kept shop around 1200 B.C.

The town of Nauplia is a small and picturesque port huddled at the foot of a tall cliff. The waterfront looks across the harbor to a small island named Bourzi, once the site of a diminutive Venetian fortress, later of a retirement home for Greek executioners (who were hated men), and now, happily, of a charming hotel and restaurant. When snack time caught up with us, a telephone call from the quay brought a launch to ferry us across the water.

If any ghosts of bygone executioners remained on the island, they did not disturb us. The restaurant was cheerful, and I ordered the pure native pick-me-up—a glass of *ouzo* and a plate of savory nibbles, slices of zesty garlic sausage, sharp *feta* cheese, oversized green olives, and pieces of deep-fried octopus tentacles *(Recipe Index)* with a delicate marine flavor.

On our return trip to Athens we stopped for dinner at a *psistarya,* or rotisserie. One goes to a *psistarya* to eat coal-roasted lamb, young and tender, seasoned only with salt and pepper. The place we chose was an open-front establishment grandly named Uncle Tom's Resort Restaurant, which provided us with a somewhat mixed experience. We relished the smoky, crusty lamb, the fresh tomato slices dressed with olive oil and lemon and the *feta* that seemed to make up the entire menu, and a smooth red wine that was so local it had no name, not even a label on the bottle. But we sat at a bare, plastic-topped table under baleful fluorescent lights, and presently acquired as fellow patrons a group of youths who seemed to believe that a silent jukebox is an unhappy jukebox. They made it rapturously, deafeningly happy.

Perhaps as an over-reaction to that experience, we determined on our return to Athens to explore a truer Greece, the Greece of ancient times. And this exploration brought to mind another Greek cuisine, a cuisine that was strange, remote—and fascinating.

The serenest place in Athens, and the noblest, is the Acropolis on a sunny afternoon. The grandest monument up there is the Parthenon, built in the Fifth Century B.C. to honor the virgin goddess Athena, the city's protectress. In the sanctum her statue, 38 feet tall, had flesh of ivory and contained more than a ton of gold. This splendor vanished long ago, but it requires no great effort of the imagination to recreate the scene at the great Panathenaic festival, when the whole city turned out to worship and propitiate Athena. Priests chanted, the populace prayed, and no doubt vendors shouted. Animals were sacrificed, then cooked and eaten, as though the people were enjoying a feast with their revered patroness.

This was the zenith of classical Athens, when her citizens had advanced not only in the arts and sciences but in the social graces of the table. Only a boor ate alone. A man customarily took his meals with his family unless he had guests; then his womenfolk stayed out of sight. There were servants or slaves to wash the feet and hands of the arriving company and perhaps to perfume their heads. Each diner lounged on a couch as food was put before him—roast pork, perhaps, or fresh fish—and ate with his hands.

The wine for the feast was always diluted with water, but no one now knows just how it tasted. It is on record that the Greeks clarified their wines with powdered marble or potter's earth, and it is probable that they sometimes flavored it with pine resin, producing an ancestor of the *retsina* so popular in Greece today—a wine imbued with the fresh smell of a stand of evergreen trees. They also occasionally added perfumes to their wine bowls, and one of their prized diluting agents was salt water, which they scooped out of a calm sea and boiled with spices until it was reduced by about two thirds. They strained the resultant whatever-it-was and stored it away for years, to be broken out for some special entertainment.

Such an occasion might be a symposium or feast, presided over by a "symposiarch," often ending in a drinking party. There were songs and jokes, and entertainment by flutists, acrobats and dancing girls. More seriously, the symposium functioned as an intellectual gathering at which each man spoke at length and was listened to by all the others.

Long before the institution of such formalized affairs, at a time when the Greeks were still close to being the barbarians they later scorned, there was a style of banqueting that might come as a shock to the contemporary American palate. In *Hercules, My Shipmate,* a fictitious evocation of the voyage of the Argonauts to recover the Golden Fleece, the poet and scholar Robert Graves attempted to reconstruct one such feast. The time was about a century before the Trojan War, and here is how the meal went.

"Soon each Argonaut found himself seated at table with a woman on either side of him. The woman on his left kept his beech-wood trencher heaped with abundance of food—fish, roast mutton with capers pickled in sour wine, roast beef with sauce of asafoetida, wild game, honey-cakes, stewed dormouse . . . asparagus, dried white figs, barley-bread soaked in olive oil, samphire (a fleshy plant of the parsley family) pickled in brine, and the hard-boiled eggs of sea-fowl. The woman on his right filled his goblet with wine and water (and the mixture contained almost as much wine as water), or milk, or beer, whichever he asked for; sometimes she mixed all together and stirred in honey."

This repast may be termed barbarous or sophisticated, according to one's preferences in food, but it presumably gratified rough-hewn heroes who had not yet outgrown the practice of human sacrifice. They also made offerings of first fruits or war spoils in their efforts to bribe or flatter the gods, but bloodletting seems to have been considered the surest shortcut to divine assistance. In this respect, at least, classical Athens took a great stride toward civilization by offering up animals rather than slaves, captured enemies, or, in some desperate hour, a child.

Many of the superstitions and even foods of those ancient times survive in modern Greece. Some of the dishes served at the Argonauts' banquet can be eaten in Greece today. And on the way down from the Acropolis, a final memory from my own past came back. In classical Greece the snake was associated with the cult of Athena, and it was considered propitious and comforting to have a snake living under one's house as an *oikouros ophis,* a home-protecting serpent. As we reached the foot of the Acropolis, I told Muriel that my grandmother had had just such a protector under her hut in Tzintzina, though I hadn't known then how deeply rooted in time the notion was. When I first saw this snake and ran to announce my discovery, she said, "Don't harm it. It belongs to the house."

CHAPTER II RECIPES

Taramosalata

CARP ROE SPREAD

To make about 2 cups

6 slices homemade-type white bread, trimmed of crusts
1 cup cold water
½ cup (4 ounces) *tarama* (salted carp roe)
¼ cup fresh lemon juice
¼ cup finely grated onions
¾ to 1 cup olive oil

Soak the bread in the water for 5 minutes, then vigorously squeeze it dry with your hands. With a large mortar and pestle or the back of a spoon, mash the bread until smooth. Then add the *tarama,* 1 teaspoon at a time, mashing and stirring constantly. Beat in the lemon juice and the grated onion and continue mashing until the mixture becomes a smooth paste.

Transfer the mixture to a large bowl and, with a whisk or a rotary or electric beater, beat in the oil, 1 tablespoon at a time; make sure each tablespoon is absorbed before adding more. When about ½ cup of oil has been beaten in, the mixture should be creamy and smooth. Pour in more oil in a slow, thin stream, beating constantly until the *taramosalata* is thick enough to hold its shape almost solidly in a spoon. Taste for seasoning and refrigerate until ready to use. *(Taramosalata* will thicken further as it chills.) Serve as part of a platter of appetizers *(meze)* accompanied, if you like, by cubes of fresh bread for dipping.

NOTE: A less authentic, but quicker, way to make *taramosalata* is to soak and squeeze the bread dry and combine it with the *tarama* in the jar of an electric blender. Blend at medium speed until the mixture is smooth. Without stopping the blender, remove the cover and add the lemon juice and onion. Still blending, pour in up to 1 cup of oil in a slow, thin stream, adding as much of it as you need to give the *taramosalata* its proper consistency. Taste for seasoning and refrigerate before using.

Garides me Saltsa

SHRIMP IN TOMATO, WINE AND FETA CHEESE SAUCE

To serve 4

4 medium-sized fresh, ripe tomatoes, or substitute 1½ cups chopped, drained, canned tomatoes
1½ pounds raw shrimp in their shells (25 to 30 medium-sized shrimp)
6 tablespoons olive oil
¼ cup finely chopped onions
½ cup dry white wine
2 tablespoons finely chopped parsley, preferably flat-leaf parsley
½ teaspoon crumbled oregano
1 teaspoon salt
Freshly ground black pepper
2 ounces *feta* cheese, cut into ¼-inch cubes

Drop the fresh tomatoes into a pan of boiling water and remove them after 15 seconds. Run them under cold water, and with a small, sharp knife, peel them. Cut out the stems, then slice the tomatoes in half crosswise. Squeeze the halves gently to remove the seeds and juices, and chop the tomatoes coarsely. (Canned tomatoes only need to be drained and chopped.)

Shell the shrimp but leave the last shell segment and tail attached to the body of the shrimp. With a small, sharp knife, devein the shrimp by making a shallow incision down their backs and lifting out the intestinal vein with the point of the knife. Wash the shrimp under cold running water and pat them dry with paper towels. Set aside.

In a heavy 10- to 12-inch skillet or shallow casserole, heat the oil over moderate heat until a light haze forms above it. Add the onions and, stirring frequently, cook for 5 minutes, or until they are soft and transparent but not brown. Stir in the tomatoes, wine, 1 tablespoon of the parsley, the oregano, salt and a few grindings of pepper. Bring to a boil and cook briskly, uncoverd, until the mixture thickens to a light purée. Add the shrimp and cook over moderate heat for 5 minutes. When the shrimp are pink and firm to the touch, stir in the cheese, taste for seasoning and sprinkle the top with the remaining tablespoon of parsley. Serve directly from the skillet or casserole. Customarily, the shrimp are accompanied by crusty loaves of bread.

Tangy *retsina* complements the rich shrimp dish called *garides me saltsa.*

To serve 6 to 8

1/4 cup olive oil
1/2 cup finely chopped onions
1/4 cup finely chopped scallions, including 2 inches of the green tops
2 pounds fresh spinach, washed, thoroughly drained and finely chopped
1/4 cup finely cut fresh dill leaves, or substitute 2 tablespoons dried dill weed
1/4 cup finely chopped parsley, preferably flat-leaf parsley
1/2 teaspoon salt
Freshly ground black pepper
1/3 cup milk
1/2 pound *feta* cheese, finely crumbled
4 eggs, lightly beaten
1/2 pound butter, melted
16 sheets (1/2 pound) *filo* pastry, each about 16 inches long and 12 inches wide

Spanakopita

SPINACH-CHEESE PIE

In a heavy 10- to 12-inch skillet, heat the olive oil over moderate heat until a light haze forms above it. Add the onions and scallions and, stirring frequently, cook for 5 minutes, or until they are soft and transparent but not brown. Stir in the spinach, cover tightly, and cook for 5 minutes. Then add the dill, parsley, salt and a few grindings of pepper and, stirring and shaking the pan almost constantly, cook uncovered for about 10 minutes, or until most of the liquid in the skillet has evaporated and the spinach has begun to stick lightly to the pan. Transfer the spinach mixture to a deep bowl and stir in the milk. Cool to room temperature, then add the cheese and slowly beat in the eggs. Taste for seasoning.

Preheat the oven to 300°. With a pastry brush, coat the bottom and sides of a 12-by-7-by-2-inch baking dish with melted butter. Line the dish with a sheet of *filo,* pressing the edges of the pastry firmly into the corners and against the sides of the dish. Brush the entire surface of the pastry with about 2 or 3 teaspoons of the remaining butter, spreading it all the way to the outside edges and lay another sheet of *filo* on top. Spread with another 2 or 3 teaspoons of butter and continue constructing the pie in this fashion until you have used 8 layers of the *filo* in all.

With a rubber spatula, spread the spinach mixture evenly over the last layer of *filo* and smooth it into the corners. Then place another sheet of the *filo* on top, coat with butter, and repeat with the remaining layers of *filo* and butter as before. Trim the excess pastry from around the rim of the dish with scissors. Brush the top of the pie with the remaining butter and bake in the middle of the oven for 1 hour, or until the pastry is crisp and delicately browned. Cut into squares and serve hot or at room temperature.

To serve 4

A 3- to 3 1/2-pound chicken, cut into 8 serving pieces
Salt
Freshly ground black pepper
4 tablespoons butter
1/4 cup olive oil
1 1/2 cups finely chopped onions
1 tablespoon finely chopped garlic
6 fresh, ripe tomatoes, preferably plum tomatoes, peeled, seeded and finely chopped *(see garides me saltsa, page 61),* or substitute 1 cup chopped, drained, canned plum tomatoes
2 tablespoons tomato paste
1/2 cup chicken stock, fresh or canned
1 four-inch-long cinnamon stick
Freshly grated *kefalotiri* or Parmesan cheese

Kota Kapama

BRAISED CHICKEN IN TOMATO AND CINNAMON SAUCE

Pat the chicken completely dry with paper towels and season the pieces liberally with salt and a few grindings of pepper. In a heavy 10- to 12-inch skillet, melt the butter in the oil over moderate heat. When the foam begins to subside, add the chicken a few pieces at a time, starting them skin side down and turning them with tongs. Regulate the heat so that the chicken colors quickly and evenly. As the pieces brown, transfer them to a plate.

Pour off all but a thin film of fat from the skillet and add the onions and garlic. Stirring frequently, cook for 8 to 10 minutes, or until the onions are lightly colored. Stir in the tomatoes, tomato paste, chicken stock, cinnamon stick, 1/2 teaspoon of salt and a few grindings of pepper. Bring to a boil, then return the chicken to the skillet and baste it thoroughly with the sauce. Reduce the heat to low, cover tightly and simmer, basting occasionally, for about 30 minutes, or until the chicken is tender. Taste for seasoning.

To serve, arrange the pieces of chicken attractively on a heated platter and spoon the sauce over them. Or serve, as is often done in Greece, with any type of cooked hot pasta. Mound the pasta in the middle of a deep platter and ladle the sauce over it, tossing the strands about to coat them evenly. Arrange the chicken around the pasta and serve at once, accompanied by freshly grated *kefalotiri* or Parmesan cheese.

Spinach, *feta* cheese and eggs go into flaky *spanakopita (opposite).*

To serve 8

A 6½- to 7-pound leg of lamb, trimmed of excess fat but with the fell (the parchmentlike covering) left on
1 large garlic clove, peeled and cut lengthwise into 8 thin slivers
1 teaspoon oregano, crumbled
2 teaspoons salt
Freshly ground black pepper
6 tablespoons fresh lemon juice
2 medium-sized onions, peeled and thinly sliced
1 cup boiling water
2 cups (about 1 pound) *orzo* (rice-shaped pasta)
½ cup canned tomato purée
Freshly grated *kefalotiri* or imported Parmesan cheese

Giouvetsi

ROAST LEG OF LAMB WITH ORZO

Preheat the oven to 450°. With the tip of a small, sharp knife, make 8 quarter-inch-deep incisions on the fat side of the lamb and insert a sliver of garlic in each. Combine the oregano, 1 teaspoon of the salt, and a few grindings of pepper and press the mixture firmly all over the surface of the lamb. For the most predictable results, insert a meat thermometer into the thickest part of the leg, being careful not to let the tip touch any fat or bone.

Place the leg, fat side up, on a rack in a shallow roasting pan and roast it uncovered in the middle of the oven for 20 minutes. Reduce the heat to 350°, baste the leg with a tablespoon or so of lemon juice, and scatter the onions in the bottom of the pan. Roast for 15 minutes more, then baste the lamb again with another tablespoon of lemon juice and pour the cup of boiling water over the onions. Basting periodically with the remaining lemon juice, continue roasting for another 40 to 60 minutes, or until the lamb is done to your taste. A meat thermometer will register 130° to 140° for rare, 140° to 150° for medium, and 150° to 160° for well done. (The Greeks prefer well-done lamb.)

Meanwhile, bring 2 quarts of water and the remaining teaspoon of salt to a boil over high heat. Pour in the *orzo* in a slow thin stream so that the water does not stop boiling, and cook briskly for about 10 minutes until the *orzo* is tender but still slightly resistant to the bite. Drain in a sieve or colander.

When the leg of lamb is done, place it on a large heated platter and let it

Pungent garlic and oregano make *giouvetsi* a distinctively Greek roasted leg of lamb, here served with *orzo,* a rice-shaped pasta.

rest at room temperature for 10 or 15 minutes for easier carving.

Meanwhile, pour off all but a thin film of fat from the roasting pan. Stir the tomato purée into the onions, scraping in any brown particles clinging to the bottom and sides of the pan. Stir in the *orzo,* return the pan to the middle shelf of the oven and bake uncovered for 10 to 15 minutes until the *orzo* is heated through. Taste for seasoning.

To serve, mound the *orzo* around the leg of lamb and pass the grated cheese separately to be sprinkled over the pasta.

Bakaliaro Tighanito

DEEP-FRIED COD

To serve 4

- 2½ pounds salt cod
- 3 cups flour
- 2 cups lukewarm water (110° to 115°)
- ½ teaspoon baking soda
- ½ teaspoon salt
- Vegetable oil or shortening for deep-fat frying
- *Skordalia* (garlic-and-potato sauce, *below*), or substitute 2 lemons, each cut lengthwise into 6 or 8 wedges

Starting a day ahead of time, place the cod in a glass, enameled or stainless-steel pan or bowl, cover it with cold water and soak for at least 12 hours, changing the water 3 or 4 times. Drain the cod, rinse under cold running water, and cut it into pieces about 2 inches long and 1 inch wide.

An hour or so before you plan to serve the cod, make the batter. In a large mixing bowl, combine 2 cups of the flour, the warm water, baking soda and salt and, with a large spoon, mix to a fairly smooth cream but do not overbeat. Then let the batter rest for about 1 hour at room temperature.

Preheat the oven to 200°. Line a large baking dish or pan with paper towels and set it aside. In a deep fryer, heat 3 to 4 inches of oil or shortening until it reaches a temperature of 375° on a deep-frying thermometer.

Pat the fish completely dry with paper towels. Dip the pieces, one at a time, into the remaining cup of flour and shake vigorously to remove any excess. Six or 7 pieces at a time, drop the fish into the batter, and when thoroughly coated, lift them out with tongs and deep-fry them for 5 or 6 minutes, turning them over frequently until they are golden brown. Transfer them to the lined dish and keep them warm in the oven while you fry the remaining fish. Serve hot, accompanied by *skordalia* or garnished with lemon wedges.

Skordalia

GARLIC-AND-POTATO SAUCE

To make about 1 cup

- 1 large or 2 small baking potatoes (about 1 pound), peeled and cut into small pieces
- 1 tablespoon finely chopped garlic
- 1 teaspoon salt
- 1 egg yolk
- 8 to 12 tablespoons olive oil
- 2 tablespoons fresh lemon juice
- White or freshly ground black pepper

Drop the potatoes into enough lightly salted boiling water to cover them completely and cook briskly until they show no resistance when pierced with the point of a small, sharp knife. Drain and return the potatoes to the pan. Shake the pan constantly over moderate heat for a minute or so until the potatoes are completely dry. Then mash them to a smooth purée.

With a large mortar and pestle or the back of a spoon, mash the garlic and salt together to a fine paste. Add the warm mashed potatoes a little at a time, stirring and mashing vigorously until the ingredients are well combined. Beat in the egg yolk, then the oil, a tablespoon or so at a time, making sure each addition of oil is absorbed before adding more. The mixture will absorb from 8 to 12 tablespoons of oil, depending on the texture of the potatoes.

Beat in the lemon juice, taste and add as much pepper and salt as you think it needs. The sauce should be highly seasoned and dense enough to hold its shape almost solidly in a spoon. If you prefer a thinner sauce, beat in a little lukewarm water a few drops at a time. *Skordalia* is traditionally served with fried or broiled seafood or with cold sliced beets.

Domates Yemistes me Rizi

BAKED TOMATOES STUFFED WITH RICE

To serve 6

1¼ cups water
½ cup uncooked long- or medium-grained rice
6 firm ripe tomatoes, each about 3 inches in diameter
2 teaspoons salt
6 tablespoons olive oil
½ cup finely chopped onions
¾ cup canned tomato purée
½ cup finely chopped parsley, preferably flat-leaf parsley
2 tablespoons finely cut fresh mint, or substitute 1 tablespoon dried mint
2 teaspoons finely chopped garlic
¼ teaspoon oregano, crumbled
Freshly ground black pepper

In a small saucepan, bring 1 cup of water to a boil over high heat. Pour in the rice in a slow thin stream, stir once or twice, and cook briskly uncovered for 8 minutes, or until the rice is softened but still somewhat resistant to the bite. Drain the rice in a sieve and set aside.

Cut a ¼-inch slice off the stem ends of the tomatoes and set aside. With a spoon, hollow out the tomatoes, remove the inner pulp and discard the seeds. Chop the pulp and set it aside. Sprinkle the tomato cavities with 1 teaspoon of salt and turn them upside down on paper towels to drain.

Preheat the oven to 350°. Make the stuffing in the following fashion: In a heavy 10- to 12-inch skillet, heat the oil over moderate heat until a light haze forms above it. Add the onions and, stirring frequently, cook for 5 minutes, or until they are soft and transparent but not brown. Stir in the rice, tomato pulp, ½ cup of the tomato purée, the parsley, mint, garlic, oregano, the remaining teaspoon of salt and a few grindings of pepper. Stirring constantly, cook briskly until most of the liquid in the pan evaporates and the mixture is thick enough to hold its shape almost solidly in the spoon.

Arrange the tomatoes, cut side up, in a baking dish large enough to hold them side by side. Fill the tomatoes with the stuffing, packing it in firmly, and cover each tomato with its reserved top. Combine the remaining ¼ cup of tomato purée with the remaining ¼ cup of water and pour the mixture around the tomatoes. Bake uncovered in the middle of the oven for 20 minutes, basting the tomatoes once or twice with the cooking liquid. Cool to room temperature and serve the tomatoes directly from the baking dish.

Anginares a la Polita

ARTICHOKES WITH DILL SAUCE

To serve 6

½ cup fresh lemon juice
¼ cup flour
1 cup water
6 medium-sized artichokes
1 cup olive oil
½ cup finely chopped onions
¼ cup finely cut fresh dill, or substitute 1 tablespoon dried dill weed
2 teaspoons salt

In a large, deep bowl, beat the lemon juice and flour together with a whisk or spoon, add the water and beat to a smooth thin paste. Set aside.

With a small, sharp knife, trim ⅛ inch off the stem end of each artichoke and peel the tough outer skin from the remaining stem. Snap off the small bottom leaves and any bruised or discolored outer leaves. Lay each artichoke on its side, grip it firmly, and with a large knife slice about 1 inch off the top. Spread the top leaves apart gently and pull out the inner core of thistlelike yellow leaves. With a long-handled spoon, scrape out the hairy choke inside. Drop the artichokes into the lemon-juice mixture, turning them about to coat them evenly and let them soak while you make the sauce.

Heat the olive oil over moderate heat in a shallow enameled or stainless-steel casserole large enough to hold the artichokes comfortably. Add the onions and cook for 5 minutes, or until they are soft and transparent but not brown. Drain the artichoke soaking liquid into the casserole, add the dill and salt and, stirring constantly, bring to a boil over high heat.

Lay the artichokes side by side in the sauce and baste them thoroughly. Reduce the heat to low, cover tightly, and simmer for 20 minutes. Then turn the artichokes over and, basting occasionally, simmer 25 minutes longer, or until their bases show no resistance when pierced with the point of a small knife. Remove from the heat and let the artichokes cool to room temperature. To serve, arrange on a platter and spoon the sauce over them.

A crusty loaf contrasts with the luscious texture of rice-stuffed tomatoes.

III

A Treasury of Turkish Delights

Seated like guests in the color-drenched stall of a rug merchant in Istanbul, Turkey, shopping tourists sip sweet, black coffee and water served by the merchant as they examine a copy of a prayer rug. Mixing coffee and business in this way is a custom throughout the Middle East where refreshments are essential preliminaries to any business transaction.

It may be that the best way to gauge the amazing range and quality of Turkish food is to go to Turkey, as we did, as tourists in the charge of fairly affluent hosts with an interest in good eating. The food we were offered by our hosts was hardly, I suppose, what every Turk eats every day, but in its scope and lavishness it encompassed Turkish cuisine at its finest. A typical evening feast, for example, would begin with an hors d'oeuvre of small, really ripe tomatoes, cut ingeniously to look like tight-petaled roses, and tiny fresh green chilies. Further to whet the appetite, there were thin slices of dark brown *pastirma,* a heavily spiced dried-beef delicacy often called, with Muslim irony, "Turkish bacon." (As good Muslims, Turks are forbidden to eat pork.) *Pastirma* is akin to the "pastrami" familiar in many parts of the United States; the Turkish way of making it is to start with a good cut of beef, add the sharpness of paprika and the lemony tang of cumin and garlic, then let the meat "cook" in the sun for weeks.

Other appetizers were more substantial. One consisted of humble broad beans (also known as fava beans, horse beans or, more elegantly, as Windsor beans) boiled and served cold—but ennobled by being cooked at the last stage of their preparation in *pilaki,* a pinkish, savory mixture of chopped onions, carrots, parsley, dill and garlic stewed in olive oil and tomato sauce. Another, also served cold, was a form of the well-loved *dolma* of the Middle East—vine leaves stuffed in a variety of ways and rolled into thumb-sized, two-bite morsels *(Recipe Index).* The *dolma* we ate in Turkey always contained rice, often currants and pine nuts, sometimes ground meat, and a cook's choice blend of aromatics, including invigorating quantities of black pepper. (Fresh young vine leaves are best for the dish because of the fragrance they add, but preserved leaves in cans or jars make perfectly acceptable substitutes.) A similar mixture, without the meat, went into steamed or boiled stuffed mussels *(Recipe Index),* which were opened, cleaned and packed tight again without wrecking their lovely blue-black shells. Finally there was hot *börek,* a sheet of thin dough filled with cheese or seasoned meat, rolled up like *dolma,* and fried to crispness in butter or oil. In its most delicate form, *börek* is not much bigger than a cigarette and is called—in Turkish—just that: *sigara böreği (Recipe Index).*

By exercising stern self-restraint in the face of such temptations, I usually managed to arrive at the table still ready to eat—only to be overwhelmed by the number of courses. At one meal the first full course was Circassian chicken *(Recipe Index),* boiled, cut into bits and dressed with an unusual creamy sauce in which the oil and pulp of pounded walnuts predominated. Next came a cup of *düğün çorbasi*—"wedding soup"—a lemony, slightly thickened mixture of lamb or veal and vegetables cooked for hours in soupbone stock, rich, meaty but tart, and so elaborate that it is usually made only for matrimonial feasts *(Recipe Index).* Lamb was served as a main course, along with fresh scallions and small browned potatoes; the meat had been cooked in its own distinctive fat and did not taste at all repetitious after the mutton soup. For salad we were each served an artichoke in a tangy vinaigrette sauce; the vegetable was upended on the plate, with about six inches of stem stabbing festively upward. The next course, which I mistook for dessert, turned out to be another part of the main meal: a "water" *börek* (so named because the dough is scalded just long enough to turn it into a broad, tender noodle) enclosing a savory meat filling—probably lamb again, but seasoned to a different taste, and briefly baked under a generous coating of butter.

At last the time came for dessert. As I have said elsewhere, the Middle East has a collective sweet tooth, but in Istanbul we found ourselves on a high plateau of the confectioner's art. At one hospitable table or another we sampled *güllâç,* soft layers of thin dough boiled in milk and enhanced with softly sweet rose water, and *sariği burma,* a cake with the texture of a doughnut, but twisted to look like a turban. Both were topped with *kaymak,* an incredibly rich clotted cream extracted from six times its volume of milk. (The word *kaymak* doubles as a flattering description of a pretty girl.)

There are many sweet shops in Istanbul, their windows piled high with enticing merchandise. In one display I counted more than ten varieties of *helva* (the Turkish spelling), all of them delectable. My wife was delighted to find trays of *kurabiye,* a rich butter cookie that she herself bakes at home, with a whole clove in each morsel and a thorough final dusting of powdered sugar. We feasted our eyes on golden, diamond-shaped *baklava (Recipe Index),* and on cubes of chewy *lokum* (a confection known in the United States as "Turkish delight"), with starch-and-sugar coatings to keep them separate from one another and offer a dry surface to the grasp of eager fingers.

To my own delight, the Turks have often been inspired to metaphor in the naming of some of their dainties. The "vizier's finger," for example, is an elongated sweet roll fried crisp in olive oil, admonitory to look at but not at all forbidding to the palate. Two other sweets bear downright erotic names: "sweetheart's lips," which are fried cookies made of rounds of nut-filled

Langouste, a variety of lobster, is the choice of most of this cosmopolitan group dining at an Istanbul restaurant on a pier under the Galata Bridge, which spans the fabled Golden Horn. The spires and dome in the distance are those of the Sülemaniye Mosque, Istanbul's largest and one of its landmarks.

dough folded to suggest a mouth, and "lady's navel" *(Recipe Index)*, a fritter with a dimple in the middle and sometimes a dab of *kaymak* in the dimple.

My picture of Turkey's lavish food often comes to a focus in the memory of one or another great meal. One was a splendid banquet served in a villa on the Bosporus: a "lunch" that lasted until 4 o'clock in the afternoon and left us logy but content. It was a chilly spring day, and our hosts' home, built some 70 years ago as a *yali,* or waterfront summer "cottage," had no central heating. There were two portable electric heaters, but a bar provided vodka, to help fight the chill. Later, Turkish wines were served, a delicate white and somewhat fruity red, and that also helped regulate our personal thermostats. So did the animated conversation. From the handsome, dark-eyed woman at my left I learned a Turkish saying: "When a moment of silence falls during a meal, somewhere a girl is born." Surely, only boys were born that afternoon.

The main dish of that meal was a spring lamb, roasted whole to a crisp and crackling brown and brought in on a tray by two men, who displayed it for all to see. An expert carver deftly took over, and I was served an ample part of the loin, tender, moist (but not pink) and uncomplicated by fancy seasonings. It was salted throughout in exactly the right proportions, as was every dish we tried in Turkey; the Turks rightly believe that merely shaking salt over the surface of cooked food does little for the rest of it.

After the flesh, the lamb's brains were served in small slices. I ate my bit and enjoyed its delicate flavor and smooth, buttery texture; Muriel, for her part, asked for the tongue and got it. Moments later someone, at her re-

Istanbul is a city of coffee houses. At establishments like the Pierre Loti *(above),* Turkish men gather to gossip, to play a leisurely game of *tavla,* or backgammon, to smoke the water pipes called narghiles—and even to conduct business.

quest, scraped the tidbits from the lower jaw into her plate—but afterward, when I teased her about eating an animal's gums, she looked astonished.

As we left the villa, the butler called her back and handed her, with a gracious bow, a "souvenir" wrapped in paper napkins. It was the lamb's jawbone.

One Sunday morning in Istanbul we slept late in our hotel room, ordered breakfast sent up, and chatted about the contrasts among old and new ways of Turkish life—contrasts in such diverse areas as food, work and leisure, and the very language itself. Turkish has borrowed a number of words from English and French for use in contemporary times: *telefon,* both *otomatik* and *manüel, tren* (train) and *polis* (police). We had crossed the Bosporus on the *feribot;* and from menus we had gleaned *omlet, sandviç, kakao* (cocoa), *çikolata* (chocolate), *bisküvit* (biscuit) and *greypfrut.*

These borrowings are a relatively recent phenomenon, which may be related to a change in the written Turkish language. Until the 1920s, Turkish was written in the beautiful but difficult Arabic script. Then Kemal Atatürk, the statesman who deposed the last sultan, adopted a modified form of the Roman alphabet as one part of his all-out program of Westernization. Atatürk campaigned against the feminine custom of wearing the veil; one rarely sees the veil today in Turkish cities, though it is still common in provincial regions. He also ordered men to discard their traditional fezzes and wear hats with brims, in the Western style.

Atatürk made Sunday the official day of rest, replacing the Muslim Friday (actually, Friday had never been seriously observed as a respite from work, perhaps because the Muslim faith maintains that the Almighty could not possibly have suffered fatigue as a result of the Creation). Thus it was that on this Sunday—after our breakfast of toast spread with a fragrant, deep amber domestic honey—we went out to mingle with the streams of people and see what they were eating on their day off. Vendors carried trays of cakes on their heads. Others sold slices of hot *kokoreç,* made from the innards of young lamb wrapped in a coil of intestines and grilled on a spit. Now and then a lad worked his way through the crowd to deliver a glass of tea or coffee, carrying it on a disclike tray suspended from three chains and never spilling a drop. Shoeshine boys sat beside boxes extravagantly ornamented with shiny brass studs and fancifully shaped finials.

Modern Turkish traffic is suicidal, and I never mastered the trick of crossing a thoroughfare through streams of cars that flowed past, bumper to bumper. The Turks, on the other hand, face this problem with complete aplomb, and cross their streets with hardly a look at the cars. One heroic man, carrying a huge sack of flour and dusted from head to foot by his work, stepped off the curb, lifted one whitened finger as a signal, and safely made it to the bakery across the street. Made uneasy by the sight, we turned away from modern Turkey for a spell, in search of another kind of scene—the older, more leisurely world of the Ottoman Turks.

We took a cab to the old part of Istanbul, where many of Turkey's historical treasures can still be seen. Our objective was the enormous palace complex of Topkapi Saray, where the Ottoman sultans once lived in splendor with their courtiers and harems. Among the most impressive parts of the palace are the rooms in which the imperial treasures are displayed. One coffee service flashes with thousands of diamonds set into the pot and the cups and saucers; I could barely imagine anyone using it, though many diners surely had. Only slightly less extravagant are the spoons once used by ladies of the court: some have handles of polished coral and bowls of ivory, tortoise shell, mother-of-pearl or solid gold.

The imperial kitchens at Topkapi are divided into 10 sections, each a large, clean, thick-walled rectangle with its own specialty—soup, bread, meat and so forth. From the outside the kitchen sections line up like a row of gigantic Turkish artichokes—actually, a row of separate dome-roofed little buildings topped by the stalks of chimneys. Inside, one sees heavy old balances for measuring food in bulk, cauldrons three feet in diameter and covered pans of similar proportions. Using these implements, a staff of about 200 fed 3,000 to 5,000 people daily, and as many as 10,000 on holidays.

No one knows exactly what was prepared in these kitchens. The palace archives give no recipes—and the cooks of that day may not have been able to read—but some idea of the cuisine may be gained from the list of kitchen stores purchased in a single year, 1640. Meat was pre-eminent, at 1,131 tons. The spinach ordered came to 92 tons; carrots, evidently not in favor, to less than a ton; and a category of unspecified "vegetables" to 94 tons. In a feat of caterer's accounting, separate entries were made for 320,350 heads of lettuce and 11,720 cabbages. Rice far outstripped wheat, 265 tons to 3. Among dairy products, 14 tons of yoghurt were listed, and 4 of cheese, along with 2,720 plates of *kaymak.* Egg purchases exceeded 18,000 dozen. And tartness apparently won out over sweetness, with 59 tons of vinegar and 19 of lemons

A vendor on a street in Istanbul totes a tank of *visne*—sour-cherry juice thickened with sugar—and a jug of water to mix to order for a customer. Such walking refreshment stands and their mysteriously elaborate equipment add color to streets throughout the Middle East.

against 10 tons of sugar (a golden abundance of honey probably corrected the imbalance, but does not appear in the record).

As for the dishes made from these ingredients, the mystery remains. Written menus of the time indicate that the soup chef alone had nearly 40 soups in his repertoire, but the very names of many of these soups, surviving in the Arabic writing of that day, have no equivalents in modern Turkish and defy translation. Some of the dishes must have been magnificent, if only for their audacity. We are told, for instance, that gold and precious stones were pulverized and added to the sultans' more ambitious cooking. Other dishes represented humbler fare for the thousands serving the sultan. Among those living on the sultan's bounty were the Janissaries, an elite, privileged troop of soldiers made up of Christian boys taken from their families and brought up as ferocious, war-hungry Muslims. An old print shows the Janissaries lined up in a forecourt of the palace, awaiting their mess call and their meal of soup and *pilav* cooked in huge iron kettles. The kettles played an unusual role in Turkish history. As the Janissaries grew in numbers and power, they took to upsetting these pots and beating on the bottoms with wooden spoons whenever they pressed for change in official policy, and they usually got their way. At last, in 1826, Sultan Mahmud II trained cannon on their barracks and blasted the corps out of existence.

It is more pleasant, in this royal precinct, to think back to the *lâle devri* or Tulip Period in the time of Sultan Ahmed III, who reigned from 1703 to 1730 (and died in jail a few years later, a victim of the unruly Janissaries). In his heyday this sensitive sovereign dined in a way that makes one daydream of being his guest. When the April moon was full and floods of tulips burst into bloom in the palace garden, Sultan Ahmed's table was set on a balcony overlooking an opulent scene. Lamps were hung about, along with caged canaries and glass globes filled with colored water. Sometimes whirling dervishes entertained the sultan with their madly spinning dance, or girls played catch with a golden ball. And lumbering among the tulip beds were turtles by the hundreds, each with a lighted candle mounted on its shell.

It was midafternoon when we emerged from Topkapi. Passing a street vendor, we bought two round buns fresh from the oven, one crisp as an American hard roll and studded with sesame seeds, the other soft and puffy as a dumpling; for a sweet, we also bought a sticky nougat edged with sugar wafers. We strolled away munching, and that was lunch—a way of saving our appetites for what lay ahead.

Having had so much of Turkey's finest cooking in private homes, we planned now to visit the city's restaurants and try more ordinary fare, the authentic dishes of average Turks. We already knew that finding them might be difficult in Westernized Turkey. As in Greece, we quickly learned not to rely on hotel kitchens for authentic native preparations—though once I ran into a curious turnabout involving a lowly hamburger. It was featured on the Americanized menu as a "Bosporus Burger," and I ordered it, specifying that it was to be cooked very rare. The headwaiter nodded agreeably—but the meat that came to the table was cooked through. I called him over and pointed this out. He seemed unable to understand how anyone could want to eat meat before it had lost every trace of color. What was more, he explained, the chef had mixed chopped veal with the beef, and worked in olive oil, onion juice and breadcrumbs—creating, in fact, a variant of *köfte,* the Turkish lamb or mutton patties broiled on skewers. "Nobody complains," he concluded.

There is good, truly Western cooking in Turkey, and the best is to be found at Istanbul's Dilson Hotel, where we were proudly shown through a newly instituted school for chefs and waiters.

A state banquet was to be held that night, and the chef and his students had done themselves proud for the event. They brought out roasted lambs with heads that sprouted tall antlers of sculptured butter, and eyes that were ringed by the pastry tube for additional decorative effect. They showed us fish with icings of mayonnaise and frillwork of shrimps along their sides; chickens under a snow-white *velouté* sauce prettied up with snips of carrot and green pepper in floral patterns; and ducks covered with a light brown glaze that blossomed with citrus-peel flowers in various colors.

Escoffier surely would have cheered, for the sophisticated dishes undoubtedly tasted as good as they looked. But what would the visiting dignitary of the evening have thought if he had hoped to taste real Turkish food? To be sure, the experienced maître d'hôtel at the Dilson declared vehemently that Turkey had to overcome its reputation for "primitive" cooking and prove that it can turn out elegant Western fare. He spoke like a culinary Kemal Atatürk, and I understood why he felt so strongly, but what I wanted was not imitation Paris but real Turkey—the very unprimitive food that delights the visitor determined enough to go after it.

We sought and found that food in several small, inexpensive restaurants. The best ones look clean even from the outside: a peek through the windows reveals rows of spotless tables, usually covered with white tablecloths protected by sheets of white oilcloth. The service is never less than diligent; in some restaurants, the table is cleared after each course and a new setting of plates and flatware brought out for the next one.

For religious reasons, many of these eating places serve no alcoholic drinks—not even beer, which goes so splendidly with Turkish food. But this minor deprivation introduced me to a drink that suits equally well: the popular and refreshing *ayran,* which is simply yoghurt diluted with water and delicately salted. The taste resembles that of buttermilk and, like buttermilk, *ayran* leaves long, threadlike lines on the inside of the glass.

Among the dishes I liked best were the cooked vegetables that are served cold. They are stewed with olive oil, tomatoes, onions, in some cases garlic, and usually masses of minced parsley. In the interplay of these flavors, the tartness of the tomato and the palate-cleansing freshness of the parsley counterbalance any oiliness, which is present but never cloying. The artichokes and green beans prepared this way were particularly good, but supreme among these dishes was a succulent preparation based on eggplant and curiously named *imam bayildi*—"the imam fainted" *(Recipe Index).* It is variously explained that the imam, or Muslim holy man, lost consciousness as soon as he sniffed the fragrance of the great dish set before him, or that he gorged on it until he passed out. Both stories are plausible; the fact that the recipe calls for an extraordinary amount of garlic may also be significant.

Some Turkish foods, such as stuffed tomatoes and bell peppers, are meant to be eaten lukewarm after being cooled in the pot. This seems strange to an

An Istanbul vendor of lemonade cruises the streets carrying his product in a brass and glass backpack, its gleaming ornateness contrasting sharply with the simple and unhygienic serving equipment: a single glass and saucer, from which each customer takes his turn.

Continued on page 82

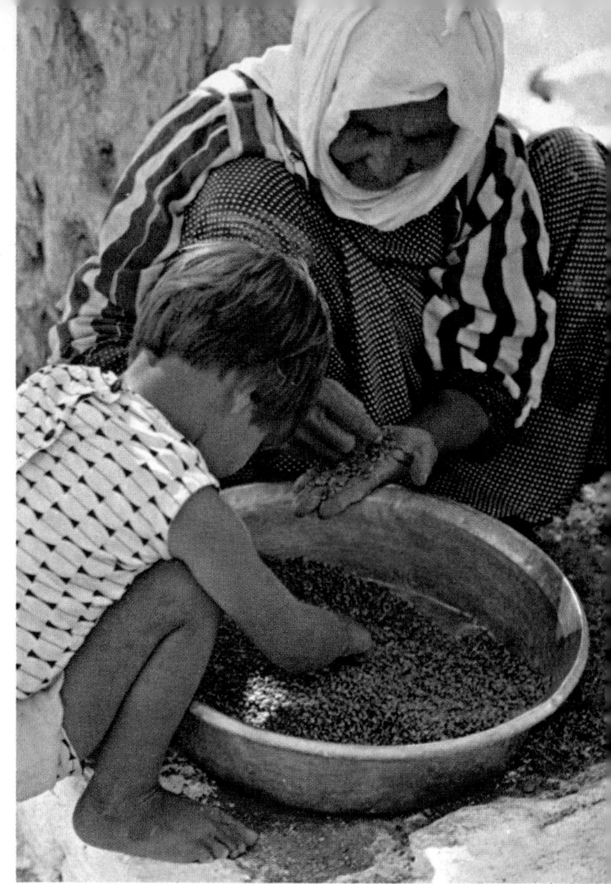

A Turkish Family's Feast and Party

Yasar Oral, a youth of the village of Bademler Koyu, about 33 miles southwest of Izmir, is leaving home to serve his compulsory military duty, and his family has planned a farewell feast and party for him. In preparation for the feast, Yasar's grandmother Fatma and his three-year-old sister Canan *(above)* pick over the wheat that will be ground into *burghul* for *pilavi,* a dish resembling rice *pilaf.* His mother Cicek, the woman of the house, is shown at left carrying wood for the oven in a wickerwork hamper; she will do most of the cooking and baking for the feast. This does not mean that the Orals are poor folk. Yasar's father Halil Oral, a 43-year-old tobacco grower, is a leading citizen of Bademler Koyu: he has served as *muhtar* (headman) of the village, and his family is one of the more affluent of the 200 living in the area. On their 280-acre farm the Orals grow not only tobacco, but enough grapes, vegetables, wheat and olives for their needs. When they interrupt their hard-working lives for a social occasion like this one, food is plentiful and spirits are high.

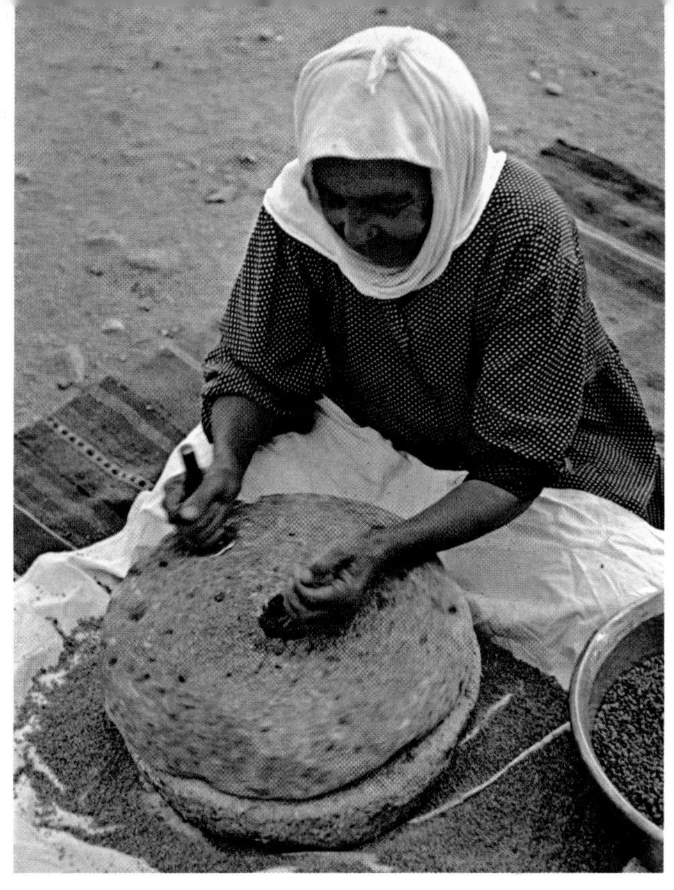

Grandmother Fatma, whose customary role in the preparation of the family's food is a supervisory one, has removed her jacket for the tedious job of grinding wheat for *burghul* on the day before the party *(left)*. Her stone handmill is little different from primitive ones, dating back to about 1000 B.C., that have been found in Mesopotamian excavations; by the time of the Hellenistic period, in the 4th and 3rd Centuries B.C., such mills had spread to the opposite end of the Fertile Crescent. To make the bread for the party, Cicek Oral *(below)* kneads wheat flour into a dough while her mother-in-law gradually adds water. The leavening agent or "starter" for her sour-dough bread is a lump of dough saved from a previous batch.

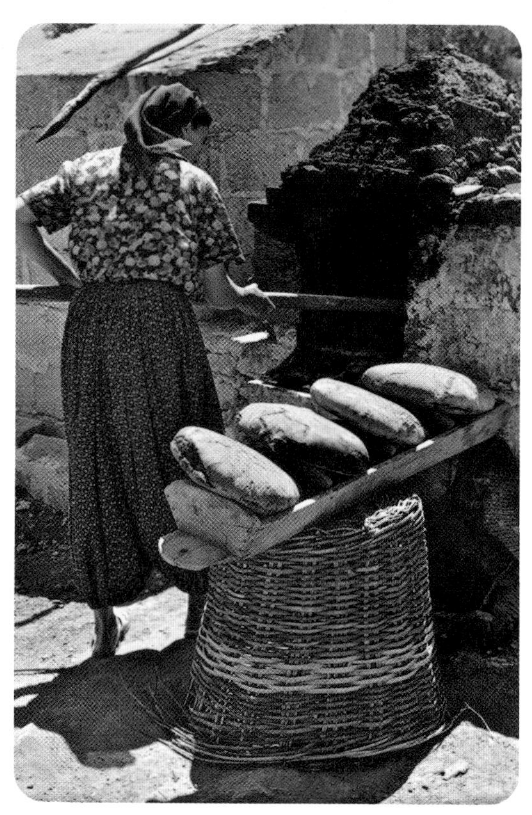

Using a long wooden paddle, Cicek adds more loaves to the outdoor oven to replace the ones she has just set out to cool on her overturned all-purpose hamper. Only part of this batch of bread is for the feast; the rest will last the family for several days. Light-textured, flavorful bread like this, made of wheat flour and leavened with yeast, has been a mainstay of the Middle East for millennia. The kind of salad that Cicek prepares for the party as Canan watches *(below)* is of lesser antiquity: it contains tomatoes and green peppers, both New World imports, along with onions and cucumbers. The party begins early, as the first guests to arrive join the Orals *(opposite)* for a 9 o'clock breakfast of bean soup, *burghul, pilavi,* fried eggplant, fried green peppers, grapes and bread—the last meal they will have before their feast in the afternoon.

At the party for Yasar, hosts and guests clap time to the music of a clarinet and a drum and Sezai Sagdic, one of the guests, performs a high-spirited folk dance. The amphora *(foreground)* holds water to refresh the dancers and players.

American at first, but the custom suits the climate and I quickly came to enjoy my meals that way. The stuffing for these dishes may be an elaborate vegetarian production involving a dozen ingredients, including rice, mint, dill, currants, allspice and a pinch of sugar, or it may emphasize mincemeat, butter rather than olive oil, a minimum of seasonings and only a little rice. The rice is prepared in an unusual and very flavorful way. The Turks often fry it raw with onions to begin with, giving it a savor that plain boiled rice lacks, no matter what other flavors it picks up from the tomato or the pepper.

Of the hot main courses we chanced upon, two stand out. One is *türlü güvec (Recipe Index),* a substantial country stew made like others the world over. Anything goes in. Pieces of lamb and sliced onions browned in butter, okra, zucchini, any other handy vegetables and the indispensable tomato are combined with just enough water to prevent burning, and baked, covered, for a couple of hours in a slow oven. It acquires its distinctively Turkish flavor from the lamb and local vegetables, as well as from the fact that, like most native dishes, it does not need a separate gravy or sauce but creates its own blend of juice in the pot.

Our second discovery was *döner kebab,* chunks of well-seasoned mutton or lamb stacked tightly on an upright spit that revolves in front of a charcoal fire. Alternating layers of fat insure moistness, and the spit turns slowly, so that some part of the meat's surface is always done well enough to be shaved off in thin slices. The knife used is about a yard long and murderous to look at, but what it delivers is blissful eating—tender strips of rich, dark mutton that satisfy the appetite they stimulate.

The standard way to end such meals is by sipping a tiny cup of hot, dark Turkish coffee. It was from Turkey that Europe first learned the pleasure of drinking coffee, in the 16th Century, and coffee remains one of the necessities of Turkish life. In earlier days, Turkish marriage vows included a promise by the bridegroom to keep his wife in coffee. How curious it is, then, to learn that when the first coffeehouse opened in Istanbul its stock in trade was quickly classified with wine, tobacco and opium as one of the Four Ministers of the Devil. Sultan Murad IV, who reigned from 1623 to 1640, is said to have executed 100,000 unfortunates who could not resist the Four. His edicts, happily, soon went the way of all Volstead Acts.

In our wanderings in old Istanbul we often went beyond restaurant-hunting to explore the fish, spice and flower markets in and near the so-called Egyptian Bazaar. This is a modern structure, dating from 1943, but it is adorned with the traditional cupolas of the Middle East, and occupies a site where spices, perfumes and drugs were traded many centuries ago. Walking toward it you find yourself in a true oriental bazaar, boisterous, colorful, uninhibited. You go past seafood stalls and restaurants, brushing by the waiters who politely but unabashedly urge you to come in for a fresh sea bass or a plate of pink boiled shrimp. One snack bar is set up on a small boat moored to the quayside; at the rail a cook presides over fish sizzling on a charcoal grill while his patrons sit facing the water and rocking gently with the swell. The stalls display the day's catch—whole small fish with gills flipped open in bright red proof of freshness, larger ones cut into steaks to be sold by the piece. I noted bonito, sea bass, bluefish, mackerel, many others I could not identify—and the prized *kalkan* or "shield," a pinkish-red flatfish marked by prominent knobs or bosses that justify its name. Someone has counted 129 edible kinds of seafood in the Bosporus, and it seemed every one of them was on display in the market every day.

The spice market bustled with hawking and haggling; shopkeepers were quick to run out and beg casual window-shoppers to step inside, and their invitations were hard to resist, for each store was fragrant with the haunting aromas of cinnamon and clove, thyme and mastic. Escaping from the spices, we looked at lovely tubs of white *peynir,* the Turkish cheese made of milk from cows and sheep, pleasantly bland when it is fresh, becoming drier and saltier as it ages. There was also *tulum,* a sharp cheese named after the goatskin in which it matures; it is usually crumbly and gray-white, but yellows if the original milk has a high butterfat content. Butcher shops displayed whole carcasses of sheep in their windows. We soon realized that the so-called spice market has become a hustling Oriental-style department store, with some stalls offering gaudy fabrics for sale, and even such antiseptic modern merchandise as electric refrigerators, kitchen ranges, hi-fi sets and phonograph records.

The fascinations of window-shopping in this exotic setting almost always held us until lunchtime, the perfect hour to find oneself in the Egyptian Bazaar with an appetite for seafood. Ours was best satisfied in the Pandeli restaurant, a widely known establishment whose proprietor, after moving his business to its present location, refused to advertise the new address, saying that his customers "will come to me wherever I am." They did indeed, and so did we, climbing up one flight from the street to a room designed to suit good eating. The walls were tiled in Turkish ceramics, with a crystal chandelier sparkling beneath a brightly colored, vaulted ceiling, and our table looked out over the crossroads where the Bosporus and the Golden Horn meet and tidal currents of pedestrians troop across the Galata Bridge.

Lunch at the Pandeli generally began with marine appetizers. We nibbled on *lakerda,* a salt-cured bonito much like the smoked salmon lox we buy back home, and on a tangy salted roe that had been dried and preserved in a wrapper of wax. There were also fresh boiled shrimp in a rich, lobster-flavored sauce. At one of our meals, no less than three fish courses followed. Two of them were new treats for us: first, deep-fried fillets of the *kalkan* we had seen in the stalls, a sort of turbot but possessing a unique flavor that sets it apart from its cousins, and second, *barbunya,* the small, tasty red mullet of the Eastern Mediterranean, pan-fried and served with a drizzle of olive oil. The third dish we knew well: swordfish *(Recipe Index).* In this case it was the preparation that was a surprise; the flesh had been cut in finger-thick squares, steeped in a marinade that held the bite of pepper, threaded on skewers with alternating bay leaves, and grilled over coals.

Invariably, we came away from the Pandeli knowing that we had eaten seafood at its best and freshest. There was never a need to apply any of the oft-repeated bits of advice to connoisseurs of good fish: make sure the scales are still snugged tight against the body, press a finger into the flesh and expect it to spring back, look the beast in the eye for signs of telltale cloudiness. Our criterion, one that every fish lover knows, was the sense of smell. For fish that smells the least bit fishy has been out of the water too long—and at Pandeli, the fish passed that test and every other.

CHAPTER III RECIPES

Çerkes Tavuğu

COLD SHREDDED CHICKEN WITH WALNUT SAUCE

To serve 6 to 8 as a first course

- A 3- to 3½-pound chicken, cut into 6 or 8 serving pieces
- 3 cups water
- 1½ teaspoons salt
- 1½ cups shelled walnuts
- ½ cup finely chopped onions
- 3 slices white homemade-type bread
- 1 teaspoon paprika
- Freshly ground black pepper
- 1 tablespoon finely chopped parsley, preferably flat-leaf parsley (optional)

In a 4- to 5-quart saucepan, combine the chicken, water and ½ teaspoon of the salt. Bring to a boil over high heat, reduce the heat to low, partially cover, and simmer for 30 minutes, or until the chicken is tender but not falling apart. Transfer the chicken to a plate, and boil the stock rapidly, uncovered, over high heat until reduced to 1½ cups.

Combine the walnuts, onions and stock in the jar of an electric blender and blend at high speed for 15 seconds. Add the bread, ½ teaspoon of the paprika, the remaining 1 teaspoon of salt and a few grindings of pepper, and blend at high speed until the mixture becomes a smooth purée.

(To make the walnut purée by hand, pulverize the nuts with a nut grinder or mortar and pestle. Transfer them to a bowl, add the onions, and, with the back of a spoon, mash them together to a smooth paste. Tear and shred the bread with a fork, then mash it into the nuts. Beat in the hot stock, a few tablespoons at a time, and continue beating until the mixture is smooth and thick enough to hold its shape almost solidly in a spoon.)

When the chicken is cool enough to handle, remove the skin with a small knife or your fingers and cut or pull the meat away from the bones. Discard the bones, and cut the chicken meat into strips about ⅛ inch wide and 1 to 1½ inches long. Place the chicken in a bowl and add 1½ cups of the walnut sauce, tossing the chicken about with a spoon to coat the pieces well.

Mound the chicken on a platter, mask the top with the remaining sauce, and sprinkle with ½ teaspoon of paprika. Garnish with parsley if desired.

NOTE: A more traditional garnish for *çerkes tavuğu* is made from paprika and the oil of ground walnuts. For this, pulverize ¼ cup of shelled walnuts with ½ teaspoon of paprika in a mortar and pestle. Place a spoonful of the mixture at a time in a garlic press, and squeeze the oil over the chicken.

Arnavut Ciğeri

LAMB'S LIVER WITH RED PEPPERS, ALBANIAN STYLE

To serve 4 as a first course

- 2 small onions, peeled, sliced ⅛ inch thick and separated into rings
- 1 tablespoon plus ¼ teaspoon salt
- ¼ cup finely chopped parsley, preferably flat-leaf parsley
- ¼ teaspoon crushed hot red pepper
- 1 pound lamb's liver, trimmed and cut into ½-inch cubes, or substitute 1 pound calf's liver, trimmed and cubed
- ¼ cup *raki*, or substitute any other anise-flavored apéritif such as *ouzo* or Pernod
- ¼ cup flour
- ¾ cup olive oil
- Freshly ground black pepper
- 2 long red Italian-type peppers, cut in half, deribbed, seeded and cut lengthwise into ⅛-inch-wide strips

Place the onion rings in a sieve or colander, sprinkle with 1 tablespoon of the salt, and turn them about with a spoon to coat them evenly. Let them rest at room temperature for 30 minutes, then rinse under warm running water and squeeze them gently but completely dry. In a large bowl, toss the onions, parsley and red pepper together until well mixed. Set aside.

Drop the liver into a bowl, pour in the *raki* and stir together for a few seconds. Then pour off the *raki*. Toss the liver and flour together in another bowl, place the liver in a sieve and shake through all the excess flour. In a heavy 10- to 12-inch skillet, heat the oil over high heat until a light haze forms above it. Add the liver and stir it about in the hot oil for 1 or 2 minutes, or until the cubes are lightly browned. Stir in the remaining salt and a few grindings of pepper. Transfer the liver to paper towels to drain.

Mound the liver in the center of a heated platter, arrange the onion-ring mixture and red pepper strips around it and serve at once.

Accompaniments for a milky *raki* apéritif include *(from top)* chicken with walnut sauce; stuffed mussels; stuffed grape leaves; and sautéed liver.

Midya Dolmasi

COLD STEAMED MUSSELS STUFFED WITH RICE AND PINE NUTS

To serve 10 to 12 as a first course

- 1 cup olive oil
- 3 cups finely chopped onions
- ½ cup pine nuts (pignolia)
- 1½ cups uncooked long- or medium-grain rice
- ¼ cup dried currants
- ½ teaspoon ground cinnamon
- ¼ teaspoon ground allspice
- 1 teaspoon salt
- 4 cups water
- 6 dozen mussels in their shells

In a heavy 10- to 12-inch skillet, heat the oil over moderate heat until a light haze forms above it. Add the onions and, stirring frequently, cook for 8 to 10 minutes, or until they are soft and lightly browned. Stir in the pine nuts, cook for 2 or 3 minutes, then add the rice, currants, cinnamon, allspice and salt. Pour in 2 cups of the water and bring to a boil over high heat, stirring constantly. Reduce the heat to low, cover tightly and simmer for 20 minutes, or until all the liquid has been absorbed by the rice. Set aside off the heat.

Meanwhile, scrub the mussels with a stiff brush or stainless-steel mesh scouring pad under cold running water. With a small, sharp knife, open them one at a time in the following fashion: Holding the mussel firmly in one hand, cut along the joint between the two shells, starting at the broadest end and leaving them hinged together at the narrow end. Carefully pry the mussel open and cut and pull off the black ropelike tufts from the shell.

Place about 1 tablespoon of the stuffing mixture in each mussel, close the shells and hold them firmly together by looping a short length of string around the center two or three times, then tying it tightly in place.

Arrange the mussels in two layers in a large, heavy casserole, pour in the remaining 2 cups of water and bring to a boil over high heat. Reduce the heat to low, cover tightly and steam for 20 minutes. Remove the cover and let the mussels cool to room temperature in the casserole.

Then remove the mussels from the casserole with a slotted spoon and cut off the strings. Discard the cooking liquid. Arrange the mussels on a large platter or individual serving plates and serve chilled or at room temperature.

Imam Bayildi

BRAISED EGGPLANT WITH TOMATOES AND ONIONS

To serve 6

- 3 medium-sized eggplants (about 1 pound each), as long and narrow as possible
- 4 tablespoons plus 2 teaspoons salt
- 6 medium-sized onions, peeled, sliced ⅛ inch thick and separated into rings
- 5 medium-sized fresh, ripe tomatoes, peeled, seeded and finely chopped *(see garides me saltsa, page 61)*, or substitute 1½ cups chopped, drained, canned tomatoes
- ½ cup olive oil
- 6 large garlic cloves, peeled
- 1 cup water
- 2 tablespoons finely chopped parsley, preferably flat-leaf parsley

With a sharp knife, cut off the stem and peel each eggplant lengthwise, leaving 4 evenly spaced 1-inch-wide strips of peel intact. Slicing between the strips, cut each one in half. Cut side up, make three or four 4-inch-long lengthwise slashes through the thickest part of each half, spacing the slashes about 1 inch apart. Sprinkle the eggplants with 1 tablespoon of the salt and arrange them in two or three layers in a large flat bowl or pan. Pour in enough cold water to cover them by 1 inch, weight with a heavy casserole, and let the eggplants rest at room temperature for at least 30 minutes.

Meanwhile, drop the onion rings into a large colander set in a deep plate. Sprinkle the onions with 3 tablespoons of the salt, turning them about with a spoon to coat them evenly. Let stand at room temperature for at least 30 minutes, then rinse the onions under warm running water and squeeze them gently but completely dry. Place them in a bowl, add the tomatoes and the remaining 2 teaspoons of salt and toss together thoroughly.

Pour 2 tablespoons of the oil into a heavy casserole large enough to hold the eggplants in one layer. Drain the eggplants, rinse them under cold water and pat dry with paper towels. Arrange the eggplants cut side up in the casserole. Force as much of the onion-tomato mixture as possible into the slashes and spread the rest on top. Place a garlic clove on each eggplant half, and sprinkle them with the remaining 6 tablespoons of oil. Pour in the cup of water and bring to a boil over high heat. Reduce the heat to low and simmer covered for 1 hour and 15 minutes, or until the eggplants are tender. Cool in the casserole to room temperature.

To serve, arrange the eggplants on a large platter or individual serving plates, spoon the cooking juices around them and sprinkle with parsley.

Kadin Budu

"LADY" MEATBALLS

To serve 4 as a first course (about 16 meatballs)

- 1 pound lean ground lamb or beef
- ½ cup finely chopped onions
- ¼ cup uncooked long- or medium-grain rice
- 1 tablespoon salt
- ½ teaspoon freshly ground black pepper
- 1 cup olive oil or vegetable oil
- 2 eggs, lightly beaten

Combine the meat, onions, rice, salt and pepper in a deep bowl. With a large spoon or your hands, mix the ingredients together and knead vigorously until they are well blended. A tablespoon at a time roll the mixture into balls about 1 inch in diameter and shape them into egglike ovals. In a heavy 12-inch skillet, bring 2 cups of water to a boil over high heat. Add the meatballs and return the water to the boil. Reduce the heat to low and simmer uncovered for 30 minutes, adding boiling water if necessary to keep the balls covered. With a slotted spoon, transfer the meatballs to a plate.

Pour the water from the skillet, add the oil in its place, and heat over moderate heat until a light haze forms above it. With tongs, dip the balls in the eggs and drop them into the hot oil. Fry the meatballs over high heat for 5 to 8 minutes until they brown on all sides. Drain on paper towels and serve.

Imam bayildi (the Imam fainted) got its name, one legend says, when a gourmet-priest swooned upon being denied the dish.

Pomegranate seeds provide a bright, edible adornment for *keşkul* (*recipe opposite*), a rich custard thickened with ground almonds and rice flour.

Sigara Böreği

DEEP-FRIED CHEESE-FILLED PASTRY "CIGARETTES"

To make 14

- 1 pound *tulum* (Turkish sheep's-milk cheese), or *feta* cheese
- ½ cup finely chopped parsley, preferably flat-leaf parsley
- 14 sheets *filo* pastry, each about 16 inches long and 12 inches wide
- 12 tablespoons butter, cut into ¼-inch bits and clarified (*see baklava, page 40*)
- 2 eggs, lightly beaten
- ⅓ cup milk
- Vegetable oil or shortening for deep frying

Crumble the cheese into a small bowl, add the parsley, and mash them together with a fork until blended into a smooth paste.

Assemble each *sigara* in the following fashion: Using a pastry brush, coat one sheet of *filo* pastry lightly but evenly with a teaspoon or so of the clarified butter. Fold the sheet in half lengthwise to make a two-layered rectangle about 16 inches long and 6 inches wide.

Place 2 tablespoons of the cheese mixture in the center of one short side of the rectangle, and, with the back of a spoon or a metal spatula, spread the cheese into a strip about 3 inches long and ½ inch wide reaching to within about ½ inch of the edge of the pastry.

Brush the outside edges of the pastry all around with another teaspoon or so of the butter, fold the long edges toward the center by about ½ inch and brush them again with butter. Fold the short end over the cheese filling and then roll up the pastry into a tight cylinder. The finished *sigara* will be about 5 or 6 inches long and 1 inch in diameter. Stir the beaten eggs and milk together, and brush the top, sides and ends of each pastry with the mixture.

In a heavy 12-inch skillet with a deep-frying thermometer, or an electric skillet, heat 1 or 2 inches of oil or shortening until it reaches a temperature of 375°. Fry 4 or 5 *sigaras* at a time, turning them once with a slotted spoon, for about 3 minutes, or until golden brown on all sides. As they brown, transfer them to paper towels to drain. Serve the *sigaras* hot, as a first course.

Keşkul

ALMOND AND RICE-FLOUR CUSTARD

To serve 6

2 cups light cream
2 cups milk
1 cup blanched almonds, pulverized in a blender or with a nut grinder or mortar and pestle
3/4 cup sugar
1/2 teaspoon almond extract
1/4 cup rice flour
1 tablespoon fresh pomegranate seeds
1 tablespoon finely chopped almonds
1 tablespoon finely chopped unsalted pistachio nuts

In a 2- to 3-quart saucepan, combine the cream, 1½ cups of the milk, the ground almonds, sugar and almond extract. Bring to a boil, remove the pan from the heat, cover, and let the almonds steep for 20 minutes. Strain the mixture through a fine sieve set over a bowl, pressing down hard on the almonds with the back of a spoon to extract their moisture before discarding them.

Return the almond-flavored liquid to the saucepan. Dissolve the rice flour in the remaining ½ cup of milk, stir it into the liquid and set the pan over low heat. Stirring frequently, simmer for about 15 minutes, or until the custard thickens enough to coat the spoon lightly. Strain through a fine sieve and spoon the custard at once into 6 individual dessert bowls. Chill in the refrigerator for about 1 hour. Before serving, garnish with pomegranate seeds ringed with circles of chopped almonds and pistachio nuts.

Kadin Göbeği

"LADY'S NAVEL" FRITTERS

To make about 2 dozen fritters

SYRUP
2 cups sugar
2 cups water
1/2 teaspoon fresh lemon juice

FRITTERS
1½ cups water
3 tablespoons butter
1/8 teaspoon salt
2 cups sifted all-purpose flour
3 eggs
Vegetable oil for deep frying
1 teaspoon almond extract
1/4 cup chilled heavy cream, stiffly whipped

To make the syrup, combine the sugar, 2 cups of water, and the lemon juice in a small saucepan and bring to a boil over moderate heat, stirring until the sugar dissolves. Increase the heat to high and cook briskly, uncovered, for 5 minutes, or until the syrup reaches a temperature of 220° on a candy thermometer. Set aside off the heat and let the syrup cool to room temperature.

In a heavy 2- to 3-quart saucepan, bring the 1½ cups of water, the butter and salt to a boil over high heat, stirring until the butter melts. Pour in the flour all at once, and beat vigorously with a wooden spoon until the mixture is blended and becomes an almost solid doughy mass. Immediately make a well in the center of the paste with the spoon. Break an egg into the well and beat vigorously until it has been absorbed. Beat in the remaining eggs, one at a time. The finished paste should be thick, smooth and shiny.

In a large deep-fat fryer with a frying thermometer, or an electric deep fryer, heat 3 to 4 inches of oil to a temperature of 360°. For each fritter, pinch off 2 tablespoons of dough and roll it into a ball 1 inch in diameter. Dip a thumb into the almond extract and press it into the center of the ball, making a depression ½ inch deep. In batches of 5 or 6, deep-fry the fritters for 10 to 12 minutes, turning them occasionally to brown them evenly. Plunge the browned fritters into the syrup, let them steep for 5 minutes, then transfer them to a platter and cool to room temperature. Before serving, drop a teaspoon of whipped cream into the depression in each fritter.

Kaymakli Elma Kompostosu

POACHED APPLES WITH WHIPPED CREAM

To serve 4

1 cup sugar
1 cup water
16 whole cloves
4 large firm cooking apples, peeled and cored
1/2 cup chilled heavy cream, stiffly whipped

In a heavy 3- to 4-quart saucepan, bring the sugar and water to a boil over high heat, stirring until the sugar dissolves. Firmly insert 4 cloves in a ring around the top of each apple. Place the apples side by side in the pan, baste with the syrup, reduce the heat to low, and cover. Basting occasionally, simmer for 15 minutes, or until the apples are tender. Cool them in the syrup. To serve, transfer the apples to individual dessert dishes. Pile whipped cream in the center of each apple and pour over it a tablespoon of the syrup.

Taking a Fish Apart – and Putting It Back Together

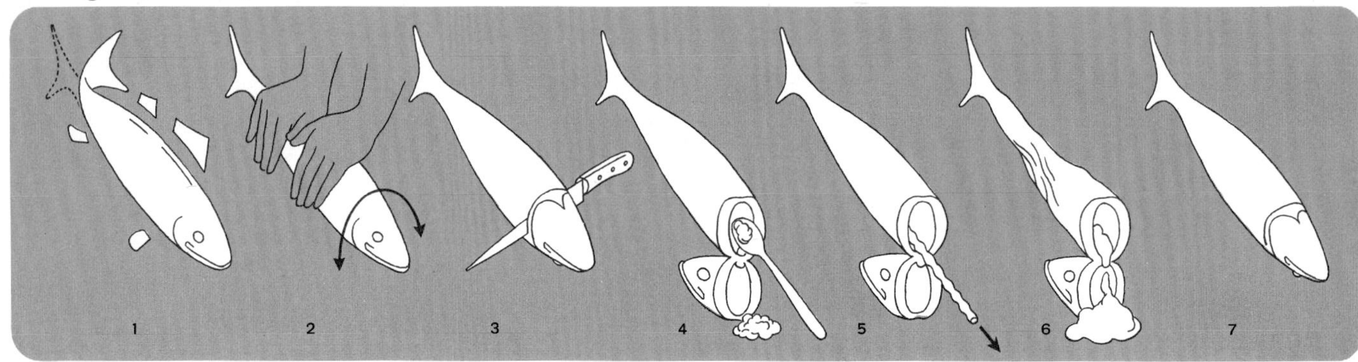

To prepare a mackerel for stuffing, trim off the protruding fins with scissors (1). Then break the backbone at the base of the tail by bending the tail sharply forward over the body. On a flat surface, roll the fish back and forth under the palms of your hands (2) for a few minutes to loosen the backbone. Turn the fish over and cut down through the throat just behind the gills (3), leaving the head attached by a hinge of skin about ½ inch wide. With a long-handled spoon (4), scoop out and discard the entrails. Wash the fish inside and out, then hold the body tightly and pull out the backbone (5). Starting from the tail, gently press the fish with your thumbs to push out as much flesh as possible (6), but keep the skin intact and the head attached so the fish can easily be reassembled (7).

An accompaniment of boiled carrots is served on a platter of *uskumru dolmasi* (baked stuffed mackerel), along with the garnish of tomatoes and lemon slices that has been baked with the fish. The raw apples are, by Turkish custom, a required conclusion to a fish meal. Until a diner eats his apple, say the Turks, "the fish will swim in his stomach."

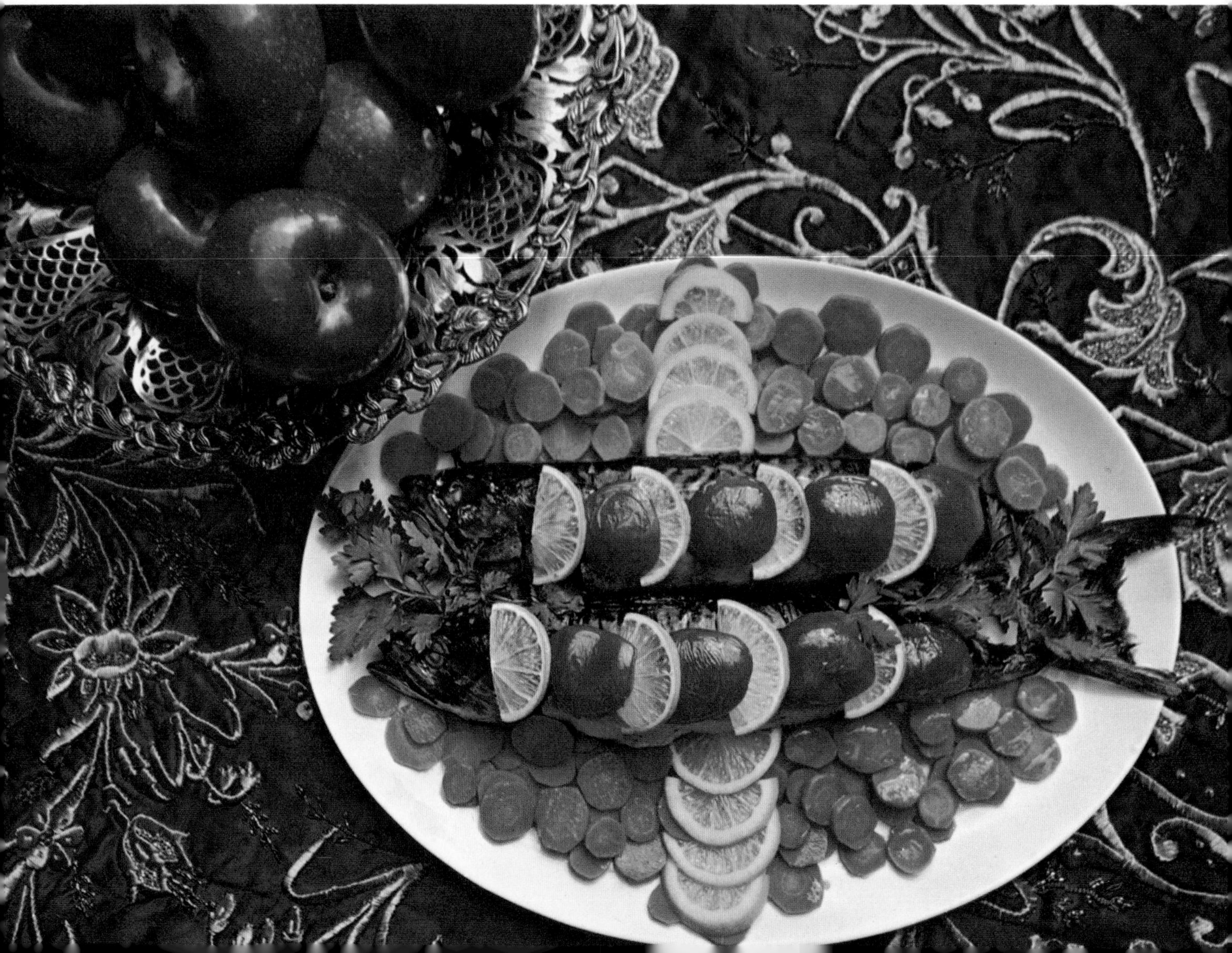

Uskumru Dolmasi

BAKED MACKEREL WITH PINE NUT, CURRANT AND HERB STUFFING

To serve 6

6 whole fresh mackerel, weighing about 12 ounces each
½ cup plus 2 teaspoons salt
½ cup plus 1 tablespoon olive oil
1 cup finely chopped onions
½ cup pine nuts (pignolia)
1 cup soft, fresh crumbs, made from homemade-type white bread, pulverized in a blender or torn apart and shredded with a fork
½ teaspoon coriander seeds
Freshly ground black pepper
½ cup finely chopped parsley, preferably flat-leaf parsley
½ cup finely cut fresh dill, or substitute ¼ cup dried dill weed
½ cup dried currants
4 to 6 medium-sized ripe tomatoes, sliced ¼ inch thick
3 lemons, sliced ⅛ inch thick
1 cup cold water

Clean and hollow out the mackerel, following the directions in the diagram at left. Place the fish in a bowl or pan large enough to hold them comfortably, sprinkle with ½ cup of the salt and cover them completely with cold water. Set aside at room temperature for about 30 minutes. Meanwhile place the fish meat in a sieve, wash under cold running water, drain and pat dry with paper towels. Set aside.

To make the stuffing, heat ½ cup of the olive oil in a heavy 12-inch skillet set over moderate heat. Add the onions and, stirring frequently, cook for 8 to 10 minutes, or until they are soft and lightly browned. Stir in the pine nuts, reduce the heat to low, and cook for another 2 or 3 minutes until they color lightly. Add the fish meat, crumbs, coriander, the remaining 2 teaspoons of salt and a few grindings of pepper. Stirring frequently, cook over low heat for about 5 minutes. Remove the pan from the heat, stir in the parsley, dill and currants, and cool to room temperature.

Preheat the oven to 450°. With a pastry brush and the remaining 1 tablespoon of olive oil, coat the bottom and sides of a flameproof baking dish large enough to hold the mackerel comfortably in one layer. Rinse the mackerel under cold running water, drain and pat them completely dry inside and out with paper towels. Using a long-handled spoon carefully fill each fish with about 1 cup of the stuffing mixture. Then pat the fish gently back to their original shape.

Arrange the mackerel side by side in the baking dish and garnish the top of each fish with a row of alternating tomato and lemon slices. Pour 1 cup of water around the mackerel and bring to a boil over high heat. Bake in the middle of the oven for 25 minutes, or until the fish feel firm when pressed lightly with a finger. Do not overcook.

Serve the fish at once directly from the baking dish or arranged on a large heated platter, and garnish with additional lemon slices. If you like, serve them with boiled, sliced carrots.

Zeytinyağli Pirasa

BRAISED LEEKS WITH RICE

To serve 4 to 6

2 pounds firm, fresh leeks, each approximately 1½ inches in diameter
¼ cup olive oil
1 cup finely chopped onions
1 teaspoon flour
1 teaspoon salt
½ teaspoon sugar
1½ cups water
3 tablespoons uncooked long- or medium-grain white rice
2 lemons, each cut lengthwise into 6 or 8 wedges

With a sharp knife, cut the roots from the leeks. Strip away any withered leaves and cut off and discard all but about 2 inches of the green tops. Then wash the leeks under cold running water, spreading the leaves apart to rid them of sand. Slice the leeks crosswise into 1-inch lengths, and set aside.

In a heavy 3- to 4-quart casserole, heat the oil over moderate heat until a light haze forms above it. Add the onions and, stirring frequently, cook for 5 minutes, or until they are limp and transparent but not brown. Stir in the flour, salt and sugar, cook for a minute or so, then add the water and raise the heat to high. Stirring constantly, cook briskly until the mixture comes to a boil and thickens lightly.

Add the rice and the leeks, turning them about with the spoon to coat them evenly with sauce. Reduce the heat to low, cover tightly and simmer for 30 minutes, or until the leeks and rice are tender but still intact. Taste for seasoning. Cool to room temperature and serve directly from the casserole, accompanied by the lemon wedges.

IV

In the Arab States, a Lavish Hospitality

Fifty-three of the countless varieties of Middle Eastern appetizers called *mazza* are displayed on a rooftop in the ancient Lebanese city of Sidon, with a Crusaders' castle, the Château de la Mer, in the background. The dishes range in complexity from raw tomatoes and cucumbers to a fried *kibbi* of seasoned lamb garnished with pine nuts *(third from bottom, left)*.

Lebanon, Syria, Jordan and Iraq form a tight Arabic hub at the center of the Middle East. Most of their peoples are devoutly Muslim; all are alike in spirit, in culture—and in cuisine. All four states are former vassals of the Ottoman Empire; taken together, they encompass the region called by historians the Fertile Crescent, where the first great civilizations of the Middle East were born and where man first learned to produce his own food.

We first explored Arabic cooking in Lebanon, the Mediterranean gateway to the three other states and a worldly place in comparison to the others, which are deeply Arabic. Short drives over good roads link three of the four capital cities: less than 70 miles inland from Lebanon's Beirut to Syria's Damascus, something over 100 to the south from Damascus to Jordan's Amman. From there, a quick jet flight takes you to Baghdad in Iraq, the eastern limit of the Arabic lands. The Z-shaped journey gives the traveler a full view of a fascinating cuisine, and by choosing selectively in each country he can enjoy a wide range of foods and eating customs.

Beirut, most accessible on the Mediterranean, was our starting point. The city is famous as an international playground, but it is also a busy seaport and banking center, for the Lebanese are entrepreneurs after the model of their seafaring ancestors, the Phoenicians, who traded in every corner of the ancient Mediterranean world. Famous from that time are the cedar forests of Lebanon, whose scented wood is said to have made up part of King Solomon's Temple in Jerusalem. Over the millennia the majestic groves have dwindled to a few hundred trees; the best-known stand, about 6,000 feet high in the Lebanon Mountains, now flourishes beside a Lebanese ski resort

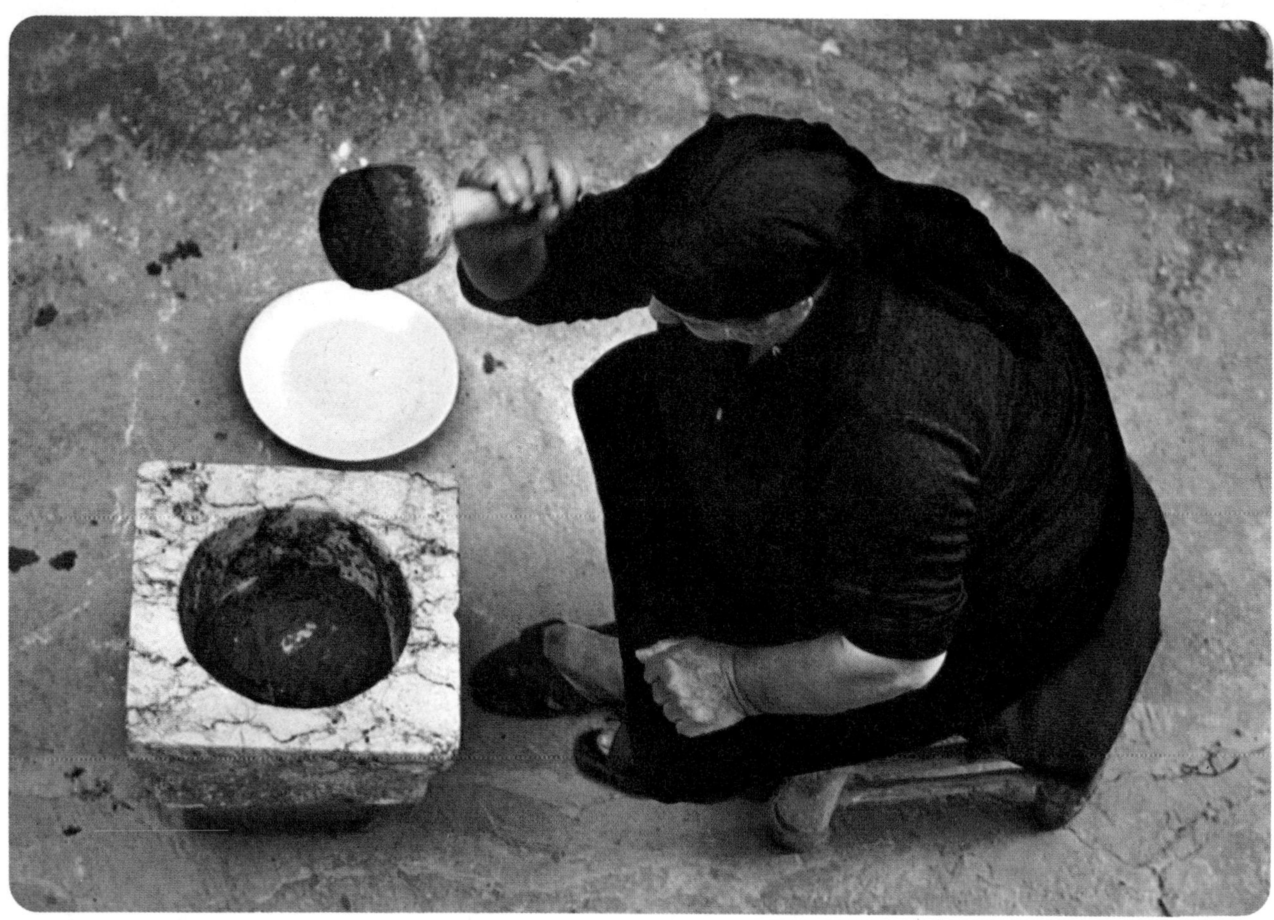

In a sunny courtyard in the village of Zahle, a Lebanese matron prepares the spicy dish called *kibbi,* which may be served either hot or cold. Into a portion of lamb already reduced to a paste with a wooden pestle and stone mortar, she pounds onions, *burghul,* salt and pepper. For a *kibbi* prepared by less arduous methods, see the Recipe Index.

with a chair lift 7,550 feet long. Lumbering is no longer allowed, but enterprise marches on.

Our own enterprise took us to Zahle, a resort community in the same mountain range but closer to Beirut. Our objective was *mazza,* the traditional Arab avalanche of appetizers, each of which comes in small portions—but 20, 40, 60, even 100 at a time. We took a table at one of Zahle's gaily painted outdoor restaurants, beside the mountain stream that bisects the town. The townsfolk live among their vineyards along the steep slopes on either side, with views of the green plain of Bekaa below.

The waiter brought a *mazza* that was modest by Arab standards but still included too many dishes to list. He set the plates down, put a little fresh golden amber olive oil on almost every one, and left us to our exploration. To begin with there was *tabbouleh,* a salad of chopped tomatoes, green and white onions, radishes, parsley and mint. Now *tabbouleh* is a fairly conventional salad until a final unforgettable ingredient is added: nutty-flavored *burghul,* which is wheat boiled to the point of splitting, parched in the sun, and cracked or ground to various degrees of fineness. In our salad the grains were medium in size, and because they had been soaked beforehand, delightfully chewy in texture.

Many of our *mazza* specialties were prepared with *tahina* (crushed sesame seeds) even more nutty in flavor than *burghul.* In the basic sauce, *tahina* is combined with garlic, salt and a little water, thinned with plenty of lemon juice, and beaten into a smooth paste. Garnished with parsley, the sauce is served separately as one dish of the *mazza*. Mixed with mashed chick-peas, it becomes *hummus bi tahina* and takes on a rich flavor. It blends well, too, with the pulp of fresh avocado, but it is best of all, to my mind, in *baba ghannooj (Recipe Index),* an eggplant dish that has a delicate smoky flavor lingering from the first step in the preparation of the eggplant, when it is broiled over an open fire. The versatile sauce also makes a tangy dressing for salads and even for fish; in one dish of our *mazza* it was used as a coating for a substantial mound of fresh parsley leaves.

Another *mazza* was *kibbi nayya,* raw ground lamb with *burghul.* The only other ingredient in this *kibbi nayya,* aside from salt and pepper, was onions, but it is often made with a great many spices added. In every version, however, the essential ingredient is a long, weary pounding, which gives a soft, doughlike consistency to the meat. The mixture is patted neatly into a flat, round cake and garnished, preferably with green scallions. *Kibbi nayya* is a great dish for anyone who loves tartar steak and is ready to try a distinctive Middle Eastern version of the dish.

We ate all these foods in the Arab manner, tearing bite-sized pieces from a disc of flat bread and using them to scoop up morsels from our plates. And we drank glass after glass of anise-flavored *arak* as an apéritif, preparing it just as the Lebanese do, by diluting it to whiteness with water and adding chipped ice. At a table near us, some Lebanese businessmen were following these same customs with a spread of *mazza* that outpointed ours by many plates, and with no stinting of *arak.* They then ordered lunch!

The appetizers had scuttled our appetites, but the businessmen put away large platters of *kibbi* prepared as a main dish rather than as an appetizer. (Some Lebanese claim *kibbi* is a national dish, but it reappears in Syria under the same name, in Jordan as *kobba,* and in Iraq as *kubba.*) Every version starts with the raw lamb and *burghul* pounded to a paste. But for its heartier role it is then often cooked. It can be shaped like a hamburger and fried, or made into hollow balls the size of large eggs, stuffed according to fancy, and baked or broiled. To me, *kibbi* as a main dish was best when baked in a pan in a three-layer arrangement of assorted *kibbis:* the middle one, lamb seasoned with sautéed pine nuts and onions and a pinch of cinnamon or allspice, the other two layers consisting of lamb and *burghul* and a glaze of golden butter on the very top.

As my wife and I left the restaurant, our neighbors finally had finished eating and were concluding their meal with another venerable Arabic custom. They began to share a narghile, the Middle Eastern pipe that cools the smoke by passing it through water, handing the mouthpiece on its long, flexible tube from man to man.

Heading back to Beirut, we drove through towns where men peddled fresh almonds, picked while the outer shell was still green and the nut-to-come a faintly flavored jelly. One vendor sold cotton candy; another dispensed licorice juice from a finely chased brass container. The men who stood idly on the sides of the road, watching the traffic, were probably independent landowners. And a man who squatted in the sun, wearing a round, white, brimless hat, was surely a priest of the Druze sect—an esoteric

Continued on page 98

Dinner in Beirut: An East-West Blend

Selma Abu Khadra, a young matron of Beirut's cosmopolitan society, entertains her guests with a dinner party *(below)* that is typically Lebanese in its sophisticated combination of Middle Eastern food with Western touches. Selma, her sister and her aunt began preparations for the meal early on the morning of the party. While the others prepare stuffed grape leaves and eggplant, Selma stuffs *kibbi,* or lamb paste, with ground lamb and pine nuts *(left). Kibbi* appears in three guises on the buffet table. Platters of fried stuffed *kibbi* balls are at the hostess' right and near the center of the table; a *kibbi* pie, garnished with parsley, sits before a platter of shish kabob; and a plate of raw *kibbi* is at the center of the table's right-hand end. The salad on romaine leaves at left, in front, is *tabbouleh* made with *burghul,* tomatoes, onion and seasoning; next to it are grilled lamb chops served on stuffed grape leaves.

At pre-dinner cocktails, a Western custom acceptable in Beirut, Selma wears an ornate gown called a *galabiyeh* and smokes a *narghile*.

Muslim faction that believes in reincarnation and scorns prayer as an arrogant human interference in divine affairs. At one point, between towns, we passed an abandoned mud-brick caravansary, or inn, its roof caved in and its walls crumbling; we remembered that this same road, now asphalt paved, had once served as a trade route to Syria, and realized that the decaying building had been one of the way stations.

A fat sheep standing outside a farmhouse meant that the family inside clung to the fading custom of preparing *kawerma*—that is, of butchering meat in the fall and preserving it for the winter. The animal would be force-fed many times a day—sometimes in the middle of the night—to make it as fat as possible. On slaughtering day, the fat would be stripped off and boiled down; the best parts of the flesh, cut small and seasoned with salt and pepper, would be fried in the same cauldron. The entire contents of the cauldron would then be turned into crocks and sealed—provisions for the cold months to come, when hearty stews and meat breakfasts with fried eggs would be welcome.

The caravan route southeastward from Lebanon leads eventually to Damascus. That ancient crossroads city, the capital of modern Syria, rises on a broad, fertile plain called the Ghuta—a 400-square-mile oasis, one of the few green expanses in all Syria. It is watered by the Barada River, which flows through the city and loses itself in Al-Utaybeh, a desert lake 18 miles to the east. All along the course of the river the soil of the Ghuta is rich, and the villagers who work it build their houses close together, saving all the land they can for farming and herding. Here livestock pasture on rich grazing land, cereals and vegetables thrive, and fruit trees bear abundantly.

Even the nearby desert contributes a delicacy, the Syrian or Middle Eastern truffle. It looks like its European cousins, resembling a small dark-brown potato, but tastes much blander. In Syrian markets these fungi are sold still crusty with the sand they grew in. After a vigorous scrubbing, they are ready to be sliced and broiled or sautéed to be eaten alone. (I have never seen them used merely as a decorative garnish in the Middle East, no doubt because their delicate aroma would be overpowered by other foods.) Whether or not to peel them is a question that can provoke a quarrel; for my part, I stand staunchly with the party that advocates retaining the skin, for a skinless truffle seems to me little more than a tasteless, fleshy tuber.

Damascus itself has always been famous for its beauty and lush setting. Muhammad, who crossed the Arabian desert to visit the city, declined to pass through its gates, saying that a man cannot enter Paradise twice and that the immortal one was worth waiting for. Through the center of old Damascus cuts the "Street called Straight," mentioned in the Acts of the Apostles as Saint Paul's dwelling place at the time of his conversion to Christianity. Nearby, another street, the Sook el-Bazooriyya, is filled with confectioners' shops selling exotic sweets that must have been traditional in Biblical times. Candied pears are infused with the spicy flavors of cinnamon, cardamom and ginger, then coated with a bright mixture of sugar and gum mastic. There are delightfully tart little balls of dried, deep-orange apricots, ground up and cooked in syrup, each piece crowned with a shiny white blanched almond and rolled in sugar. Rather similar balls of confectionery are made of pounded almonds sweetened and strengthened with almond extract and with

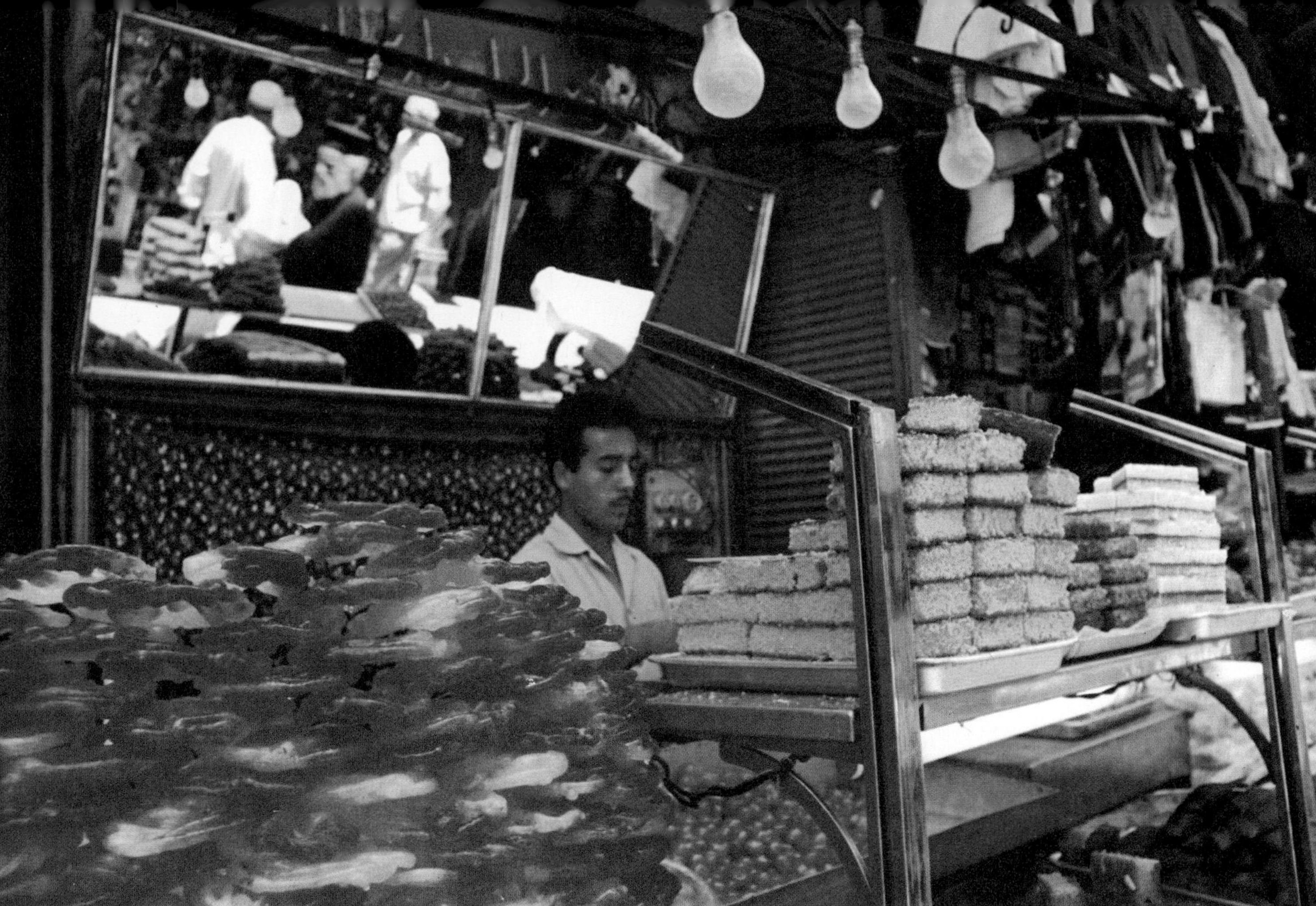

An open-front sweets stall in Beirut, its huge mirror reflecting the busy street scene, offers passersby a variety of square, honey-rich cakes and a tray of candied dates. The heaped pile of confections at the left is a simple taffy made by boiling sugar, water and lemon juice together; the colorless, amorphous product is then dyed and shaped into rings.

essence of rose petals; as you bite into one of them you find, for good measure, a brilliant red maraschino cherry.

Obviously, the food of Syria is made for the eye as well as the palate. Bright green coriander leaves, strongly scented, often garnish a main-course platter. Pomegranate seeds glow pinkly in green salads and in a number of dishes based on ground meat. But behind the vivid appearance of the food stands an equally bright flavor, contributed by a skilled hand in the kitchen.

I saw this skill at its best demonstrated by a Syrian cook who invited my wife and me to dinner and allowed us to watch her at work. Her deftness was visible even in what seemed to be minor details of technique. To remove the seeds from a pomegranate, she halved the fruit with a knife and placed each half in her left palm, cut side down. Then she gave the skin a whack or two with the handle of the same knife, and the seeds fell into her hand. When she squeezed lemons (which she used abundantly), her hand served as a strainer, the fingers held together just close enough to trap the seeds but let the juice run through—an effective kitchen shortcut that I had never seen elsewhere.

Between such acts of expertise, she often stopped to check the oven, in which a leg of lamb was roasting. The lamb was seasoned simply and well, with slivers of garlic inserted here and there—"to breathe all through it," she said—and onions scattered around the meat. (Some Syrian cooks, I am sorry to say, rub a roast with a needlessly rich—indeed, a reprehensible—variety of herbs and spices.) A little water went into the roasting pan toward the end, to become thin gravy.

The highlight of the meal, however, was not so much the excellent lamb but her *sfeeha,* a peppery little meat pie that Syrian housewives turn out by the dozen. As with all dishes good enough to survive for generations, this one takes various forms. The version we had used a dough containing olive oil. The filling was coarsely chopped lamb mixed with a little of its own fat, then with pine nuts, chopped onions and a dab of yoghurt, and made hot with pepper and fragrant with allspice. The mixture was set on thin, flat rounds of dough, and the edges of the dough were crinkled up to form irregular cups. Almost all of the meat was left uncovered for the double cooking that was to come—first a light baking, then a stage of crisping and browning under the broiler.

The more pepper used in *sfeeha,* the more welcome its side dish of yoghurt, homemade, of course, with an almost lemony tartness that is missing in the commercial yoghurt sold in the United States. Dinner ended with Arabic coffee, the strong, thick "wine of Araby." Our hostess told us that she could read our fortunes if we upended our demitasse cups on their saucers and let the sediment flow down, forming patterns prophetic of our future. I declined, quoting the English wit Sydney Smith: "Fate cannot harm me; I have dined today." My wife accepted and was told, among other things, that she would cross a body of water. It had rained that day, and as we took our leave, she stepped out the door and into a puddle.

There is precious little water between Syria and Jordan; instead, there is an endless succession of brown furrowed hills. When we got to Jordan's capital city of Amman, almost the first thing I did was to go looking for Jordan almonds, the crunchy white sweets with a smooth coating of sugar over a core of almond. What better place on earth to buy them than here, in the land of their name. We wandered through the center of the city, looking at shop windows and fruit stands and sniffing the spicy smoke of sausages grilling in alley restaurants. Then, in the window of a candy store, we saw Jordan almonds, went inside and bought some. They were good, all right, but then I asked what they were called. Their name in Arabic turned out to be *mulabbas ala loz,* or "confectioner's almonds." Later, I looked into the history of the English name—and discovered that the "Jordan" in Jordan almonds derives from the French *jardin,* or "garden." Even so, what we bought in ignorance we ate in delight.

Amman is a clean, gray-white city rising within a cup of hills. At the upper levels of town, the houses have architectural touches of blue and pale rose, and broad picture windows and balconies cascade down the slopes, taking advantage of the views. But close by these homes of the well-to-do are simpler dwellings. From one perch high in the hills I remember looking down to the swimming pool of a luxury hotel, with bright bikinis among the yellow poolside umbrellas. Alongside the hotel was a tiny concrete cube that housed an Arab family with at least three children. Their laundry was drying on a pile of twigs and branches and the children played in a courtyard they shared with some chickens, a goat and a donkey.

What they would eat that night only their mother knew, but it could not have been more typical of the region than our dinner. We went with a Jordanian companion to a restaurant that specialized in skewered meats—the *kebabs* that rank among the glories of Middle Eastern cooking. To me they always conjure up images of hungry prehistoric shepherds sitting outside a cave as they broiled pieces of meat impaled on a stick or of encamped warriors grilling their meat on spears and swords. Our restaurant was an efficient establishment with a grill on which meats were charcoal broiled to order.

When an Arab speaks of meat, of course, he means lamb or mutton, and that is what we had in four skewered versions. One was the familiar succulent *shish kebab,* chunks of leg of lamb hardly seasoned at all—a relatively modern way of making a *kebab. (Kebabs* highly seasoned by long marinating are throwbacks to older times, before refrigeration, when the steeping mixtures were designed to preserve the meat as well as tenderize and flavor it.) But another skewer of *kebab* was quite different; it bore oblong meatballs with enough pepper to punish the tongue. And there was one of spicy variety meats—little pieces of heart, kidney and liver as pungent as the Latin *anticuchos.* Our final *kebab* was *tuhal,* made up of tender medallions of lamb two or three inches thick, slit and stuffed with a blend of parsley, pine nuts and hot green peppers. Our companion, straining his inadequate English, told us that the cut came from "behind the liver." From this anatomical clue, and the meat's tenderness, I guessed that he meant the loin.

Knowing that as part of our visit to Jordan we would attend a *mansaf*—a dinner in the desert as guest of a Bedouin sheikh—I had boned up on Arab manners for the occasion. The meal, I learned, properly begins with a ceremonial washing of hands. Then grace is said: *bismi'l-Lāhi'r-Rahmāni'r-Prahīm*—"In the name of God the Merciful and Compassionate." (In all, the "names of God" number no less than 100—of which only 99 are said to be known to mankind.) The only utensil laid out is a huge communal dish in which the meat and rice are served to the entire company. This is placed on the floor, which is also where you place yourself, for desert nomads travel light and chairless from camp to camp.

The food must be eaten with the right hand, preferably with the first three fingers. The correct method is to grasp a handful of rice, toss and squeeze it lightly into a ball, and bring it to the mouth without dropping a grain and without touching fingers to lips. The meat, handled in the same way, is expected to be tender enough to be plucked from the bones. According to my informants, much lip smacking and at least one well-rounded belch are expected from the guest as proof that he has eaten well. At the end, God is praised—*al-hamdu li-Lhah*—and the hands are washed again.

We expected to be welcomed with a hospitality more rigidly codified than we had experienced before. In the hostile desert, anyone from prince to beggar can present himself at any home and ask for a meal and a night's lodging knowing that he will never be turned away. The poor will serve what they can, if only a few dates; there is a popular legend about a penniless widow who slaughters her only goat—the nanny that provides her and her children with their sole source of milk—to feed a passing stranger. The well-to-do will invariably provide meat and rice. The guest, if he has the means, shows his gratitude by leaving or sending gifts—coffee, sugar, dress materials for the womenfolk. The host stands apart while his visitor is eating, and dines later with his family.

Continued on page 108

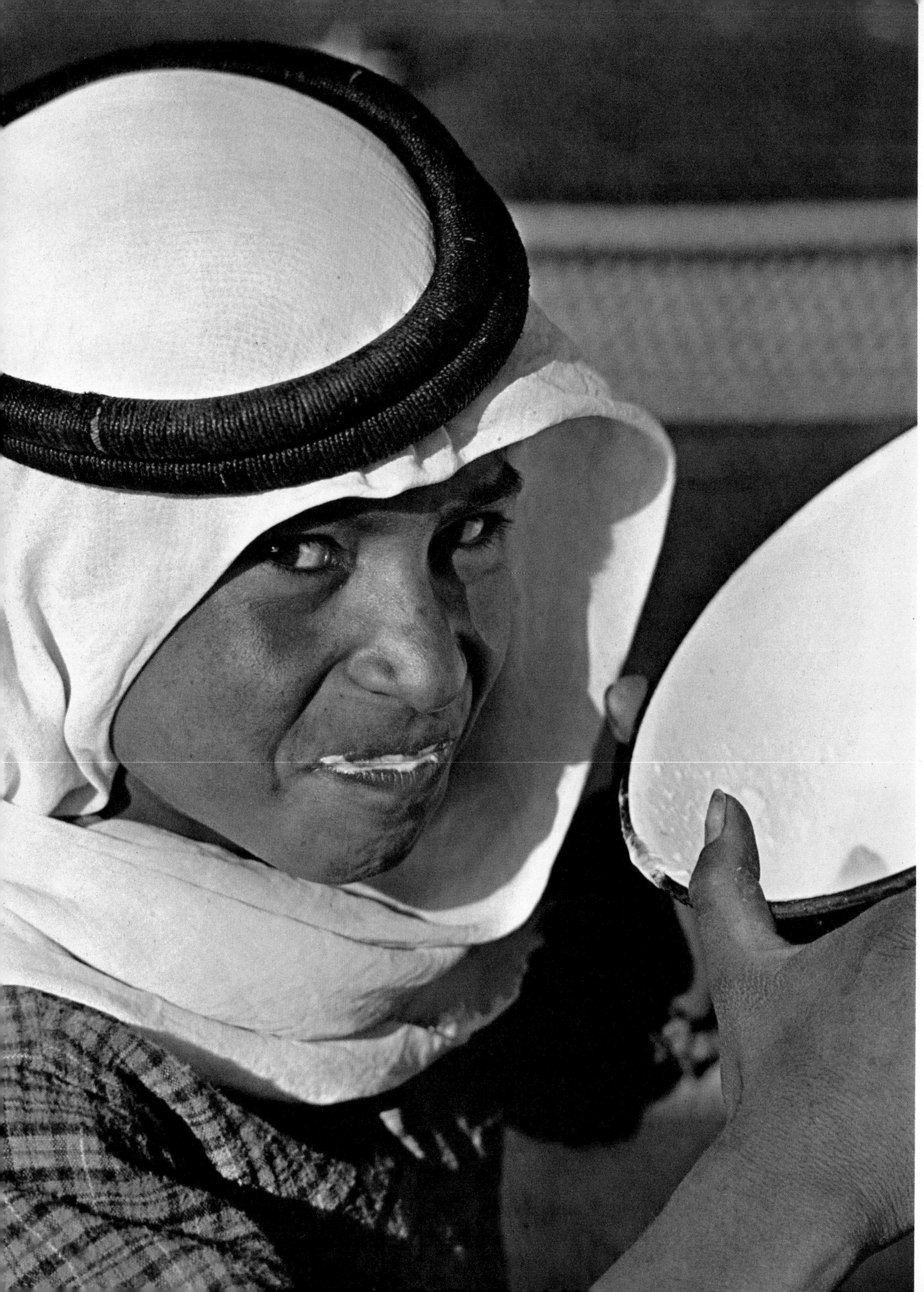

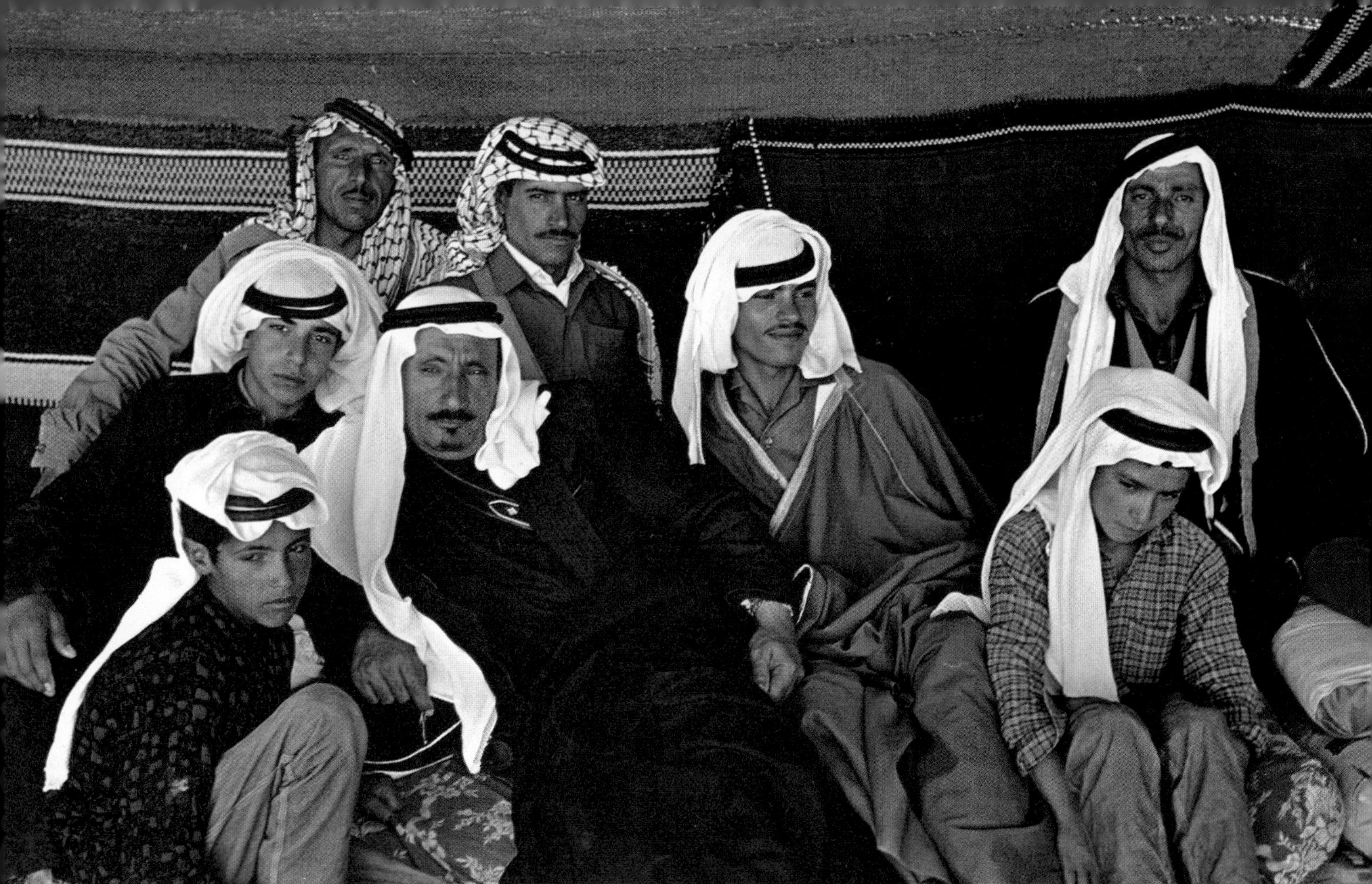

Some of the family of Sheikh Faisal ibn Yasi *(second from left, front row)* gather in his tent to discuss a *mansaf* planned for the afternoon. Even the younger members of the group will serve as co-hosts, since they are closely related to Faisal: the youth at his right is a son, Satam Faisal Hamd; the one at the far end is Mamduh Hamd, one of the sheikh's brothers. Though the al Yasis have substantial meals every evening, their breakfast, like that of less affluent Bedouins, consists mainly of *laban,* a yoghurtlike food. In the picture at left, the youth appreciatively tipping his *laban* bowl is Mamduh Hamd.

Ancient Civilities in a Bedouin Tent

The most gracious compliment a Bedouin can offer is an invitation to a *mansaf,* or formal dinner, in his desert tent. The fare is simple—the meal consists essentially of boiled lamb and rice, served together—but the etiquette involved in serving and eating the meal has been elaborated over the centuries almost into a ritual. Sheikh Faisal ibn Yasi, who with his family *(above)* leads the 73,000-member Huwaytat tribe, is no primitive, unsophisticated man (he is a skilled administrator and has served in the Jordanian parliament), yet a *mansaf* in his tent today is much like the ones that fascinated the Westerners who first observed them generations ago. For example, the women of the sheikh's entourage, who do much of the hard work of preparation, are not permitted to be present at the banquet. (Along with the smaller children, they eat the leftovers.) Any man, on the other hand, whether a stranger or even an enemy, is welcome to share whatever the Bedouin host has to set forth for his guests. Other *mansaf* customs appear on the following pages, in pictures that show a *mansaf* and the preparations for it in Sheikh Faisal's desert camp 20 miles south of Petra.

A tribeswoman bakes *shrak*—a whole-wheat crust on which food will be served at the *mansaf*—on a domed "oven" made of cast iron.

Naif Hamd ibn Yasi, one of the sheikh's brothers, spreads cooked, seasoned rice on the flat *shrak (left)*. For a *mansaf* several of these rice-covered sheets are assembled on a large platter, and boiled lamb is piled on top of the rice. The final ingredient of the dish, a sauce of seasoned butter, is poured over the lamb and rice *(above)* just before the diners begin eating.

At a pre-meal ritual in which each diner ceremoniously washes his hands *(left)* Sheikh Faisal's elegant wristwatch and Western tailoring contrast sharply with the utensils passed among the company by one of his relatives. When all the hosts and guests have washed, the meal begins *(below)*. A diner uses no table implements; with his right hand alone—the left hand must not touch food—he pulls off a lump of tender lamb, dextrously rolls a ball of rice around it and pops the mixture into his mouth. When the group of men shown here have finished eating, their platter will be refilled and another group will take their place. Finally, when all have eaten, they will drink coffee together.

As one member of the al Yasi family pours coffee, holding two cups at a time, another heats water for more on a fire in the background.

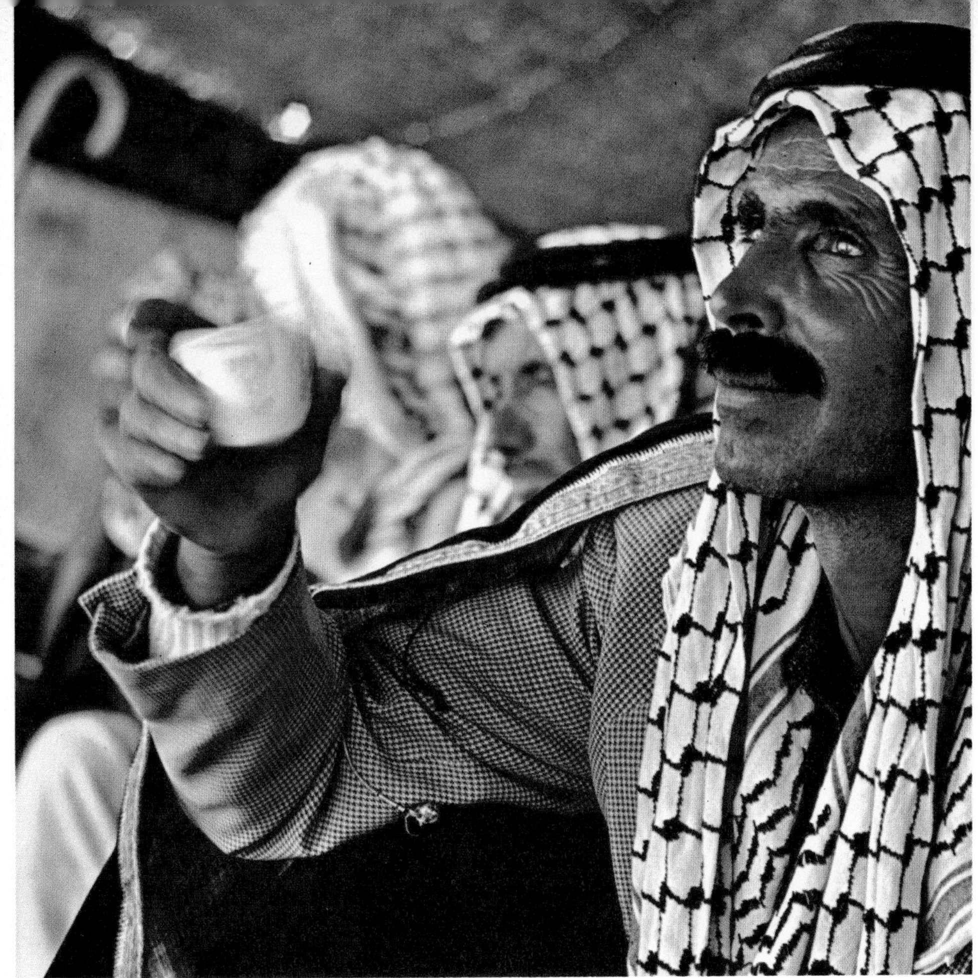

Beaming gratitude, a guest shakes his cup from side to side—a gesture meaning "No more."

Tent poles and a metal coffee service gleam in the light of oil lamps and an open fire as the men of the al Yasi family and their guests form a circle, chatting and sipping coffee far into the night *(below)*. For all its splendor, the setting is utilitarian. The rugs and cushions on the tent floor make up the major part of the sheikh's household furniture. Even the Bedouins' romantic headdresses *(kuffiyyahs)* are as essential a part of their attire as their trousers or robes. They never remove *kuffiyyahs* at meals, though they may toss the ends of the scarves back from their faces when indoors.

According to the Bedouin's strict rules of hospitality, the stranger must not be asked his business, or where he came from or where he is bound. Even the host's enemy must be given asylum for as long as 48 hours, with safe conduct assured to the border of the local chief's territory. Since thirst is the grimmest of the hazards in desert travel, the rules specially require that a guest be provided all the tea or coffee he wishes.

Our own *mansaf* missed out on some of the traditional niceties, but all in all it went quite well. We were greeted by the sheikh, a tall young man, lithe and handsome in his long gray robe. On his head he wore the Arab *kuffiyyah,* a square of white cloth secured by a double cord, with the corners hanging gracefully to his shoulders. A curved dagger, sheathed in silver, flashed at his belt, and a pistol hung in a holster at his hip, but the warmth of his smile made us welcome. We stepped inside his tent, woven from the hair of black goats, and shook hands with about a dozen men, exchanging mutually unintelligible pleased-to-meet-you's. The interior was cool, and the bare ground was half covered with bright-patterned Jordanian rugs. With relief I observed a row of bolsters arranged along the far side; I had not relished the prospect of sitting unpillowed on the ground throughout the meal.

This dinner was an occasion to be shared, and the sheikh went out to gather a considerable party—many of them total strangers. He hailed a couple of passing soldiers and invited them in. He even flagged down a policeman patrolling the desert highway, and the roundup went on until our group had grown to about 25. Meanwhile we were served coffee in tiny porcelain cups. The long-beaked pot, richly enameled in blue, was brought around again and again—and I had been told never to refuse this token of Arab hospitality. Presently I learned from watching others the polite way to signal "enough." After six or seven servings I waggled my emptied cup and one of the servants took it away.

Just before the meal began, warm water was poured over everyone's hands, a basin held below catching the runoff. Then two enormous trays appeared, heaped with rice mixed with browned pine nuts and almonds, and adorned with big pieces of boiled baby lamb. The one set before us, on a rectangle of blue-patterned oilcloth, was crowned with a knob of fat from the tail, which in this part of the world can reach a weight of 20 pounds. In the most literal sense we dug in, some of us up to the wrist, in search of the hottest rice. As we ate, the sheikh's servants repeatedly poured a sour-milk sauce over the tray, adding a pleasant sharpness to the mild food.

After another washing of the hands, more coffee came along, followed by glasses of sweet tea. Between the two, a bowl of rice pudding went the rounds. Meanwhile the big dinner trays were carried outside the tent, and the men who had served us sat cross-legged around them, dining on our ample leavings. The women and children would have their turn next.

Later, comparing what I had expected with what had actually taken place, I realized that the classic banquet script had not been followed to the letter. The prayers had been omitted—a needless concession, really, to the American guests. Our sheikh joined us around the tray instead of standing alongside as protocol required. Neatness in eating was honored more in the breach than in the observance: Everyone wound up with rice in his lap, fingers did touch lips at times, and a few of the diners used their left hands to gather stray grains of rice from chin or cheeks. No one belched—and my wife and I had *practiced* belching in private just for this public moment.

We went on to Iraq looking forward to the romance of its capital, Baghdad. The city itself is not old as time is reckoned in Mesopotamia; it was built only 12 centuries ago, although it lies not far from some of the fabled places of ancient times. Northward lies ruined Nineveh, a powerful city in pre-Christian times. Southward lies partly excavated Babylon, where Belshazzar, in the middle of a drunken feast during the 6th Century B.C., saw the ominous handwriting on the wall. Down near the Persian Gulf, where the Tigris and Euphrates Rivers meet, romantics locate the Garden of Eden. But Baghdad, so much younger than these cities, glimmers with remembered stories of Aladdin, of Ali Baba, and of Scheherazade herself spinning night-long tales to the caliph.

My wife and I landed there one sunny morning half expecting to be met by the ghost of Harun al-Rashid, one of the greatest of the caliphs, who ruled around 800 A.D. "Open sesame," I thought. What actually opened was the skies; a steady rain began. Marooned in our hotel room, we looked out at the swollen Tigris River, the flooded highway beside it, and steady perpendicular rain, and made uneasy jokes about the Deluge. But at last the rain let up, and next morning we set out on dry sidewalks to see the city. In the street we heard a melodious chant from the grounds of a private home; we peeked in and saw the gardener on his knees, invoking Allah with every seedling he planted. Farther along we ran into a pair of soldiers holding hands (an innocent custom in the Middle East) and asked them for directions to the Copper Bazaar. The bazaar sounded with hand-hammering as its artisans made water jugs, shaped souvenirs in the form of Aladdin's lamp, and incised trays in exquisite Arabic letters quoting the Koran. Great factories are beginning to turn out mass-produced goods all over the Middle East, but I truly believe that the tiny workshops on these noisy, narrow lanes will never go out of business.

Nearby was a restaurant whose stock in trade was *pacha,* the boiled heads, stomachs and trotters of sheep. Outside, a boy cracked bones on a small anvil. Inside, a huge aluminum kettle steamed in anticipation of the midday rush. An early customer ordered a bowl of broth and a second bowl containing broth-soaked bread; he helped himself to side dishes of onion and *turshi,* a mixture of pickled vegetables made attractively pink with beets or beet juice. His meal looked like a balanced, nourishing one, and I reckoned that it cost about 30 cents; for another 15 cents, he could have had pieces of tongue or stomach as well. It suddenly occurred to me that Iraq could be a bargain paradise for retirement.

We passed the *pacha* shop to lunch in a humble restaurant. The dishes began arriving almost all at once, beginning with big bowls of white rice topped attractively with red spaghettini that had been boiled in thin tomato sauce. There was a very un-Southern fried chicken, first parboiled then fried without batter in clarified butter, a plate of giblets, and tender lamb boiled and then glazed in ghee, the clarified butter that keeps for months without refrigeration (the proprietor spoke scornfully of cooks who use vegetable oils, and the rich flavor of his foods left no doubt he avoided them). Our *turshi* consisted of pickled turnips and green squash with skin ribbed like that of celery. With it came the best tasting *dolma* I have ever had: an enormous onion hollowed out and stuffed with rice and meat.

Baghdad has its cosmopolitan restaurants, too. In one where we dropped in for a drink with a Baghdadi couple, a five-piece band played softly, and I heard *Bésame Mucho* crooned for the first time in years. Few couples took to the dance floor, though one young pair burst into a frantic frug when the music quickened. At our table a bottle of *arak* was waiting—in this case, a distillate of dates, flavored with gum mastic rather than anise. Under its influence our conversation strayed to odd Iraqi sayings and customs. I learned, for instance, that when a girl is born in Iraq, people say to her parents, "May Allah be kinder to you next time"—not because the infant is not loved, but because she may someday disgrace the family. I learned, too, that in Iraqi entertaining it is customary for the guests to leave as soon as dinner is finished, and that many hostesses therefore serve dinner very late—midnight is not an unusual hour—to make the evening last as long as possible.

The best food in Baghdad is *masgoof,* fish barbecued beside the Tigris and eaten outdoors along the riverbank. So we left the showy restaurant and sought it out. The place for *masgoof* is Abu Nuwas Street, a broad thoroughfare lined with cafés strung with colored lights, flickering cook fires and tables set in tiers down to the water's edge. With our host and hostess we looked into several fish stalls and chose a live *shabboot,* a round, red-gilled fellow weighing about six pounds. It was split and cleaned, seasoned with rock salt and paprika, and placed beside the fire with nine or ten others, all impaled on sticks arranged in a circle around the crackling twigs. The cook used a long stick to push the burning wood toward one fish or another as the breeze shifted the flames.

It takes an hour for the fish to cook, and we strolled to our table and chatted over bottles of beer. At last the *shabboot* was brought on a large, oval platter, garnished with tomato slices and wedges of raw onion and accompanied by several loaves of Arab bread. "You must eat the fish with your hands," said our hostess, "so you can feel the bones." But I remembered a better explanation of the custom: "Eating with a knife and fork is like making love through an interpreter." We all tore off pieces of bread, searched out succulent morsels of *shabboot* and ate, alternating mouthfuls of fish with bites of tomato or onion. Our hostess, who knew the anatomy of the fish well, selected choice bits for Muriel and me.

The Tigris flowed silently beside us. A cricket rasped somewhere nearby. I looked up the embankment at the lights of Baghdad, their many colors a reminder of the bright romances of Scheherazade. Farther off in the darkness were the dead cities of Nineveh and Babylon. This sense of belonging to a distant past was strong here. The very spot where we were sitting had been inhabited almost as long as men have been living in settled communities, raising their food instead of hunting it. Some of the same foods we were enjoying could have been enjoyed long ago by the dimly known people of this land who invented herding and farming. For it was in Iraq, millennia ago, that agriculture began. That great accomplishment—the foundation of civilization—is also the foundation of the cooking we call Middle Eastern. It is a story more exciting than any in the *Arabian Nights,* and it is all the more worth telling in the following pages because it is real.

Clear, cool water and colorful sweet syrup make a summer drink that refreshes sweet-toothed Middle Easterners. The syrup is a solution of sugar and the juices of fruits or flowers—roses in this case—and it is so concentrated that only a small amount *(foreground)* is needed to flavor a tumblerful of water.

CHAPTER IV RECIPES

Khoubz Araby

ARAB BREAD

To make 8 eight-inch round loaves

2¼ to 2¾ cups lukewarm water (110° to 115°)
2 packages active dry yeast
A pinch of sugar
8 cups all-purpose flour
2 teaspoons salt
¼ cup olive oil
1 cup cornmeal or flour

Pour ¼ cup of lukewarm water into a small bowl and sprinkle it with the yeast and sugar. Let the mixture rest for 2 or 3 minutes, then stir to dissolve the yeast completely. Set the bowl in a warm, draft-free place (such as a turned-off oven) for 5 minutes, or until the mixture doubles in volume.

In a deep bowl, combine the flour and salt, make a well in the center, and pour in the yeast mixture, the olive oil and 2 cups of lukewarm water. Gently stir the center ingredients together, then incorporate the flour and continue to beat until the ingredients are well combined. Add up to ½ cup more lukewarm water, beating it in a tablespoon at a time, and using as much as necessary to form a dough that can be gathered into a compact ball. If the dough is difficult to stir, work in the water with your fingers.

Place the dough on a lightly floured surface and knead by pressing it down, pushing it forward several times with the heel of your hand and folding it back on itself. Repeat for 20 minutes, or until the dough is smooth and elastic. Shape the dough into a ball and place it in a lightly oiled bowl. Drape loosely with a towel and set aside in the warm place for 45 minutes, or until the dough doubles in bulk. Punch it down with a blow of your fist and divide it into 8 equal pieces. Roll each piece into a ball about 2½ inches in diameter, cover the balls with a towel and let them rest for 30 minutes.

Preheat the oven to 500°. Sprinkle 2 large baking sheets with ½ cup of the cornmeal or flour. On a lightly floured surface, roll 4 of the balls into round loaves each about 8 inches in diameter and no more than ⅛ inch thick. Arrange them 2 to 3 inches apart on the baking sheets, cover with towels and allow them to rest for 30 minutes. If you have a gas oven, bake the bread on the floor of the oven for 5 minutes, then transfer the loaves to a shelf 3 or 4 inches above the oven floor and continue baking for 5 minutes, or until they puff up in the center and are a delicate brown. If your oven is electric, bake the bread on the lowest shelf for 5 minutes, then raise it 3 or 4 inches and continue baking until the breads are puffed and browned.

Remove the bread from the baking sheets, wrap each loaf in foil, and set aside for 10 minutes. Sprinkle the pans with the remaining ½ cup of cornmeal or flour and bake the remaining 4 loaves of bread in a similar fashion.

When the loaves are unwrapped the tops will have fallen and there will be a shallow pocket of air in their centers. Serve warm or at room temperature.

Taratoor

SESAME SAUCE

To make about 1½ cups

3 medium-sized garlic cloves, peeled and finely chopped
1 cup *tahina* paste (ground, hulled sesame seeds)
¾ to 1 cup cold water
½ cup fresh lemon juice
1 teaspoon salt

In a deep bowl, mash the garlic to a paste with a pestle or the back of a large spoon. Stir in the *tahina*. Then, with a whisk or spoon, beat in ½ cup of the cold water, the lemon juice, and salt. Still beating, add up to ½ cup more of water, 1 tablespoon at a time, until the sauce has the consistency of thick mayonnaise and holds its shape almost solidly in a spoon. Taste for seasoning.

Taratoor can be served as a sauce with baked fish or fried cauliflower, and is used as an ingredient in *hummus* and *baba ghannooj* *(Recipe Index)*.

Samakah Harrah

BAKED FISH WITH WALNUT AND POMEGRANATE-SEED STUFFING

To serve 6 to 8

1 cup olive oil
A 4- to 4½-pound whole striped bass, cleaned and scaled but with head and tail left on, or substitute any other firm white whole fish
3 teaspoons salt
1 cup finely chopped onions
1½ cups finely chopped green peppers
1 cup shelled walnuts, wrapped in a towel and finely crushed with a rolling pin
½ cup plus 1 tablespoon finely chopped parsley, preferably flat-leaf parsley
3 tablespoons fresh pomegranate seeds
1½ teaspoons freshly ground black pepper
Taratoor *(opposite)*
1 lemon, cut crosswise into ⅛-inch-thick slices

Preheat the oven to 400°. Pour ¼ cup of the oil into a shallow baking-and-serving dish large enough to hold the fish comfortably. Wash the fish under cold running water, and pat it dry with paper towels. Sprinkle inside and out with 2 teaspoons of salt. Lay the fish in the dish, pour ¼ cup of the remaining oil over it, and let it marinate at room temperature for 15 minutes.

Meanwhile, in a heavy 10- to 12-inch skillet, heat the remaining ½ cup of oil over moderate heat. Add the onions and, stirring frequently, cook for 10 minutes, or until they are soft and golden brown. Stir in the green peppers and walnuts and cook for 2 or 3 minutes until the peppers are soft. Off the heat add ½ cup of parsley, 2 tablespoons of pomegranate seeds, the remaining salt and the black pepper. Taste for seasoning.

Fill the fish with the walnut stuffing, close the opening with small skewers, and crisscross kitchen string around them to secure them. Bake in the middle of the oven for 40 to 50 minutes, basting the fish every 15 minutes with its accumulated cooking juices. The fish is done when it feels firm to the touch. Do not overcook. Remove the fish from the oven and spread it evenly with the *taratoor*. Sprinkle with the remaining parsley and pomegranate seeds, garnish the top with a row of lemon slices and serve hot or cold.

Tangy *taratoor,* a sesame-seed sauce, blankets striped bass richly filled with pomegranate seeds, nuts and seasonings *(foreground).*

Tabbouleh

CRUSHED WHEAT, TOMATO, MINT AND PARSLEY SALAD

To serve 4 to 6

- ½ cup fine *burghul* (crushed wheat)
- 3 medium-sized fresh, ripe tomatoes, finely chopped
- 1 cup finely chopped parsley, preferably flat-leaf parsley
- 1 cup finely chopped onions
- ⅓ cup fresh lemon juice
- 2 teaspoons salt
- ⅓ cup olive oil
- 2 tablespoons finely cut fresh mint or 1 tablespoon dried mint, crumbled
- Romaine lettuce leaves (optional)

Place the *burghul* in a bowl or pan and pour in enough cold water to cover it completely. Let it soak for about 10 minutes, then drain in a sieve or colander lined with a double thickness of dampened cheesecloth. Wrap the *burghul* in the cheesecloth and squeeze it vigorously until completely dry.

Drop the *burghul* into a deep bowl, add the tomatoes, parsley, onions, lemon juice and salt and toss gently but thoroughly together with a fork.

Just before serving, stir in the olive oil and mint and taste for seasoning. Mound the salad in a serving bowl or spoon it onto romaine lettuce leaves.

Hummus bi Tahina

COLD CHICK-PEA AND GARLIC PURÉE

To make about 2½ cups

- 1⅓ cups dried chick-peas (garbanzos), or substitute 2 cups drained, rinsed, canned chick-peas plus ½ to 1 cup cold water
- 2 teaspoons salt
- 3 medium-sized garlic cloves, peeled and finely chopped
- ¼ cup fresh lemon juice
- 1 cup *taratoor* sauce *(page 112)*

If you are using dried chick-peas, start a day ahead. Wash the peas in a sieve under cold running water, then place them in a large bowl or pan and add enough cold water to cover them by 2 inches. Soak at room temperature for at least 12 hours. Drain the peas and place them in a heavy 2- to 3-quart saucepan. Add the salt and enough fresh water to cover the peas completely. Bring to a boil over high heat, reduce the heat to low and simmer partially covered for about 2 to 3 hours until the peas are very tender. Replenish the liquid with boiling water from time to time to keep the peas covered throughout the cooking period. Drain the peas and reserve the cooking liquid.

In a small bowl, mash the garlic to a paste with a pestle or the back of a spoon. Add the peas and ½ cup of the reserved cooking liquid or water, and mash vigorously to a smooth purée. (Alternatively, mash the garlic with a pestle or the back of a spoon, then force the garlic, peas and ½ cup of the cooking liquid or water through a fine sieve or a food mill set over a bowl.)

With a large spoon, beat in the lemon juice, a few tablespoons at a time. Beating constantly, pour in the *taratoor* in a slow thin stream and continue to beat until the mixture is smooth. *Hummus* should be thin enough to spread easily; if necessary, add up to ½ cup more of the chick-pea cooking liquid or water, beating it in a tablespoon at a time.

To serve, spread the *hummus* on a plate, or spoon it into a bowl.

Baba Ghannooj

COLD EGGPLANT PURÉE WITH LEMON JUICE

To make about 2 cups

- 1 medium-sized eggplant (about 1 pound)
- ¼ cup fresh lemon juice
- 2 tablespoons *taratoor* sauce *(page 112)*
- 1 large garlic clove, peeled and finely chopped
- 1 teaspoon salt
- 1 tablespoon olive oil
- ¼ cup finely chopped onions
- 1 tablespoon finely chopped parsley, preferably flat-leaf parsley

First, roast the eggplant in the following fashion: Prick it in 3 or 4 places with the tines of a long-handled fork, then impale it on the fork and turn it over a gas flame until the skin chars and begins to crack. (Or, if you have an electric stove, pierce the eggplant, place it on a baking sheet and broil 4 inches from the heat for about 20 minutes, turning it to char on all sides.)

When the eggplant is cool enough to handle, peel it, cutting away any badly charred spots on the flesh. Cut the eggplant in half lengthwise and chop it finely. Then mash the pulp to a smooth purée, beat in the lemon juice, *taratoor,* garlic and salt. Taste for seasoning.

To serve, spread the purée on a serving plate or mound it in a bowl and sprinkle the top with the olive oil, chopped onions and parsley.

Three exotic Middle Eastern appetizers often served with Arab bread are *(from top) tabbouleh, hummus bi tahina* and *baba ghannooj (recipes above).*

Sfeeha

BAKED LAMB PIES

To make about 16 pies

DOUGH

- 2¼ to 2¾ cups lukewarm water (110° to 115°)
- 2 packages active dry yeast
- A pinch of sugar
- 8 cups all-purpose flour
- 2 teaspoons salt
- ¼ cup olive oil

FILLING

- 2 cups finely chopped onions
- 1 tablespoon plus 2 teaspoons salt
- 4 tablespoons olive oil
- ½ cup pine nuts (pignolia)
- 2 pounds lean boneless lamb, coarsely ground
- 2 medium-sized fresh, ripe tomatoes, peeled, seeded and finely chopped
- ½ cup finely chopped green pepper
- ½ cup finely chopped parsley, preferably flat-leaf parsley
- ½ cup fresh lemon juice
- ¼ cup red wine vinegar
- 1 tablespoon tomato paste
- 1 teaspoon cayenne pepper
- 1 teaspoon allspice
- 2 teaspoons salt
- Freshly ground black pepper

Make the dough in the following fashion: Pour ¼ cup of the lukewarm water into a small, shallow bowl and sprinkle it with the yeast and sugar. Let the mixture rest for 2 or 3 minutes, then stir to dissolve the yeast completely. Set the bowl in a warm, draft-free place (such as a turned-off oven) for about 5 minutes, or until the mixture almost doubles in volume.

In a deep mixing bowl, combine the flour and the 2 teaspoons of salt, make a well in the center and into it pour the yeast mixture, the ¼ cup of olive oil, and 2 cups of the remaining lukewarm water. Gently stir the center ingredients together with a large spoon, then slowly incorporate the flour and continue to beat until the ingredients are well combined. Add up to ½ cup more lukewarm water, beating it in a tablespoon or so at a time, and using as much as necessary to form a dough that can be gathered into a compact ball. If the dough is difficult to stir, work in the water with your fingers.

Place the dough on a lightly floured surface and knead it by pressing it down, pushing it forward several times with the heel of your hand and folding it back on itself. Repeat for about 20 minutes, or until the dough is smooth and elastic. Sprinkle it from time to time with a little flour to prevent it from sticking to the board.

Shape the dough into a ball and place it in a lightly oiled bowl. Drape loosely with a kitchen towel and set aside in the warm, draft-free place for 45 minutes to 1 hour, or until the dough doubles in bulk. Punch the dough down with a single blow of your fist and divide it into 16 equal pieces. Roll each piece into a ball about 1½ inches in diameter, cover the balls with a towel and let them rest for 30 minutes.

Meanwhile, prepare the filling. Drop the onions into a deep bowl and sprinkle them with 1 tablespoon of the salt, turning them about with a spoon to coat them evenly. Let the onions rest at room temperature for at least 30 minutes, then squeeze them dry and return them to the bowl.

In a small skillet or saucepan, heat 1 tablespoon of olive oil until a light haze forms above it. Add the pine nuts and, stirring constantly, brown them lightly. Add them to the bowl of onions, along with the lamb, tomatoes, green pepper, parsley, lemon juice, vinegar, tomato paste, cayenne pepper, allspice, 2 teaspoons of salt and a liberal grinding of black pepper. Knead the mixture vigorously with both hands, then beat with a wooden spoon until the mixture is smooth and fluffy. Taste for seasoning.

Preheat the oven to 500°. With a pastry brush, coat 3 large baking sheets or jelly-roll pans with the remaining 3 tablespoons of oil.

On a lightly floured surface, roll each of the balls into a round about 4 inches in diameter and no more than ⅛ inch thick. To make open-faced pies, spoon about ½ cup of the lamb filling mixture on the center of each round. Then, with a spatula or the back of the spoon, spread the filling to about ½ inch of the edge.

To make closed pies, spoon about ½ cup of the filling on the center of each round. Pull up the edge from 3 equally distant points to make a roughly triangular-shaped pie and pinch the dough securely together at the top.

With a metal spatula, arrange the pies on the baking sheets. Bake in the lower third of the oven for 30 minutes, or until the pastry is lightly browned. Serve hot, or at room temperature, accompanied, if you like, with yoghurt.

Spicy ground lamb and yeast dough make the Syrian appetizers called *sfeeha*.

To serve 6

SAUCE
7 medium-sized fresh ripe tomatoes, peeled, seeded and finely chopped *(see garides me saltsa, page 61),* or substitute 2½ cups chopped, drained, canned tomatoes
1 cup finely chopped onions
2½ cups water
1 teaspoon salt
Freshly ground black pepper

SQUASH
6 medium-sized zucchini or other summer squash, each about 7 to 8 inches long
2 teaspoons salt
2 teaspoons finely cut fresh mint or 1 teaspoon dried mint

STUFFING
1 pound lean ground lamb
⅔ cup uncooked long- or medium-grain white rice, thoroughly washed and drained
1 teaspoon salt
¼ teaspoon ground nutmeg, preferably freshly grated
½ teaspoon ground allspice
Freshly ground black pepper

Kousa Mahshi

STUFFED SQUASH WITH TOMATO SAUCE

To make the sauce, combine the tomatoes, onions, 2½ cups of water, 1 teaspoon salt and a few grindings of pepper in a heavy casserole large enough to hold the squash in 1 or 2 layers. Stirring frequently, bring to a boil over high heat, reduce the heat to low, cover and simmer for 20 minutes. Set aside.

Meanwhile, scrub the zucchini under cold running water. Pat them dry with paper towels and, with a small, sharp knife, cut about 1 inch off the stem ends. Carefully tunnel out the center of each squash leaving an ⅛-inch-thick shell all around. The best utensil for this is the Syrian *munara,* or squash corer, but you can use an apple corer almost as effectively. As the squash are cored, drop them into a large bowl containing 2 quarts of water, 2 teaspoons of salt and the mint. Let the squash soak for 5 or 10 minutes.

To make the stuffing, combine the lamb, rice, 1 teaspoon salt, nutmeg, allspice and a few grindings of pepper. Knead vigorously with both hands, then beat with a wooden spoon until the mixture is smooth and fluffy. Spoon the stuffing into the squash, tapping the bottom end lightly on the table to shake the stuffing down, then filling the squash to their tops.

Place the squash in the tomato sauce, laying them flat. Bring to a boil over high heat, reduce the heat to low, cover tightly and simmer for 30 minutes, or until the squash show only the slightest resistance when pierced with the point of a small, sharp knife. Do not overcook.

To serve, carefully transfer the squash to a heated platter or individual serving dishes and spoon the sauce over them.

To make 14

½ pound (2 quarter-pound sticks) butter, cut into ¼-inch bits and clarified *(see baklava, page 40)*
3 ounces shelled unsalted pistachios, finely chopped (about ¾ cup chopped)
2 tablespoons sugar
14 sheets *filo* pastry, each about 16 inches long and 12 inches wide, thoroughly defrosted if frozen

SYRUP
2½ cups sugar
1¼ cups water
1 tablespoon fresh lemon juice
½ teaspoon rose water

Farareer

BAKED "BIRD'S NEST" PASTRIES

Preheat the oven to 400°. With a pastry brush, coat a large baking sheet with 1 tablespoon of the butter. Coarsely chop half of the pistachios and set them aside. Chop the rest of the nuts finely and combine them with the 2 tablespoons of sugar.

To assemble each "bird's nest," brush one sheet of *filo* evenly with about 1 teaspoon of the butter. Fold the sheet in half crosswise to make a two-layered rectangle about 12 inches by 8 inches. Brush the top with about ½ teaspoon of the butter. Following the directions opposite, fold over the long closed side of the pastry by 1 inch. Brush the top of the fold lightly with butter and sprinkle a teaspoon or so of the finely chopped pistachios in an even row along its length. Roll and shape the bird's nest as shown opposite.

Arrange the pastries on the baking sheet and brush the tops lightly with the remaining butter. Bake in the upper third of the oven for 20 minutes, or until the pastries are crisp and a delicate brown. Slide them gently onto a large platter and sprinkle the hollow in each one with a teaspoon or so of the coarsely chopped nuts.

Meanwhile, make the syrup. In a small, heavy saucepan, bring the sugar, water and lemon juice to a boil over high heat, stirring until the sugar dissolves. Cook briskly, uncovered and undisturbed, for about 5 minutes, or until the syrup reaches a temperature of 220° on a candy thermometer. Add the rose water and pour the syrup into a heatproof bowl or pitcher and let it cool to lukewarm. Serve the syrup separately with the platter of warm pastries.

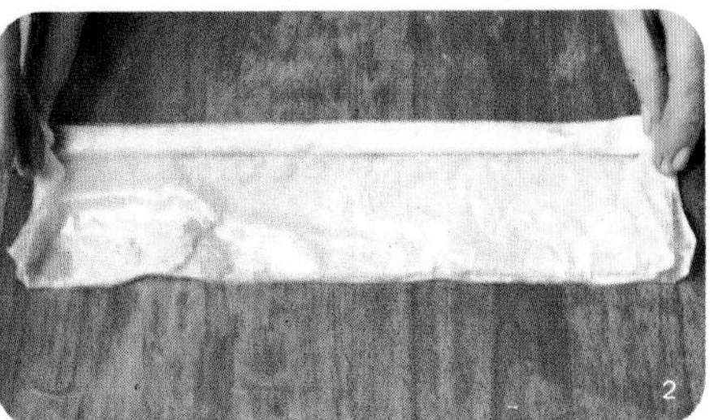

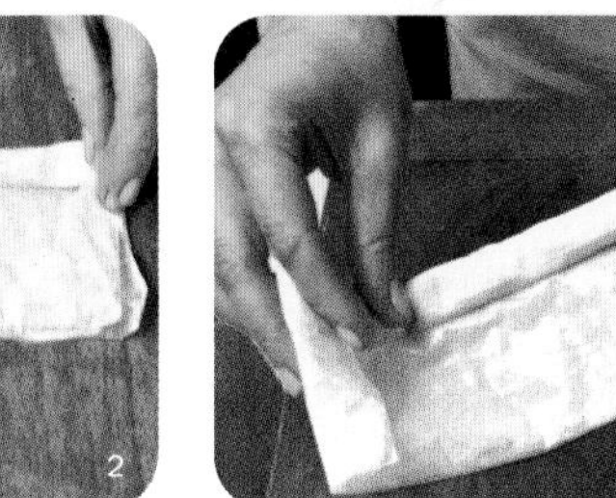

Before adding the filling to *farareer* or "bird's nest" pastry *(recipe at left)* spread a sheet of *filo* pastry flat and brush the top with melted butter. Gently fold the sheet in half crosswise and butter the top again. Turn over the closed edge by about one inch, butter it; then, as shown above, spread it evenly with a spoonful of the pistachio mixture you have prepared for the filling.

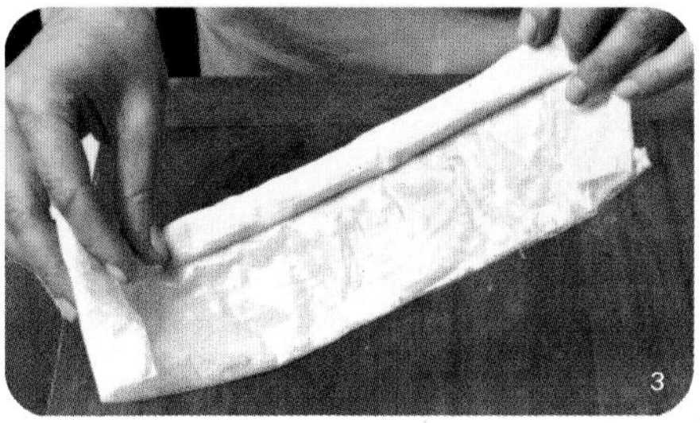

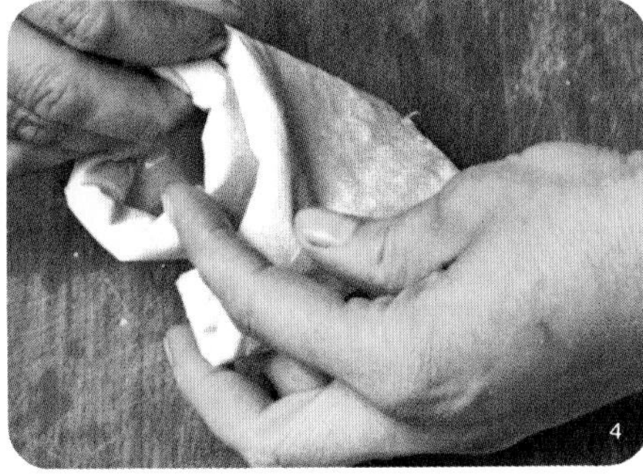

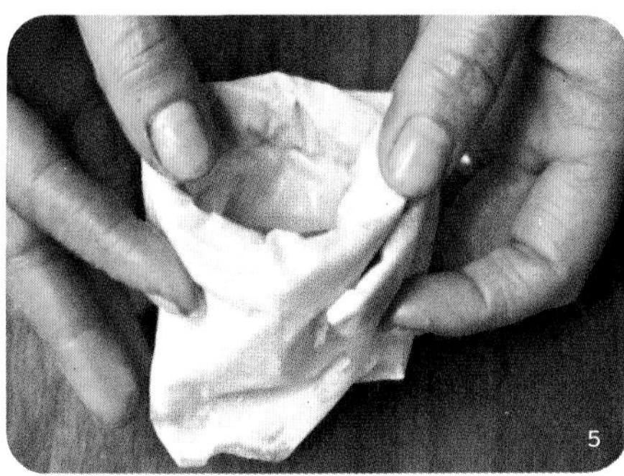

Starting at the fold, roll the pastry to within 2 inches of the opposite edge and turn the short ends over (2). With the filled side facing upward, lift the ends of the pastry in both hands (3) and lap them over one another to make a ring about 3 inches in diameter (4). Crumple the loose pastry up into the hollow center of the ring (5) to form a nest.

Gracefully shaped and baked to a golden crisp, "bird's nest" pastry is sprinkled with nuts and sweetened with syrup *(below)* before serving.

V

The Food That Launched Civilization

Wheat picked from an Israeli field is arranged to show the green-to-gold color change that indicates ripening of this staple Middle Eastern foodstuff, man's oldest cultivated crop. First domesticated at least 9,000 years ago in the region between southeastern Turkey and northwestern Iran, it has developed from a wild grass to the most widely grown grain in the world.

North of the modern city of Baghdad begins Kurdistan, a hilly, grassy region in Iraq, Iran and Turkey with a pleasant, cool climate. It has few important modern cities or spectacular ruins; its peasants lead lives that for centuries have changed hardly at all. But historically Kurdistan is in a class by itself. What makes the region unique is an ancient event in the history of food and of mankind—the domestication of plants and animals. According to all available archeological evidence, this great achievement first took place here. It gave man his first dependable and manageable food supply, and it provided the foundation upon which was built all civilization: villages, cities, nations, empires, writing, literature, law, science.

No one knows what those first farmers of Kurdistan looked like, what color their faces were or what sort of language they spoke. They were forgotten thousands of years before the beginning of recorded history and are known today only through scanty remains found under the mounds of debris, called tells, that dot the Middle East. But the old bones, tool fragments and seeds reveal that these men and women turned mankind from total dependence on the accidental gifts of nature to control over sources of food.

For hundreds of thousands of years after men appeared on earth the way they got their food changed hardly at all. They lived in small bands, eating what nature offered. The women and children gathered fruits, nuts and seeds, dug up roots and collected slow-moving game such as tortoises and snails. The men hunted almost any animal they could kill. Sometimes they ate well, but hunger was an ever-present danger. When the band had eaten all the natural food in one locality, it moved on.

Very, very gradually, over a period of tens of thousands of years, man's foraging techniques improved. He devised better tools and weapons, hunted more skillfully and made better use of wild vegetable foods. About 9,000 B.C. some of the bands learned to live fairly well without continual wandering. This could be done only in favored parts of the earth, and one of these natural Gardens of Eden was in what is now northern Iraq, where wild sheep ranged the plains and several kinds of coarse grass—the ancestors of modern wheat and barley—produced heads of edible seeds.

It is no accident, then, that sheep and wheat—two basic foods of the modern Middle East—were tamed first. In both cases the process was slow, for primitive people are stubbornly conservative. Most experts believe that sheep were man's first controlled source of food and that their domestication was an outgrowth of systematic hunting. At intervals, men and boys would string out in lines, shouting and waving their arms to drive wild sheep into narrow places in the hills where they could be killed easily. The next step was to pen captured animals in a steep ravine with a fence across its mouth.

For centuries, perhaps for a thousand years or two, such sheep-keeping was a hit-or-miss thing, and most of the captive sheep were eaten when winter came on. Eventually, presumably during especially mild winters, a few sheep were kept alive until spring, grazing when there was grass, fed with stored hay when there was not. In this way they began to reproduce their own kind in captivity and gradually evolved into domestic sheep. The strongest and least tractable animals may have been killed first, so the breed became tamer and tamer. At last the once-wild sheep were tame enough to graze peacefully in flocks, making no attempt to escape.

The acquisition of domesticated sheep made a dramatic change in man's food supply and his way of life. The flocks produced more meat than wild sheep had done, and the supply was more dependable. People no longer went meatless when a few hunts failed.

Even more important was the cultivation of plants, for it provided a previously unknown abundance of food, and most significant of all, it permitted men to live in permanent settlements. This feat may have been first accomplished by women, and its first triumph was wheat, which still grows wild in Kurdistan and is harvested in the ancient food-gathering way. *Triticum dicoccoides,* the ancestor of nearly all cultivated wheat, thrives best on moist uplands between 2,000 and 4,300 feet in altitude. A field of *Triticum dicoccoides* looks rather like a thin stand of domesticated wheat, but there are important differences. The heads of the wild wheat are shorter and the grains smaller, and each grain is tightly enclosed in its scratchy husk. When a head ripens, its grains tend to break away from the central stem, to be dispersed by wind or animals.

At first the women gathered wild wheat merely by breaking off the heads or pulling the grains from them. Later they used wooden or bone sickles set with small flints, which would cut several stalks at a time. Ancient sickles have been found in the region, with flints that are polished just back of the edge—polished millennia ago by silica particles in the wheat straw.

Gathering wild wheat, even with a cleverly made sickle, is not agriculture. Gradually, however, the women came to realize that their wheat supply could be increased by *planting* some of the grain they had gathered in places

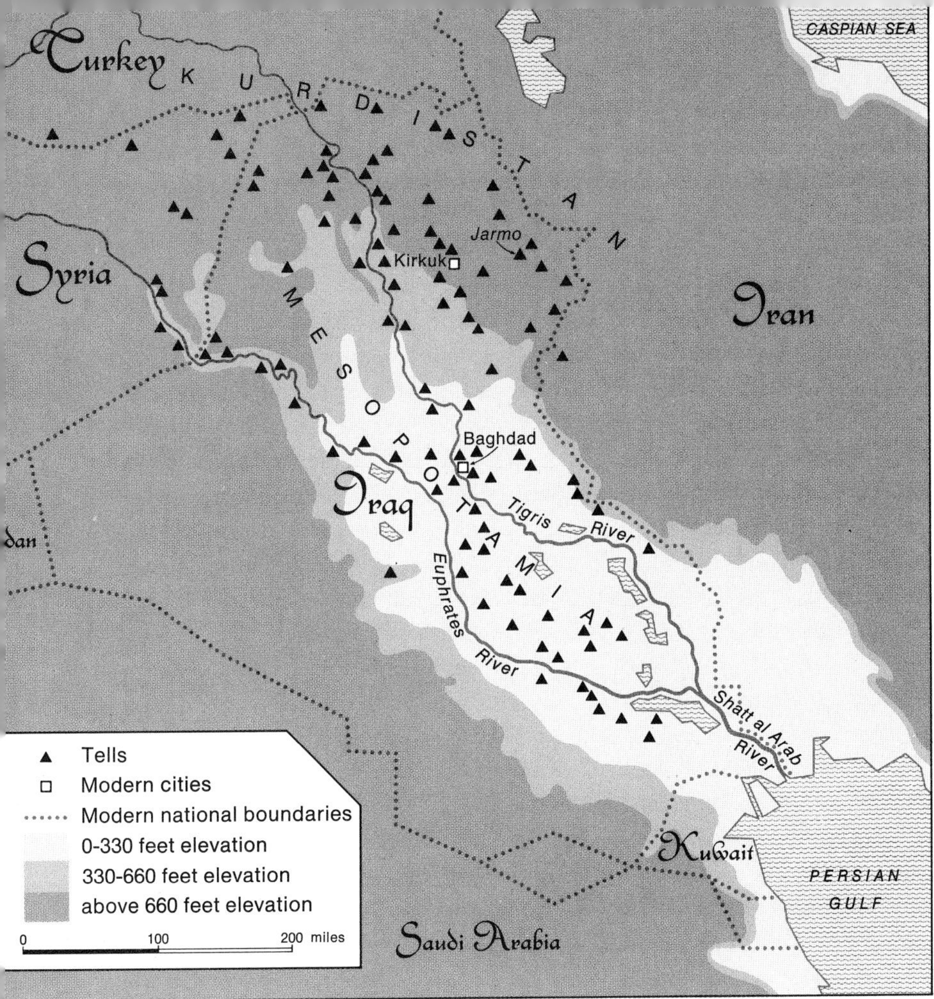

The map at left shows man's extent of settlement after he first became a farmer in the uplands of Kurdistan *(top)*, the area where plants and animals—wheat and sheep—were first domesticated in the Middle East. The black triangles mark the sites of the earliest settlements, now reduced to mounds of ruins. These ruins, called tells, trace the progress of the early farmers to low-lying lands to the south in Mesopotamia, the region between the Tigris and Euphrates Rivers. There the land was far more productive; population soared, and men developed complex systems of law, religion and writing—the basic elements of a civilized society.

where wild wheat did not grow naturally. They may have gotten this radical idea by observing that wet kernels often sprouted, forming small, green plants like the ones they saw growing wild.

It is anyone's guess what those earliest cultivated fields were like. Perhaps the women first sowed the seed in places where floods had covered the ground with bare silt, or they may have looked for patches of thin sod and spaded them after a fashion with their root-digging sticks. Either way would have worked, and when they gained a little confidence they learned that wheat did not have to grow in the higher uplands alone. It would also grow well if planted lower down, on more fertile plains and foothills.

Man's first controlled food supplies, sheep and wheat, became the basis of a truly agricultural life. As soon as the sheep were docile enough to be driven to pasture in the morning and back to safety at night, they could range over a considerable area, turning into nourishing meat the plentiful grass and weeds that human stomachs could not digest. Wheat was even more valuable, partly because it made food abundant but also because it made food that could be stored for a long time. Two or three acres of good land planted in wheat would, with luck, provide the major part of a family's food for a year. A village of several hundred people could live on its sheep and wheat and never go more than a mile from its center.

It was not quite as simple as that, of course. Not all the land was good, and little was known about how to keep it productive. Also, there was defense to think about; a village of well-fed farmers was likely to be raided by hungry nomadic hunters. But villages did flourish on domesticated animals and wheat. The most famous of them is Jarmo, first excavated in 1948 by an expedition from the University of Chicago led by Robert J. Braidwood.

The Jarmo tell is a low mound in the foothills of northern Iraq east of the oil town of Kirkuk. Like many other Middle Eastern mounds it is mud mixed with debris from successive villages built on its site. Braidwood found at least 15 distinct levels, each representing a somewhat different stage of development. In the deepest level, 25 feet down, he found the oldest, most primitive culture of all, a village that had barely achieved the agricultural way of life. It was built about 6800 B.C. In a sense, this date can be said to mark the start of man's slow progress toward civilization.

The original Jarmo had about 30 houses covering three acres. It may have had something like 200 inhabitants, and they were certainly farmers. Many sheep bones were found in what must once have been unpleasantly reeking refuse heaps, and a large proportion of them were of yearlings. This is a likely age for the slaughter of domestic sheep, but an unlikely result of hunting, which brings in animals of all ages.

Jarmo's wheat had a great disadvantage from the primitive housewife's point of view; the husk encasing each kernel was rough and tough, laborious to remove from the grain. Modern peasants pound wheat in a mortar and winnow off the husks, and the women of Jarmo probably did the same. What they did next is known with some certainty. They put the cleaned grain on curved, hollowed-out stones and ground it to flour with smaller stones. Such "saddlemills" were used for thousands of years with little change. The earliest bread was baked in thin cakes on the flat, fire-blackened stones found on many ancient hearths. Even today, if you walk into a peasant's cottage in modern Kurdistan, you will find the woman of the house making delicious bread in this 9,000-year-old way, though she is apt to bake it on metal sheets over a small fire instead of on hot stones.

The first people of Jarmo had no metal, of course, and not even pottery, only baskets and stone bowls. It is not likely that they often set their bowls on the fire, but they may have cooked grain in water in depressions lined with baked clay, heating the water by adding hot stones until it boiled. The product was probably an undercooked porridge. Meat may also have been added, but much patience and many hot stones would be needed to tenderize it much by this sort of boiling. Roasting over the coals—a cooking method much older than agriculture—would yield a better-tasting dish.

Well above the bottom level of the Jarmo mound pottery appears, and with it came new cooking possibilities. Now boiling could make the toughest meat tender and produce satisfying soups and stews. Wheat could be made into nutlike-flavored *burghul* by boiling the grains, as is still done in the Middle East. Tough roots could be softened, taking a heavy task off human teeth. "Beehive" ovens of clay also appear at the upper levels of the Jarmo mound. At first they may have been used for drying or roasting wheat, but the same ovens could roast meat or bake bread.

Peas, lentils and other crops came to supplement wheat. Goats were domesticated not long after sheep, but cattle and pigs came much later. Jarmo's cuisine could not have been elegant, but except for the lack of chicken and certain dairy products, it did not differ much from the food of peasant villages in the Middle East today. In fact, the basic dishes of a typical meal in a

Opposite: The sheep domesticated by the Middle Eastern originators of farming belonged to a spiral-horned type called the mouflon—some of whose descendants still roam wild through the forests and rocklands of the islands of Sardinia and Corsica. Although the mouflons survive in the isolation of the islands, they have disappeared from the Kurdistan homeland of the first farmers.

Olives, along with figs among the first fruits cultivated by man, are shown in this early-19th Century print as they grow in clusters of three or more on the twigs of the trees. Mature trees, which vary in height from 10 to 40 feet, reach a great age —some are believed to be 1,000 years old. Olives were first cultivated for their oil alone, which by 2500 B.C. had become an important export product for Syria, Palestine and Crete. No one knows when people discovered that the hard, bitter fruit was also edible when cured, but the Romans nibbled green and ripe olives as early as the time of Christ.

Syrian restaurant in New York—stewed mutton, *burghul* and thin sheets of bread—could have been served in ancient Jarmo.

The simple but reliable wheat-and-mutton diet had a profound effect on the lives of the first farmers. In the earliest agricultural villages, such as the Jarmo mound, houses were much alike; there were no identifiable workshops or luxury quarters. But as farming improved, it yielded more than enough food for the farmers, and they began to barter their surplus for goods produced by nonfarmers who had special skills. Later villages supported specialized potters who produced much better pottery than the farmers could make in their spare time. Other specialists turned out superior stone, bone or wooden tools, received a share of the village's surplus and formed a growing class of skilled artisans. Still others, the precursors of the merchant class, made long journeys to exchange the village's products for things it did not have, such as obsidian to make sharp stone knives.

Soon after farming began, the farmers were confronted with the troublesome problem of who owned what. People who are hunter-gatherers generally have little concept of property. They own their tools, weapons, clothing

Fresh figs, shown growing on the tree and cut in half in the picture at left, are delicious but highly perishable; they are rarely eaten outside the region in which they grow. One of the advantages of figs, however, is that they can be dried in the sun and stored for later use. Largely for this reason, figs have been cultivated around the Mediterranean for millennia (Adam and Eve used fig leaves to clothe themselves when they were expelled from Eden), and Mediterranean peoples were so dependent on figs and olives that the fig tree and olive branch symbolized peace and plenty.

and other personal objects, but hunting territory is shared by all alike and shelter is too temporary to be considered important. Farmers are different; they live in permanent houses, and they need to know what land to cultivate and where to graze their animals. As population increased, law and government were called for to settle conflicts over land and other property rights.

Archeologists do not know in detail what kind of government the farmers first developed. In the beginning it was probably quite informal; public policy may have been argued out before the whole community or before a council of elders. Elsewhere in the Middle East, villages came to include what appear to be temple premises in their centers. Temples imply an established priesthood, and when priests can convince the people that they have influence with the gods, they quickly gain both property and power. So the first rulers of the villages may well have been priest-chieftains who performed mysterious rites in the temples and acted as judges over the people.

The people of the small villages in the hills of Kurdistan did not travel far or fast on this road to advanced civilization. They soon achieved a way of life that fitted the environment and had little need to change, but eventually their population overflowed the available land in the cool hill country. Some began to move out of the hills, and one of the places they went was Mesopotamia, the low, flat plain of the Tigris and Euphrates Rivers that now makes up southern Iraq. The climate there was hot, and the rainfall was too little to grow crops dependably, but about 5500 B.C. the pioneers on the flatlands learned to irrigate their fields with water diverted from small tributary streams. The new technique unlocked a treasurehouse of food, and a dense population began to grow along the river valleys.

Once again, at this point in the history of the Middle East, ways of obtaining food fostered great advances in civilization—advances that, on the face of it, seem to have very little direct connection with food itself. Irrigation-farming cannot be done on any considerable scale by farmers working as individuals. Establishing and maintaining a complicated network of dams, watergates and ditches require many men and a strong government to plan the work and operate the system. In Mesopotamia, government may have retained its primitive democracy at first, but soon a horde of officials, religious and secular, dominated the farmers and claimed a large share of their crops. It was these large-scale governments that planned and directed what even modern engineers would describe as large-scale public works.

The burden of this agriculturally based bureaucracy may not have been welcome (except to the bureaucrats), but it helped to trigger another important advance in civilization: the invention of writing. And once again, the new advance had a great deal to do with food. Officials and landowners needed some way to keep track of rents and taxes—usually paid in grain—and they gradually developed a system of meaningful marks incised on clay tablets. The first marks were pictographs, simplified pictures of material objects. They were clumsy, but later they evolved into purely conventional signs that were as effective as the letters of an alphabet.

Writing proved a powerful tool of civilization. Traditions, laws and records were no longer dependent on human memory. They could be written down permanently, and complicated messages could be sent without risk of error. Plans were decided upon, committed to writing and adhered to. Rulers governed effectively at a distance by means of written rules and instructions. Written literature began. Literate people became a professional class, and schools were founded to train them.

By 3000 B.C. Mesopotamia, then called Sumeria or Chaldea, was a highly civilized land dotted with cities surrounded by towering walls and crowned with elaborate temples. Its poets wrote religious epics; its astronomers recorded the motions of the planets. Its artisans made beautiful things in silver, copper, textiles, ceramics and gold, and its merchants carried them to far distant lands. Along with the merchants traveled the great ideas on which civilization rests: writing, government, law and a host of technologies. Far more than Egypt, its first rival, Mesopotamia influenced all the peoples of the ancient world. The Hebrews acquired much of their culture there, as symbolized by the story of Abraham, who emigrated from Ur of the Chaldees. Mesopotamian skills and ideas spread to Greece and Rome in the west and to India and China in the east. And it all came from a revolution in the way man got his food—a revolution set off by those first farmers who tamed sheep and wheat in the hills of the Middle East.

Olive trees in the highlands of Biblical Samaria, on the Jordan's west side, grow on rocky terraces much as they did in the days of the ancient kings of Israel. In this aerial photograph, the random lines and blobs creating an abstract design upon the landscape are collections of stones cleared from the ground to permit the growth of other crops, such as wheat and barley, between the olive trees. The continuous walls mark off property boundaries.

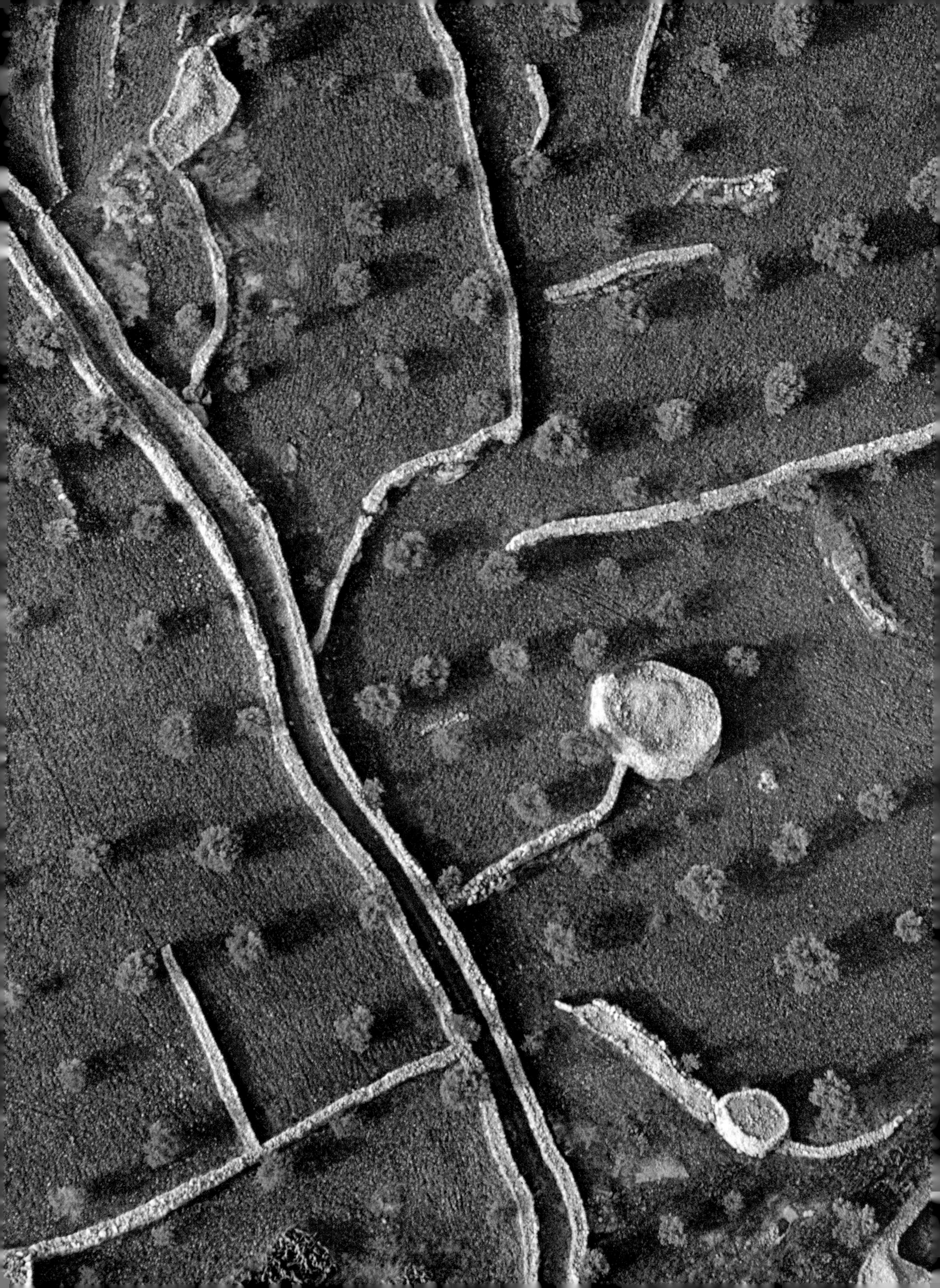

ושמחת
בחגך

VI

New Dishes for a New Nation

Eating lunch in a bowerlike hut, Israeli children celebrate the Jewish harvest festival of Succoth, or the Feast of Tabernacles. On these holy days the specially built, fruit-draped hut, or tabernacle, recalls the temporary dwellings used by the Israelites during their 40 years in the wilderness. The Hebrew sign above the table reads, "Blessed Be Your Coming."

Immigrants from 80-odd nations joined to make up the modern state of Israel, and they all brought along their own native dishes to add to an indigenous Arab cuisine. My Israeli cookbook turns up recipes from far-flung lands: Tunisian chicken, Dutch pancakes, an avocado soup from Chile. And a walk along the streets of Tel Aviv and Jaffa takes you past restaurants offering Polish, Italian, French, Viennese and Chinese food.

What we wanted, though, was Israeli food that was truly Israeli and that could be eaten there and nowhere else. Accordingly, we began our trip with a visit to Tel Aviv's Tadmor Hotel, which houses a government-supported school of cooking and hotel management. There we knew we could see and taste for ourselves some of the fascinating culinary innovations that are beginning to take root in Israel.

Located in Herzlia, a quiet upper-class suburb of Tel Aviv, the Tadmor is close to the Mediterranean shore, in a setting of flowers and trees. The guiding genius of the establishment is a trim and most distinguished man of about 60 named Izchak Niran Nikolai—or simply Nikolai (within moments after we were introduced I was addressing him by his last name alone, just as everyone else does). The school, Nikolai told me, instructs more than 100 young people in the arts of cooking, housekeeping, table service and hotel management. In the 13-month kitchen course, students learn, in Nikolai's words, "what goes on inside the pot." Graduates find jobs quickly, often as full chefs. Through these graduates Nikolai hopes to introduce the Israeli people to a modern cuisine that fits Israel's food products and climate —a cuisine more nutritious than the native Arab food, yet less overwhelming than the heavy dishes generally favored by immigrants from Central Europe. He himself has so far developed about two dozen original dishes based on ingredients easily available to the Israeli housewife—chiefly fowl and fish, which in Israel are more abundant and less expensive than red meat. In effect, Nikolai and others like him have been, perhaps for the first time in history, consciously creating a new national cuisine. The experiment is unique, and I was eager to see it in operation.

In the course of our visit we enjoyed two superlative meals in the Tadmor's dining room. During both of them, we were fascinated by the earnest young waiter-students practicing the rules of elegant service. Every movement was slow and infinitely careful, as though they were rehearsing unfamiliar rituals in which no mistakes were permitted. There was not one careless clink of silver or glassware. Indeed, the only mistake was committed by me. At the start of our first meal, I ordered a Martini without specifying that it be made American style. It was served unchilled, in the Continental proportions of equal parts of gin and vermouth. After one sip I quietly put my glass aside. Just as discreetly, the young waiter removed it.

The food that followed, with its combinations of unexpected ingredients presented in novel ways, made it easy for me to forget my misbegotten Martini. First came a compote of grapefruit sections mixed with sliced almonds and julienne strips of boiled tongue, and a sauceboat containing a nondairy, imitation cream sauce in which I caught a hint of olive oil. The main course was a rich mélange of chicken stewed with olives and pieces of orange. Dessert took the form of a double-folded crepe, crisp at the edges and filled with raisins and diced fruits—bananas, apples, figs—accompanied by a sauce with a tangy fresh-orange flavor made tangier by slivered orange peel.

At our second Tadmor meal Nikolai presided in person, and the service was even more elegant. This time we began with an imaginative first course consisting of a stuffed avocado half: the flesh had been scooped out, chopped and mixed with walnuts, pistachios, halved and pitted sour cherries, and strips of marinated herring. We went on to a crisp fillet of fish fried in olive oil, topped with half a banana, sliced lemon and chopped almonds and dill, and set briefly under the broiler. The sauce was a heady blend of onions, apples, carrots, raisins, curry powder and white wine.

It is a tribute to Nikolai's light touch that I, normally a diner of small appetite, found room for more than that fish course. And there was more to come. The next dish set before us was an assembly of strips of tender turkey breast with sour cherries and bits of pineapple—a delightful combination of colors, flavors and textures. I even did justice to a side dish of green squash, boiled but still crisp, and touched with garlic and dill; and to a mixed salad of peeled tomatoes, crunchy cucumbers and lettuce leaves, all of them tasting as if they had been picked and tossed within the hour.

For dessert we were served figs *en surprise,* a dish whose inspiration was Continental, but whose execution was clearly Nikolai's. It looked like golden puff pastry, piping hot and sprinkled with powdered sugar. Actually, it was nothing of the kind. When we forked into it we encountered the surprise—crisp-skinned fresh figs that had been simmered in sugar syrup and stuffed with what looked and tasted like ice cream of various flavors and colors. Why hadn't the stuffing melted, we asked. Because of a last-minute quick-fry technique, Nikolai explained. The figs are simmered, stuffed and frozen, then dipped briefly in very hot oil just before serving.

The "ice cream" in Nikolai's figs *en surprise* and the "cream sauces" in some of his other dishes contained no milk or cream, nor did his dinners include such milk and cream derivatives as butter and cheese. In Nikolai's kitchen the Jewish *kashrut* or dietary laws are devoutly observed, just as they are in most eating places in Israel. These laws, first laid down in such Old Testament books as Leviticus and Deuteronomy and later amplified in Jewish Biblical commentaries, provide that meat and dairy products must not be eaten at the same meal. Further, two separate sets of dishes must be kept by a housewife or restaurant chef, one for meat and the other for dairy dishes. Only "neutral" or *pareve* foods, such as margarine and eggs (the actual basis of Nikolai's "cream" and "cream sauces"), can be part of both the meat and dairy cuisines. Other *pareve* foods include fish and fish products, vegetables, grains, fruits, and bread and cookies made with vegetable shortening.

Many of the dietary laws contain flat prohibitions against eating certain foods in any form or at any meal. To qualify for the meat cuisine, for example, four-footed animals must fulfill two conditions: they must chew their cuds and have cloven hooves. This rule eliminates such animals as the pig (no cud) and the camel (wrong feet), but allows cattle, sheep and goats. What is more, *all* meat must be thoroughly drained of blood before it is eaten. Every animal must be ritually slaughtered by a specialist, who delivers a swift slash to the jugular vein with a keen knife, so that the blood can drain out as completely as possible. Then the meat is soaked in water for half an hour or so, kept under salt for another hour, and finally rinsed in water several times. One corollary of the stern taboo against blood is that liver must be cooked until it is well done. Another is that hindquarters —say, a leg of lamb, in which remaining blood can easily infuse from the veins and arteries into the flesh during cooking—may not be eaten unless the blood vessels have been removed, a tedious, costly process.

Of all the *kashrut* prohibitions, those against certain kinds of seafood are by far the most sweeping. Again, the law is explicit: an orthodox Jew is not permitted to eat any creature that lives in the water unless it has scales and fins. Many Israelis pay little attention to the law, but for the pious ones who do, this prohibition means: no eel; no crustaceans, and thus no shrimp, no crab, no lobster; no mollusks, and thus no clams, no oysters, no scallops, no mussels, no periwinkles; no octopus or squid.

Happily, the fish that *are* permitted under Judaic law are delicious in Israel. One kind, called Saint Peter's fish, has special associations because it is caught in the Sea of Galilee. The scientific name of Saint Peter's fish is *Tilapia galilaea;* its large dorsal fin has earned it the unscientific name of "combfish," and because its body is thin, legend has it that its ancestors were cloven in two when the Red Sea was parted by the Lord. With all this going for one fish, we felt we had to journey to its native habitat for a taste.

Our road led out of Tel Aviv, first north and then northeast, under a blue sky dotted with fleecy clouds. We drove past tanned young men cultivating fresh-turned fields and wearing the characteristic clochelike worker's hat called a *kova tembel,* which translates literally as "idiot's hat." Presently the lovely, fertile Jezreel Valley fell behind us, and we entered the Galilee re-

Continued on page 136

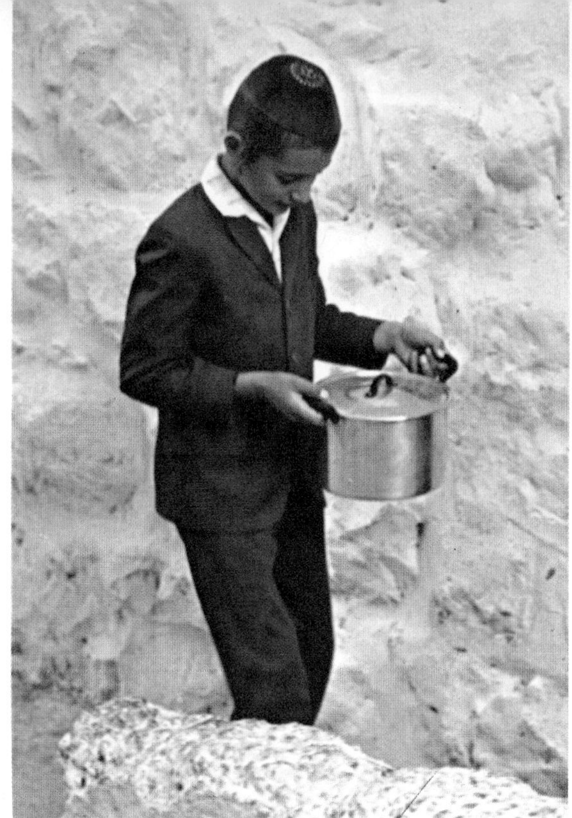

A Dinner for Sabbath

According to religious law, Orthodox Jews may not light a fire on their Sabbath (Saturday). But Jewish mothers like Mrs. Moshe Cheshen *(right)* see to it that their families enjoy hot noonday meals nevertheless. They prepare slow-cooking dishes the day before and leave them in a hot oven overnight; like New England baked beans, the dishes gain extra flavor from the extended cooking process. Perhaps the most popular of these long-cooked Sabbath dinners is a homely, hearty stew called *cholent* that originated centuries ago in the ghettos of Europe. The old-fashioned *cholent* usually contained beans, potatoes, rice and meat. Today however, Israeli cooks, busily marrying the dishes of many regions to create a cuisine of their own, have added eggs, an ingredient in a kind of *cholent* popular among North African Jews. It is this adapted dish that was prepared by Mrs. Cheshen of Jerusalem. She begins her *cholent* on Friday by first dropping rice into a bag so that it will not stick during its long baking. She then places the rice bag into a pot with a lid, and adds the remaining ingredients. By sundown Friday, when the Sabbath begins, the *cholent* is ready for long slow cooking in the communal oven *(above right)*, and by the time the Cheshens return from the synagogue the following day a hot and flavorful dinner will be waiting.

Most housewives complete the cooking of their *cholents* at home. Better than a kitchen stove, however, is a bakery oven with banked fires dying out after baking Friday's bread. In the picture at far left, ten-year-old Elie carries the family's *cholent* to a neighborhood bakery. At left, the baker removes hot meat dishes on Saturday, among them the Cheshens' *cholent.* With the family seated at the table, Mrs. Cheshen distributes the still-warm *cholent;* the only accompaniments are a salad of peppers *(center)* and a sweetened vegetable stew called *tsimmes.*

gion, the lushest land in Israel. Now we had arrived in Biblical country.

The "Sea" of Galilee is actually a harp-shaped lake of fresh water. To reach it one drives down past a sign that marks the general level of the world's seas, and continues downward for about 700 more feet to Tiberias, the lakeside health resort founded during Jesus' lifetime and still popular for its hot sulphur springs. Here again, thoughts from the Bible press in. Somewhere along these banks Saint John the Baptist preached to and purified his followers, Jesus among them. Along this lake shore Jesus found two fishermen brothers, Andrew and Simon called Peter, casting their nets, and said to them, "Follow me, and I will make you fishers of men." North of Tiberias lies Tabgha, where the multiplication of the loaves and fishes took place. And a couple of centuries later, Jewish scholars in Tiberias compiled the Mishnah, which includes the first written codification of oral traditions relating to agricultural offerings, dietary laws (including many of the laws of *kashrut*) and other culinary matters governed by religion.

Obviously, even a traveler intent upon food must make an effort hereabouts in order to stay in the present, but our appetites soon began to say *now,* and we drove on to keep our rendezvous with Saint Peter's fish. We chose an open-air restaurant, painted in bright colors, on the Galilean shore. There we sat directly beside the water, overlooking a small stone jetty that sheltered thousands of fingerling St. Peter's fish. The sight of this potential food was heartening. Not long ago the Sea of Galilee was being overfished; the catch dropped so sharply that experts were summoned to devise a remedy. They came up with a simple answer, and one that worked: Throw back the smaller fish in every catch, the "seeds" of meals to come.

For an appetizer at our lakeside restaurant, we were served a brisk salad of tomatoes and pickles, moistened with a little pickle juice; I missed the dill and garlic that flavor "Jewish" pickles sold in Stateside delicatessens, but there was a stimulating tartness in every bite. The fish itself arrived whole, deep fried, with the skin crisp and the flesh moist—exactly as fried fish should be done. In flavor it was like a somewhat bland salt-water porgy. With it came masses of French fried potatoes, an almost universal mealtime ballast nowadays; mine went mostly to the fingerlings, but I ate enough to recognize the Israeli potato as slightly sweeter than our own. Our real sweet, of course, was the dessert: plain fresh dates, with a fruity moist pulp that we popped into our mouths as we do Concord grapes at home, setting the skins aside. I doubt that I shall ever eat a dried date again.

In the hill country north of the Sea of Galilee, our excursion led us to an institution that has become world famous—the *kibbutz,* or collective agricultural settlement. The *kibbutz* at which we spent a night, Ayelet Hashahar (Morning Star), is one of the oldest in Israel, founded in 1918, and may be taken as typical of the nation's nearly 300 *kibbutzim.* Its members own their agricultural enterprise—every crop, animal, tractor and building—collectively, and are paid no wages for their work. In return, all their needs are attended to: housing, meals, doctors and hospital care, movies, concerts, plays and lectures, newspapers, even haircuts; they receive cash allowances for clothing, shoes and books. (Israel is a nation of dedicated readers.) Children are reared and educated communally, by age groups, and see their parents only after working hours and on the Sabbath. Though the total population of the *kib-*

butzim is only about 90,000—while that of the nation is 2,800,000—these farms produce almost a third of Israel's agricultural yield.

Over the years the communal austerity of the *kibbutz* has been relaxed in various ways—in some *kibbutzim,* for instance, children now sleep in their parents' homes—and the original concept has been modified to permit families to work individual homesteads. A good many *kibbutzim* have also set up commercial enterprises on the side. They manufacture such products as machines or plywood, operate restaurants (the restaurant at which we had our Saint Peter's fish was *kibbutz*-owned), or establish public rest houses, like the one at Morning Star (Morning Star also grows cotton, keeps beehives and runs a bookbinding shop). But the *kibbutz* idea remains Israel's unique contribution to contemporary social life. Perhaps no other nation in modern times has succeeded so well in an experiment of communal endeavor, with each member working for all the others as well as for himself.

We arrived at Morning Star in good time for dinner, and took our places in a spacious, informal dining room staffed with waitresses who bantered breezily with patrons they knew from former visits. The food itself was farmhouse fare, simple and satisfying. There was a savory, filling chicken-liver pâté. There was also pickled fish, a traditional European-Jewish preparation of fish fillets simmered in a spicy fish stock, sprinkled with onion rings and grated carrot and chilled until the stock becomes a delicate aspic. Several kinds of fish can be used; ours was fresh carp from Morning Star's private pond, and we sprinkled it with the tart juice of lemon wedges. The rest of the dinner included freshly killed chicken and roast beef. For dessert I chose the apple sauce, a greenish, tart purée that proved a perfect complement to the rich flavors and textures of the hearty main meal.

Next morning, up at 7 a.m., we avoided the guests' dining room and made our way to the huge communal dining hall to sample the free-wheeling morning meal that has come to be known as the "*kibbutz* breakfast." This is a sort of do-it-yourself operation, with no fixed menu, offering *kibbutz* members an ample selection of whatever is available from the fields day by day. At Morning Star the dining hall—which also serves as movie theater, concert hall and meetinghouse—seats about 300 at long, plastic-topped tables. On each table was an array of homemade bread, butter, herring marinated with onion rings, a huge bowl of raw tomatoes and onions, and dishes of fruit conserves. But these were only nibbles; soon after our arrival a stainless-steel cart came by, pushed by an attendant who dispensed bowls of porridge and boiled eggs, and he was followed by a second attendant carrying a large kettle filled with scrambled eggs. Around 8 o'clock farmhands began to stream in from the fields. They had been at work since 5 or 6 o'clock, and their appetites were impressive. So were their spirits; a rapid fire of loud and jolly kidding flew from table to table. It was obvious that life in a *kibbutz,* however unrewarding in cash, provides deep fraternal satisfactions.

The *kibbutz* philosophy, its sense not only of the dynamic present but of a hopeful future, came through most clearly and movingly when we looked in on the little children at breakfast. We barely more than peeked at them, because the motherly attendants rightly feared that our intrusion might disturb their charges. Yet we did catch a glimpse of healthy three-year-olds sitting four to a table and eating French toast, while a good thick carrot soup sim-

Continued on page 144

Fulfilling the Promise of an Ancient Land

After arid centuries the Biblical land of milk and honey flourishes once more. The state of Israel is now dotted with productive farms which once were wastes of desert, swamp and rock—a feat largely accomplished by building large irrigation networks and introducing modern machines, plants and livestock breeds. Much of this pioneering centered around farm collectives, which began as social experiments but also served, like Nahalal *(left)*, as frontier outposts. Despite harassment from hostile Arabs, Israeli settlers have made their harsh land yield abundantly. In 1948, when the state of Israel became independent, it imported three fourths of its food. Now, with a population three times greater, it is not only largely self-sufficient but exports over $140 million worth of food annually. Today a youngster like the sturdy boy picking a pomegranate *(right)* knows nothing other than the land of plenty that is his home.

Israeli farmers have multiplied production six times over in two decades by applying the most recent discoveries of agriculture at the same time they retained old practices. The sleek cattle at right are Santa Gertrudis stock from Texas, a breed that produces top quality meat in semiarid country. In Israel, Santa Gertrudis are being crossed with Arab, Turkish and Brahman (Indian) strains. The new breed is already producing some of the tenderest beef in the world, in part because of carefully balanced, high-protein feed. Enclosing ripening dates in bags *(below)* to protect them from birds is a practice centuries old, but dates, like bananas and other fruits, also benefit from modern fertilizers, pesticides and irrigation. Since Israel became a state in 1948, date production has soared from 50 tons to 1,900 tons; banana production has risen from 3,500 tons to a high of 56,000 tons; and harvest yields of citrus fruits increased from 272,700 tons to over 1 million tons.

The men preparing these modern beehives for winter are performing one of the oldest tasks in Middle Eastern agriculture, for honey has been a delicacy in this region since before Biblical times. Today the ancient art of beekeeping has been modernized, too, for on many farms, the bees are kept busy continuously as hives are trucked from place to place so that they are always near flowers. Completely new to tables in this dry country, however, are fresh fish and ducks from farm ponds like the one at left, built at a collective farm operated by boys and girls who are learning the techniques of scientific agriculture.

Dining together *(right)*, sharing labor, 1,000 or more people may live and work in one of the farming collectives called a *kibbutz*, the type of communal settlement that is a distinctive element in Israeli society. In a *kibbutz* children usually live in dormitories and visit their parents after school. Jobs are assigned on the basis of skills, and a specially trained staff prepares food for the whole *kibbutz* in the large restaurant-style kitchen *(above)*. The meals served in this *kibbutz*, one of the few that observe religious traditions, must conform to strict Jewish dietary laws, including the requirement for separate utensils for meat and dairy dishes. The rule is met with a practical simplicity typical of *kibbutzniks*. They bore holes in the handles of tableware used for dairy food *(left)* so that they can never be mixed with the unbored tableware.

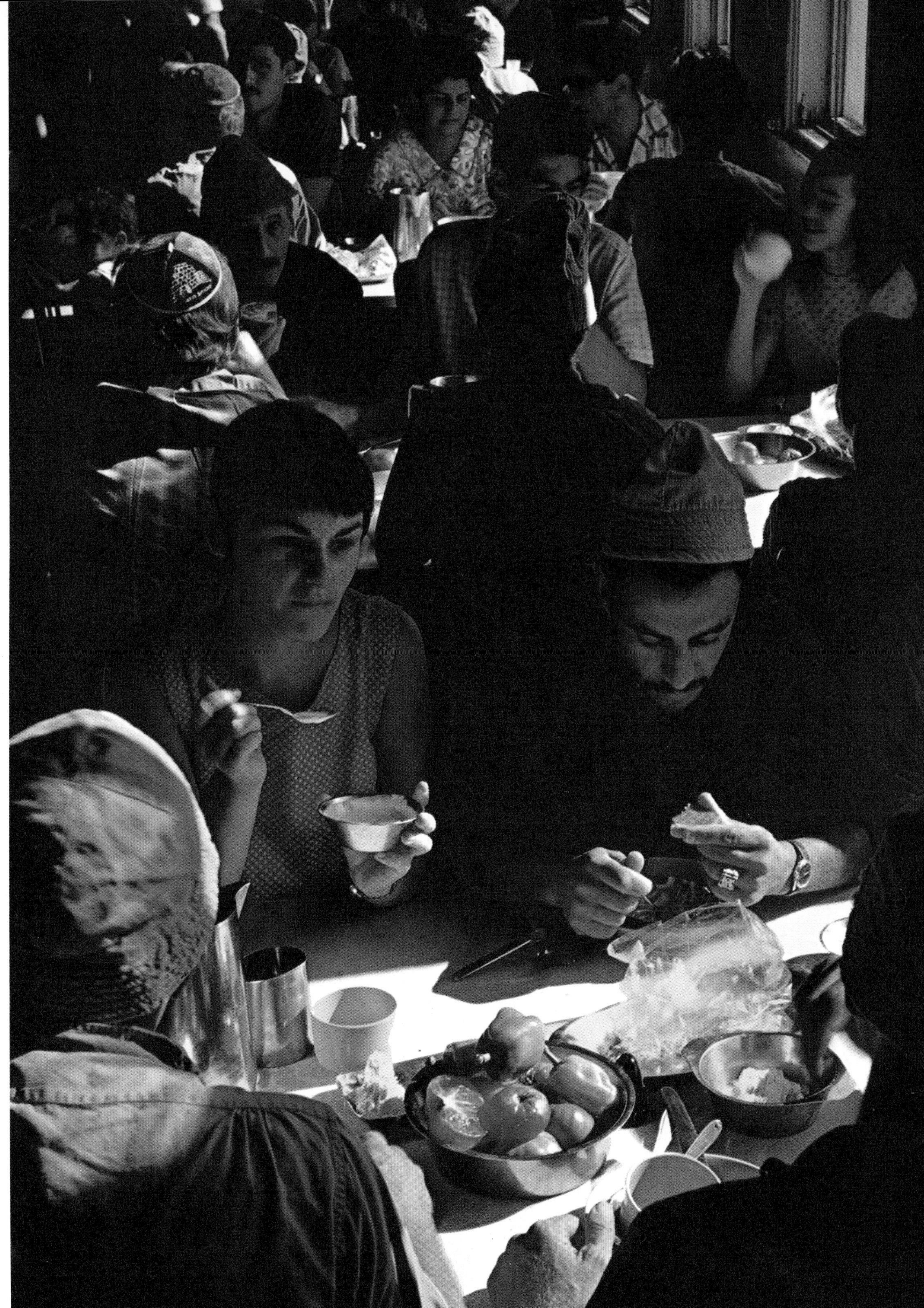

mered in a special children's kitchen, in preparation for their lunch. The slightly older kindergarteners we visited had not yet been served their scrambled eggs. These boys and girls were having raw radishes with their eggs—radishes that they themselves had raised from seed in their own "private" plot, and had pulled up for breakfast that very morning.

During our return trip to Tel Aviv, rural Israel flashed by our car windows. We drove beside fields of wild yellow daisies accented with small red poppies. We passed lemon groves, then ranks of orange trees, with their irregular mosaics of glossy green leaves and ripening, vividly colored fruit. One village on our way was inhabited entirely by vegetarians. (Many Israelis refuse to eat meat, but some atavistic craving for it has inspired such dishes as "mock liver," a savory imitation improvised from eggplant, eggs and onions.) And soon afterward we reached an olive grove with trees that have been certified by Israeli officials as being 2,000 years old. This meant that some trees had been cut down so that the scientists could count their growth rings. But many trees remained, rooted in the red soil, incredibly gnarled and twisted, some with trunks that had split in two over the long centuries, others carrying embedded rocks absorbed and lifted from the ancient earth.

Other trees along our route, nearly all young ones, gave evidence of Israel's massive program of reforestation. On her hills and plains and along her highways, some 85,000,000 trees have been planted during the past 30 years. Most of these trees are eucalyptus, pine and cypress, which thrive in Israel's semiarid climate, living through the year on the winter's precipitation. Any visitor can start a personal reforestation program at such sites as the John F. Kennedy Peace Forest in the Judean Hills outside Jerusalem. He takes a sapling from the nursery, plants it in a prepared hole, and tamps in some earth; then he can compare his baby with those in an earlier row, already rooted, and envision the stately tree to come. Or, on a grander scale involving a large number of plantings, such an occasion may call for music, public speeches and school children on parade in their Sabbath best.

Once back in Tel Aviv, we began to seek out a culinary occasion that would make a fitting close to our visit in Israel. We knew what we wanted: a domestic meal of traditional dishes—something less impersonal than the communal dining of the *kibbutz,* less innovative than the cuisine of Nikolai and the Tadmor Hotel. We wanted food that reflected an Israeli life with its roots at home, in Asia, rather than the Jewish life of European traditions. Our opportunity for just such a meal came when we had the honor of being invited to dinner in a Yemenite home.

The Yemenites of Israel, some 50,000 strong, are Jews who came to the nation in the late 1940s after 25 centuries of exile in the southwestern corner of the Arabian peninsula. Their return, in a way, was a dramatic fulfillment of their ancient faith, for they came in on modern airplanes—flying "with wings as eagles," as promised in the Bible. To their new-yet-old home the Yemenites brought a hotly spiced diet and such specialties as *kat,* a narcotic shrub whose leaves are chewed or brewed into a tea, and the seeds of a pungent, aromatic spice called fenugreek, which belongs in every proper curry and which they use in sauces. These people, I had been told, also eat such delicacies as *kahal,* an animal's udder grilled to rid it of all its milk, and thus avoid any violation of the dietary laws. The desert locust, too, is said to rank high on their list of edibles; it is baked in the oven, dried in the sun for a day, and stripped of the head, wings and legs just before serving.

Not knowing what to expect, but certain of something different and highly flavored, we showed up at our host's suburban home bearing a small gift. We were cordially received, not by the small family gathering I had anticipated but by a welcoming committee of 30 fellow diners! There was no way of communicating with them, except through the English-speaking companion who had come with us; but I have found that in such situations a little smiling makes up for many unspoken words, and the friendly faces around us quickly put us at ease.

This was a pious household. The meal could not begin until all the men, hosts and guests alike, had donned *yarmulkes,* or skullcaps, and the bread and wine had been blessed. This ceremony was performed by the eldest among us, a short, powerful-looking patriarch with a graying black beard, who intoned the sacred Hebrew words in a strong, musical voice. As he sang, he broke the bread. My wife and I, as honored guests, were the first to be offered wine, and then the food began to arrive.

Already on the table was a dark green appetizer called *hilbeh,* a sauce used as a dip for bread. In any scale of hotness, *hilbeh* must be rated *fortissimo.* Its preparation begins innocuously enough, with fresh puréed tomatoes and ground fenugreek seeds. Then the mischief is added: a mixture called *zhug,* consisting of garlic, coriander leaves, caraway seeds and cardamom, all stoked satanically with black pepper and hot chilies. A little water may go in to thin the sauce, but that doesn't help an unsuspecting diner.

What followed had its exotic moments, too, though the chicken soup and the boiled chicken were comparatively bland (we learned later that our host and all the others, thinking of our sensibilities, had subjected themselves to unspiced food—a high point in hospitality). Still, there was the *hilbeh* to dunk into and there were other traditional foods on the table prepared to the company's liking—and to mine. One was *kubaneh,* a brown, bunlike yeast bread served warm. Another was *zalabi,* a festive snail-shaped fritter sweetened with brown sugar. Best of all I liked the unfamiliar flavor of *shawil,* a powerful stew made mainly of beef liver and lungs cooked with garlic, lemon, parsley and cardamom. It was served after the main course, along with a flotilla of side dishes that we nibbled at for the rest of the evening —toasted sesame seeds, shelled almonds, sunflower seeds, popcorn. Finally, there was fresh fruit, and at almost everyone's elbow a bottle of brandy to help our after-dinner mood to bloom.

The group slipped easily from feasting to joking, and to dancing in the ancient way, usually man facing man in a lively shuffle, with hands placed at the small of the back and much bending of the knees. A round drum, shaped to fit under one arm, was tapped to help keep time. There followed a sort of community sing, with chants and songs that drew heavily on the Psalms for their words. About 11 o'clock, the evening drew to a close. We were served glasses of hot tea strongly infused with ginger, and just as we emptied them, a final chant filled the room with ancient melody. Our patriarch was thanking God for the food we had been given.

We all rose and left, exchanging many a *shalom,* the Hebrew word of both greeting and farewell that means "peace."

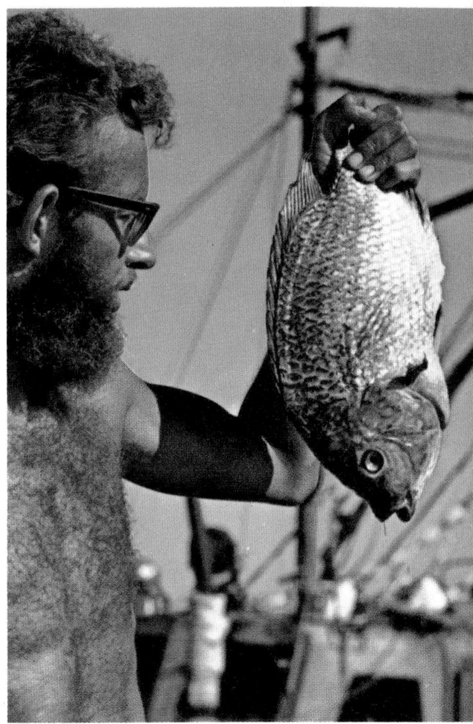

St. Peter's fish is the name Christians in Israel give to *mushat,* a plump variety of combfish being held by this bearded fisherman. The nickname refers to a Biblical episode. As related in the 17th Chapter of Matthew, Jesus told the disciple Peter to hook a fish and promised it would contain money needed to pay taxes. Legend says the fish was a *mushat,* perhaps because these surface swimmers are easy to hook.

CHAPTER VI RECIPES

Because this book deals with Israel as part of the Middle East, most of the recipes in this chapter are drawn from either indigenous food of the region or the new cuisine that has been created since the founding of the modern state of Israel. (For example, "felafel"—often called the "Israeli hot dog"—is a dish that shows the strong Arab influence on Israeli food, while the braised chicken with kumquats represents the emerging national cuisine.) A comprehensive treatment of the traditional Jewish cuisine forms part of another volume in this series.

Challah

BRAIDED WHITE BREAD

To make one 14-inch loaf

- 1 cup lukewarm water (110° to 115°)
- 3 packages active dry yeast
- 4 teaspoons sugar
- 5 to 6 cups all-purpose flour
- 2 teaspoons salt
- 3 eggs
- 1/4 cup plus 1 teaspoon all-purpose vegetable shortening
- 1 egg yolk combined with 2 tablespoons water

Pour 1/2 cup of the lukewarm water into a small, shallow bowl and sprinkle it with the yeast and 1 teaspoon of the sugar. Let the mixture stand for 2 or 3 minutes, then stir to dissolve the yeast completely. Set the bowl in a warm, draft-free place (such as a turned-off oven) for about 5 minutes, or until the mixture almost doubles in volume.

In a deep mixing bowl, combine 4 cups of the flour, the remaining 3 teaspoons of sugar and the salt. Make a well in the center, pour in the yeast and the remaining 1/2 cup of lukewarm water, and add the eggs and 1/4 cup of the vegetable shortening.

Gently stir the center ingredients together with a large spoon, then beat vigorously until all the flour is absorbed. Add up to 2 cups more flour, beating it in 1/4 cup at a time and using as much as necessary to form a dough that can be gathered into a soft ball. If the dough becomes difficult to stir, work in the flour with your fingers.

Place the dough on a lightly floured surface and knead by pressing it down, pushing it forward several times with the heel of your hand and folding it back on itself. Repeat for about 15 minutes, or until the dough is smooth and elastic. Sprinkle it from time to time with a little flour to prevent it from sticking to the board.

Shape the dough into a ball and place it in a lightly greased bowl. Drape loosely with a kitchen towel and set aside in the warm, draft-free place for 45 minutes, or until the dough doubles in bulk. Punch the dough down with a single blow of your fist and knead it again for a few minutes. Set the dough aside to rest for 10 minutes.

With a pastry brush, coat a large baking sheet with the remaining teaspoon of vegetable shortening. Divide the dough into 4 equal pieces. On a lightly floured surface, roll each piece into a rope about 22 inches long. The ropes should be about 2 inches in diameter at the center and taper to about 1/2 inch at both ends. Interweave the ropes into a four-part braid; the diagrams in the Recipe Booklet illustrate the technique.

Carefully place the *challah* on the baking sheet and let it rise in a warm place for about 30 minutes.

Preheat the oven to 400°. Brush the top of the loaf with the egg yolk and water mixture and bake in the middle of the oven for 15 minutes, then reduce the heat to 375° and continue baking for 45 minutes longer, or until the *challah* is golden brown and crusty. Cool on a cake rack.

Challah, wine for a blessing, and candles welcome a Jewish Sabbath.

The traditional almond-decorated honey cake is given a new flavor in Israel with a tradition-shattering ingredient—instant coffee.

To make one 9-inch loaf cake

1 teaspoon plus 1/4 cup vegetable oil
2 1/4 cups all-purpose flour
1/4 cup seedless raisins
1/4 cup chopped candied orange peel
3 egg yolks
3/4 cup honey
1/3 cup sugar
2 teaspoons finely grated lemon peel
4 1/2 teaspoons instant coffee dissolved in 1 tablespoon boiling water
1 teaspoon baking powder
1/4 teaspoon baking soda
1/4 teaspoon ground cinnamon
1/4 teaspoon ground allspice
A pinch of ground cloves
1/4 teaspoon salt
3 egg whites
1/2 cup sliced blanched almonds

Ugat Dvash

HONEY CAKE

Preheat the oven to 325°. With a pastry brush coat the bottom and sides of a 9-by-5-by-3-inch loaf pan with 1 teaspoon of the oil. Sprinkle the oiled pan with 2 tablespoons of the flour, tipping the pan from side to side to spread the flour evenly. Then invert the pan and rap the bottom sharply to remove the excess flour. Combine the raisins and orange peel in a bowl, add 2 tablespoons of the flour and turn the fruit about with a spoon until it is evenly and lightly coated. Set aside.

In a deep bowl, beat the egg yolks with a whisk or a rotary or electric beater until frothy. Then beat in the remaining 1/4 cup of oil, the honey, sugar, lemon peel, and the dissolved coffee. Combine the remaining 2 cups of flour, the baking powder, soda, cinnamon, allspice, cloves and salt and sift them into the egg-yolk batter, 1/4 cup or so at a time, beating well after each addition. Stir in the raisins and orange peel.

Wash and dry the whisk or beater, and in a separate bowl beat the egg whites until they form unwavering peaks when the beater is lifted from the bowl. With a rubber spatula, gently but thoroughly fold the egg whites into the batter, using an over-under cutting motion rather than a stirring motion.

Pour the batter into the loaf pan and spread it out evenly. Decorate the top with the almonds, arranging the slices to make simple daisy shapes in the center of the cake and leaving enough almonds to make a small stripe at each end. Bake in the middle of the oven for 1 hour and 15 minutes, or until a cake tester or toothpick inserted in the center comes out clean. Cool in the pan for 4 or 5 minutes, then run a sharp knife around the edges and turn the cake out on a rack. Cool completely.

Honey cake is often served with unsalted butter.

Maafeh Of Vematza Metubal Beshamiz

BAKED MATZOH, CHICKEN AND DILL CASSEROLE

To serve 4

6 eggs
½ cup finely chopped onions
½ cup finely cut fresh dill, or substitute 2 tablespoons dried dill weed
¼ cup finely chopped parsley, preferably flat-leaf parsley
2 teaspoons salt
Freshly ground black pepper
3 cups cooked chicken meat cut into strips about ¼ inch wide, ¼ inch thick and 1½ inches long
½ cup vegetable oil
3 plain square matzohs
2 cups chicken stock, fresh or canned

Matzohs are a special version of unleavened bread associated with the Jewish "Pesach" or Passover ceremonies, which commemorate the flight of the Israelites from Egypt to the Promised Land of Canaan. Escaping Egypt so abruptly, they were unable to leaven or bake their bread beforehand, and had to make a simple flour and water dough for baking in the sun, thus producing the crisp flat matzoh.

Preheat the oven to 400°. In a deep mixing bowl, beat the eggs with a whisk or a rotary or electric beater until frothy, stir in the onions, dill, parsley, salt and a few grindings of pepper, then add the chicken. Turn the pieces gently about with a spoon until they are thoroughly coated.

Heat the oil in a small saucepan until a light haze forms above it, then pour a teaspoon of it into an 8-inch-square shallow baking dish, tilting the dish to spread it evenly. Set the remaining oil aside off the heat.

Dip a matzoh into the chicken stock until it is well moistened. Lay it in the bottom of the baking dish, spread half of the chicken and egg mixture evenly over it, moisten a second matzoh in the chicken stock and place it over the chicken. Spread the remaining chicken and egg mixture on top and cover with the third moistened matzoh. Pour about half the remaining oil evenly over the last matzoh and bake in the middle of the oven for 15 minutes. Then sprinkle with the rest of the oil and continue baking for 15 minutes longer, or until the top is browned. Serve at once.

NOTE: If you do not have cooked chicken meat on hand, prepare it by poaching 3 pounds of chicken, a sliced onion, 2 celery tops, a bay leaf and a teaspoon of salt in 2 cups of water. Bring to a boil, cover and simmer over low heat for 1 hour. Remove the chicken and when cool bone and skin it. Strain the broth. You should have about 3 cups of meat and 2 cups of broth.

Hilbeh

YEMENITE HOT RELISH

To make about 1½ cups

3 tablespoons fenugreek seeds (reddish-brown seeds with a currylike aroma, from a plant of the pea family)
3 medium-sized firm, ripe tomatoes, coarsely chopped
2 tablespoons finely chopped garlic
½ teaspoon salt
3 whole cardamom pods, crushed, or ⅛ teaspoon cardamom seeds
1 teaspoon caraway seeds
½ teaspoon coriander seeds, or ¼ teaspoon ground coriander
½ teaspoon ground hot red pepper

With a mortar and pestle or the back of a spoon, crush the fenugreek seeds to a fine powder. Pour in 1 cup of boiling water and steep for 2 or 3 hours. Then drain the fenugreek in a fine sieve. Purée the tomatoes through a sieve set over a bowl and stir the fenugreek into them.

With the back of a spoon or with a mortar and pestle, mash the garlic and salt to a paste. Add the cardamom, caraway, coriander and red pepper and mash them vigorously until the mixture is smooth. Stir it into the tomato and fenugreek.

Serve at once or store tightly covered in the refrigerator. *Hilbeh* is a traditional fiery accompaniment for *felafel (Recipe Index)* or a dip for bread.

Tarnegolet Bemizt Hadarim

OVEN-BRAISED CHICKEN WITH KUMQUATS

To serve 4

A 2½- to 3-pound chicken, cut into 6 to 8 serving pieces
Salt
1 cup fresh orange juice
2 tablespoons fresh lemon juice
¼ cup honey
2 tablespoons drained, rinsed, seeded and finely chopped canned or bottled hot chili peppers
10 preserved kumquats
Lemon or orange slices

Preheat the oven to 375°. Pat the pieces of chicken completely dry with paper towels, sprinkle liberally with salt, and arrange them side by side in a baking dish large enough to hold them in one layer. Mix the orange juice, lemon juice and honey together and pour it over the chicken, turning the pieces about in the mixture until they are well moistened.

Rearrange the chicken pieces skin side down in the baking dish and scatter the chopped peppers over them. Bake uncovered and undisturbed in the middle of the oven for 15 minutes. Turn the pieces over, add the kumquats and baste thoroughly with the pan liquid. Basting occasionally, bake the chicken 30 minutes longer, or until the leg or thigh shows no resistance when pierced with a fork.

To serve, arrange the chicken and kumquats attractively on a heated platter, pour the pan juices over them and garnish with lemon or orange slices.

Felafel

DEEP-FRIED CHICK-PEA AND CRUSHED WHEAT BALLS

To serve 4 to 6 as an appetizer (about 30 one-inch balls)

½ cup fine *burghul* (crushed wheat)
1½ cups coarsely crumbled Arab bread, or substitute 1½ cups coarsely crumbled homemade-type white bread
1½ cups dried chick-peas (garbanzos), soaked, cooked and drained, or 2 cups drained, canned chick-peas, rinsed under cold water
¼ cup fresh lemon juice
2 teaspoons finely chopped garlic
2 tablespoons finely chopped fresh coriander *(cilantro)*
1 teaspoon crushed red pepper
1 teaspoon ground cumin
1 teaspoon salt
Freshly ground black pepper
Vegetable oil or shortening for deep frying

Place the *burghul* in a small bowl, pour in enough cold water to cover it completely, and let the wheat soak for about 15 minutes. Drain thoroughly in a sieve or colander. Meanwhile, drop the crumbled bread into another bowl, add cold water to cover, and soak for 15 minutes or so. Drain the water from the bread and vigorously squeeze the pieces completely dry. Set the *burghul* and bread aside.

In the jar of an electric blender, combine the chick-peas, lemon juice, garlic, coriander, red pepper, cumin, salt and a few grindings of black pepper. Blend at high speed for 1 minute, or until the mixture is reduced to a smooth purée. Transfer the mixture to a deep bowl.

(To make the purée by hand, mash the garlic and ½ teaspoon of the salt with a large mortar and pestle or the back of a spoon to a smooth paste. Beat in the coriander and red pepper, then add the chick-peas and lemon juice and continue mashing until the peas are finely puréed. Stir in the cumin, the remaining salt and a few grindings of black pepper. Or, less arduously, force the chick-peas, lemon juice and garlic through a food mill set over a bowl and beat in the coriander, red pepper, cumin, salt and a little black pepper.)

Stir the wheat and bread into the chick-pea purée. Moistening your hands occasionally with cold water, shape the mixture into balls each about 1 inch in diameter. Arrange the balls on wax paper or a plate and let them dry at room temperature for about 1 hour.

In a heavy 10- to 12-inch skillet with a deep-frying thermometer or in an electric skillet or deep fryer, heat 2 to 3 inches of the oil or shortening until it reaches a temperature of 375°. Fry the balls in the hot oil a dozen or so at a time for 2 to 3 minutes, or until they are golden brown. As they brown, transfer them with a slotted spoon to paper towels to drain while you fry the remaining batches. Regulate the heat if necessary to keep the oil at 375° during the entire cooking process.

Mound the *felafel* on a heated platter and serve hot as an accompaniment to drinks or as a first course.

A new dish for a new nation is Israel's glazed chicken and kumquats.

VII

Iran: A Tradition of Subtlety

An Iranian craftsman specializing in the repair of antique tiles interrupts work to share lunch with his nephew (and assistant) on a scaffold in Isfahan's 17th Century royal mosque, whose richly ornamented tiles are among the most beautiful in the Middle East. The tiler, member of a family that has followed this trade for eight generations, enjoys a properly traditional meal: a local specialty of saffron rice and lamb cooked and served with yoghurt.

The basic food of Iran is rice. It is eaten in quantities that stagger the Westerner—and especially a calorie-conscious Westerner like my wife, who all but counts the grains when she cooks rice, getting eight servings from a pound. An Iranian recipe may call casually for two and a half pounds of rice to serve four. And the Iranians clean up their plates of rice, sometimes at all three of their daily meals. The nation grows it own supply, mainly in the region around the Caspian Sea, where the long-grained variety flourishes.

Fortunately, Iranian rice is prepared in too many ingenious and unexpected ways to become monotonous. When cooked, it has a delicate aroma of its own and tastes only faintly of starch. And among all the rice dishes we sampled in Iran, we never received a poorly prepared serving. Every Iranian considers himself a rice expert, but like wine connoisseurs, the experts often disagree. One housewife told us that rice should never be washed before it is cooked, nor rinsed afterward. Others insisted that it should first be soaked overnight, or at least for a couple of hours, and set under the spigot after boiling. The choice of method may depend on how long the grain has been aged —no time at all, one year or two years.

The Iranian cook has at her command a complex catalogue of rice dishes, but all belong to one or the other of two basic types: *chelo* and *polo*. Both are initially cooked in much the same way; the difference between them lies in the ways they are served. *Chelo (Recipe Index)* is plain rice, boiled and buttered, topped by a *khoresh* of varied sauces and meats. *Polo* resembles a pilaf, in that the accompaniments are mixed and cooked with the rice. Whatever the type, the rice in each dish is boiled, drained and turned in a heavy pan, covered, and either baked in a moderate oven or gently steamed over a low flame as long as another three quarters of an hour. In this phase of cooking, the rice is mounded into a cone, and the tip of the cone is often indented deeply with a long-handled spoon. The ultimate refinement, however, lies in producing a crunchy brown crust called *tah dig* on the bottom of the rice. This is achieved by binding the bottom layer of rice with egg yolk, yoghurt, paper-thin potato slices or simply melted butter or oil; the crisp result is served triumphantly as proof of the cook's skill.

The *khoresh* that surmounts *chelo* rice is hardly ever missing from the Iranian table. To some extent it is a seasonal mixture; the housewife may combine whatever fruits or vegetables are available in the market with almost any meat she pleases. Domestic beef tends to be sinewy, and lamb and mutton are the traditional favorites throughout the Mideast, but chicken, wild fowl and fish are also used. (No pork, of course—if an Iranian cook chooses to prepare this forbidden food to please a Westerner, he may call it by such euphemisms as "nightingale's flesh" to cover his embarrassment.) The sauce may be sweetened by the taste of fresh quinces, pomegranates, apples or black cherries, or a grab bag of dried fruits—prunes, peaches, plums and apricots. Blanched nuts, chopped and toasted, may figure in it. Sautéed onions contribute pungency. A half teaspoonful of pepper goes with a single pound of meat, as does an equal amount of the aromatic spice called turmeric. Verjuice (the sour juice of unripe grapes), lemon or lime juice, or dried limes do their part to kill excessive sweetness imparted by the fruits. Slivers of dried tangerine peel add a citrus-grove essence. And somehow—possibly by instinct, more likely by mother-to-daughter tutelage—the right choice and proportions of such ingredients fuse into a glorious stew to spoon over one's rice.

Polo rice may come with many of the same ingredients that go into *khoresh,* and is just as variable. A good idea of the range of *polo* dishes may be gained from two of its forms. One is *tah chin (Recipe Index),* which is rice and meat with yoghurt; the second is *shekar polo,* or sugar pilaf, a sweet version served at weddings and on holidays.

Tah chin begins with pieces of lamb marinated as long as 10 hours in a blend of saffron and yoghurt (the curdled, fermented milk not only lends flavor but also acts as a tenderizer). Just before the rice for the dish finishes boiling, a little of it is mixed with yoghurt and a couple of beaten eggs to become the crisp layer of *tah dig* at the bottom of the dish. Over this go layers of meat, marinade and rice, and after additional slow cooking the *polo* is ready for the serving platter. Saffron butter may be dribbled over the rice, the spice having first been swirled in hot water to help its flavor bloom. This colorful, savory mixture is the standard *tah chin,* but the standard dish is not the only version; one cook who prepared it for us added thin layers of finely cut spinach.

The sugar pilaf turns *polo* into a rich confection that is eaten as a main course. *Shekar polo* calls for as much as a cup of heavy sugar syrup to coat a pound of boiled rice, and it comes to the table topped colorfully with the yellow of saffron in melted butter or chicken fat and a green-and-white speckling of chopped pistachios and almonds. Its sweetness is offset by an accompaniment of spicy meat—either marble-sized meatballs, sautéed and then buried in the rice during the final cooking, or rich-gravied *kameh,* a separate dish of finely ground meat fried and then boiled with split peas and sour cherries and given a dusting of pulverized cloves.

Festive preparations of *shekar polo* are made in celebration of the Iranian New Year, called *no-ruz* or "new day," when spring returns to gladden the earth. The holiday begins at the moment when the sun reaches the sign of Aries in the Zodiac, and Iranian families await that moment gathered around the *haft sin* or "Seven S's"—a table adorned with food and symbols appropriate to the occasion (in Persian, the names of all of them begin with the letter *sin).* There are also shoots of young wheat, which stand for the roots of life. The most interesting item of all, perhaps, is a group of eggs that rest on a mirror and are supposed to jiggle at the instant the new year arrives. According to an ancient Persian myth, the earth is supported on one horn of a bull, and every year the bull switches the burden to its other horn to gain a little relief. When the eggs respond to the mighty toss of the bull's horns—I suppose that someone always "sees" them move—the new year is at hand.

There follows a 13-day jubilee when schools are closed, visits, gifts and greetings are exchanged, and mountains of sweets are consumed. The nationwide party traditionally ends in day-long picnics. Spring has come and has been welcomed joyously, and everyone goes back to work.

We caught a glimpse of another Iranian picnic tradition in the provincial capital of Isfahan. It was a Friday morning, the Muslim day of rest, and we were in the company of an affable young Isfahani. I noticed a station wagon go by with a man at the wheel and at least 10 or 12 women crammed into the other seats, and asked what this odd carload might signify. With an air of elaborating the obvious, our companion explained that the driver was taking his womenfolk—who might include sisters, sisters-in-law and aunts—for a picnic in the country. Brothers take turns performing this pleasant family duty, he added, and he concluded his explanation by announcing that he would have to leave us soon because it was his turn that day.

Left to ourselves before lunchtime, we strolled among the sights that make Isfahan one of the most beautiful cities in the world. The Maidan-e-Shah, or Royal Square, a plaza nearly 1,700 feet long and over 500 feet wide, holds a quiet pool in its center now, although back in the early 17th Century it was often noisy with polo games. It is lined with mosques and other buildings covered in intricate tilework, their delicate domes and minarets thrusting up into the turquoise sky. To walk among these masterpieces is to come upon a truly legendary city.

Isfahan seemed the right place to try *chelo kebab (Recipe Index),* the Iranian national dish, and we had no trouble finding a restaurant that served it. I know of no other country on earth where so many restaurants operate without a menu; in Iran, it is simply because a great many of them serve nothing but *chelo kebab.* We chose a busy one with a spread of tables set on a sunny patio—only to encounter another Iranian custom. This area was for men only, we were told, and we were directed to a crowded indoor dining room where couples and families were admitted.

Once seated, we got our *chelo kebab* with all the ritual fixings—a big pat of sweet butter, a raw egg with the top of its shell cut away, and a little bowl of sumac, the sour, woodsy-flavored spice derived from a benign cousin of our poison sumac. All were for mashing into the *chelo,* or plain rice, which ap-

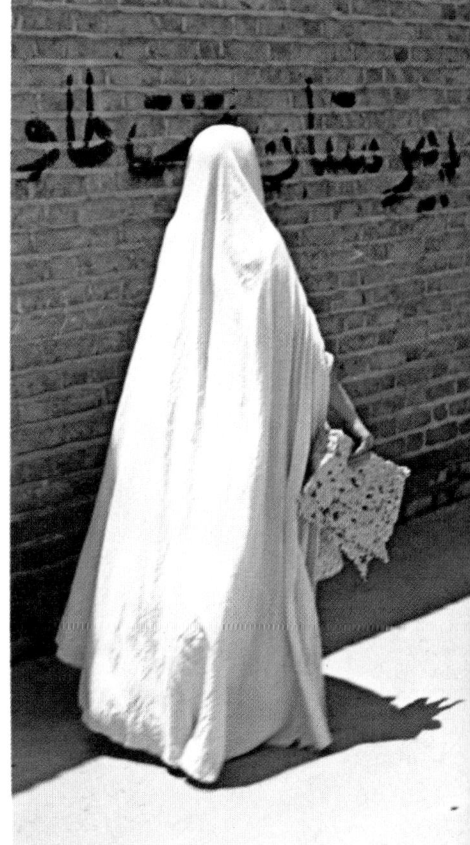

Shrouded in her *chadur* an Iranian housewife glides homeward with a meal's worth of the coarse bread called *sang-gak.* Popular with all classes for its full flavor, this whole-wheat bread is baked over hot stones in neighborhood shops that operate from 4 a.m. to 9 p.m., providing fresh *sang-gak* for every meal. One strip of the bread, usually about a yard long, sells for about three cents.

Continued on page 160

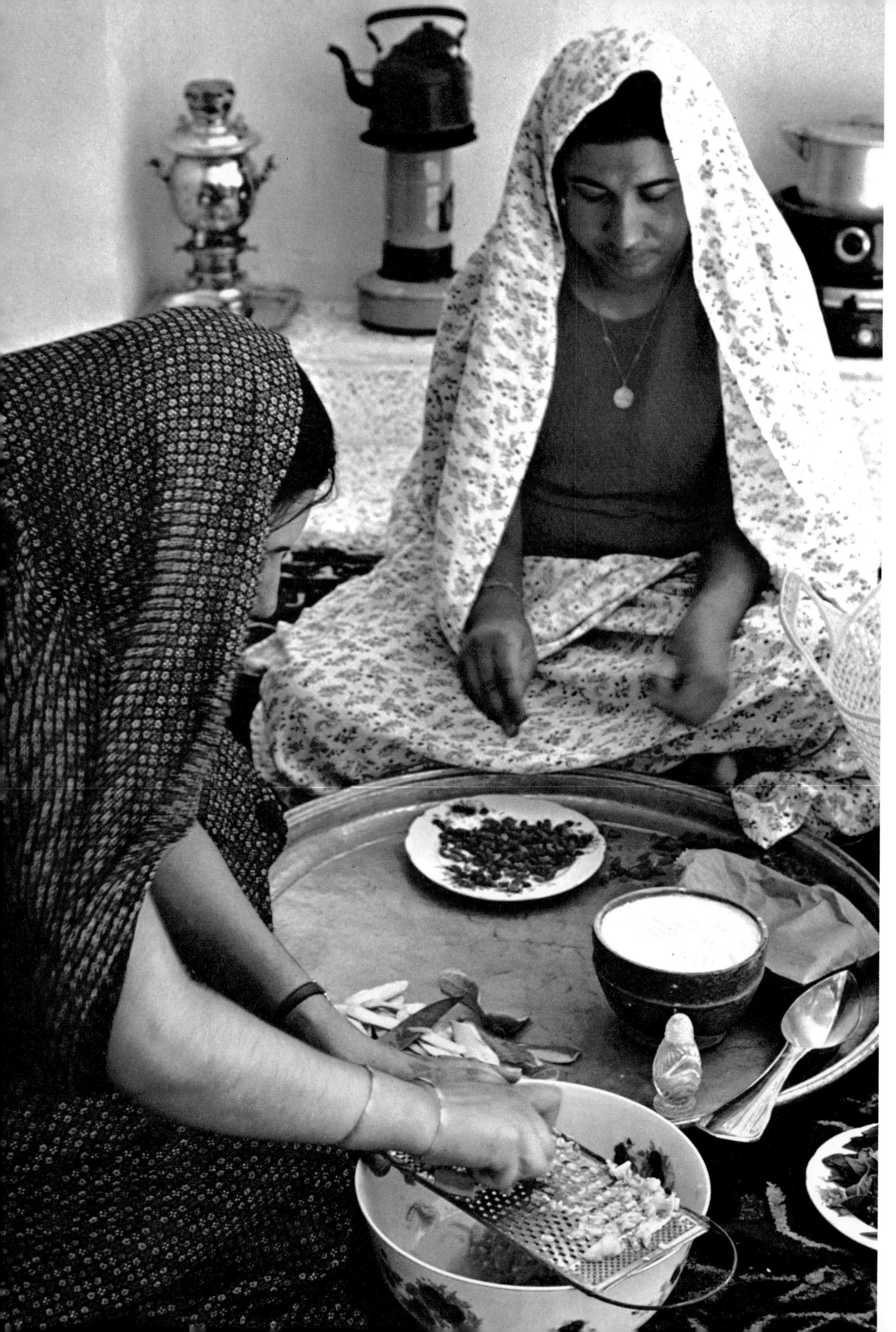

Dinner in Iran: Festive Rice "Polo"

The chilled yoghurt soup being prepared at left will be the first course for a colorful Iranian meal. But the main course, and the one most characteristic of the land, will be based on rice. Rich in bountiful crops of rice from the area of the Caspian Sea, Iranians have made this grain a staple of their daily fare and have become gourmets in its preparation. One of the most popular of their unique rice dishes is *polo,* a casserole of steamed rice with vegetables, fruits, nuts, meats or poultry. A fine *polo* is usually characterized by a crisp bottom crust of rice. The pictures here and on the following pages show the family of Hussein Mossadeghzadeh, a tilemaker of Isfahan—he is shown on page 152—as they prepare and enjoy a dinner of *alo-balo polo,* made with sour cherries and chicken.

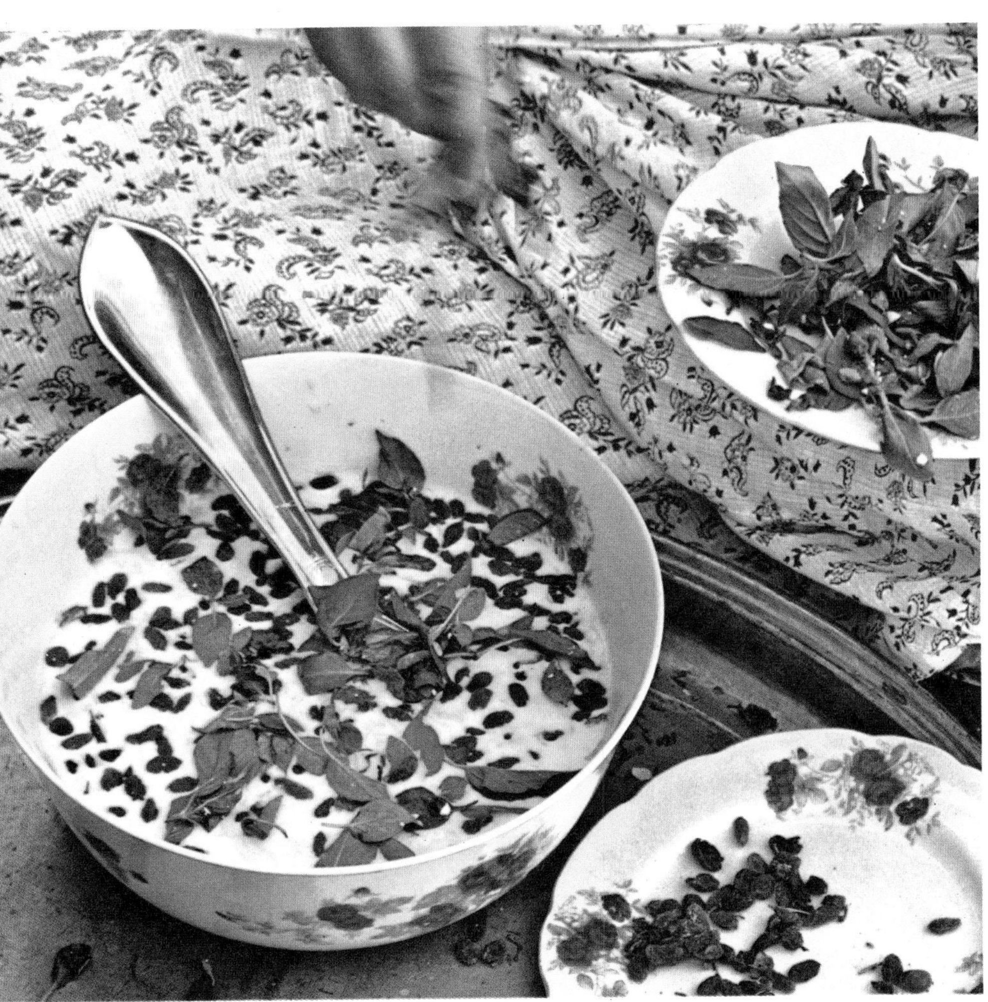

A light soup—yoghurt, grated cucumber, chopped onions, thinned with water and seasoned only with salt—is favored by Mrs. Mossadeghzadeh, who in the picture at left cleans raisins for it while her sister Aghdas *(left)* grates cucumbers. Just before serving the soup, she stirs in ice cubes and sprinkles the top with the raisins and with chopped fresh mint. (For another version, see the Recipe Index.)

To start her *polo* pot, Mrs. Mossadeghzadeh cooks sugar with fresh sour cherries—purchased that morning at Isfahan's outdoor market—until she has a thick, bittersweet preserve. While the cherries are simmering, she braises a chicken in water *(top of picture)* and parboils rice.

The finished *alo-balo polo (above)*, colorful and festive, consists of layers of rice, chicken and sour cherries, cooked to tempting tenderness. To embellish the dish Mrs. Mossadeghzadeh mixes some rice with saffron, which turns the grains a vivid yellow.

The hearty midday meal is a family affair shared on this occasion by Mr. and Mrs. Mossadeghzadeh *(top and right)*, their children, two sisters-in-law and a company of nephews and nieces. Along with *polo* and yoghurt soup, dinner included melon, cucumber and bread.

peared in huge mounds on our plates. The *kebab,* or meat, lay on top—thin slices of lamb, which had been marinated in lemon juice and grated onion, perhaps for as long as three days, then broiled over charcoal until it is done but not dry. Fillets are considered best; when tougher cuts are used, the slices are first scored lightly with a knife to be sure they will be tender.

This meat was tender. There are no knives in the customary Iranian place setting; we simply pinned down each slice with a fork and used the edge of a spoon to cut or tear away each bite. The spoon then becomes the vehicle for the rice mélange, topped by a morsel of meat. As side dishes we had cups of tart yoghurt under a buttery-yellow skin (some diners mixed it into their *chelo)* and a salad of raw onions, the green parts of scallions, and a refreshing grasslike herb—I never learned its name—with a taste like that of anise. With lunch we drank *dugh,* a tingly soft drink made of yoghurt whey mixed with water—or in this case, with sparkling mineral water. And our dessert was *bastani keshi,* Iran's clotted, sherbetlike ice cream, flavored with rose water. But the jewel of the meal was that *chelo kebab,* a combination of soft and crusty rice, tangy yet tender meat, and piquant spice.

Having had *chelo kebab* at one of Iran's great inland cities, we journeyed to the Caspian Sea to try another precious commodity, caviar. It is available in Iranian cities, of course—and a bargain at seven to twelve dollars a pound—but we wanted to see the fisheries and the Caspian itself, the world's largest landlocked body of water and its largest salt lake, fertile with sturgeon and their tiny eggs for caviar. The southern rim of the sea is very nearly the only dependably green and forested region of Iran, much of whose territory consists of a desert of dust-bowl erosion and salt-pan sterility.

To reach Bandar Pahlavi, the headquarters of Iran's state-owned fishing industry on the Caspian, we drove some 240 miles out of Tehran, the national capital, and over the Elburz Mountains, a forbidding barrier crossed from Tehran to Pahlavi by only two paved roads. Our driver, a chatty and patriotic man, took the lower, easier route for the outbound trip. Along the way he proudly pointed out a prosaic nail factory, a symbol of Iran's growing industrialization; and when we passed a stand of pistachio trees he spoke poetically, like a Persian of the past, of how sweet they smelled when in bloom. (He could have added that his nation grows some of the plumpest, meatiest pistachios in the Middle East.) At the summit of the pass the car bored into wisps of mist—the ground was "breathing," the driver said—and then the descent wound through country that grew lusher by the mile.

Arriving in Pahlavi in time for lunch, we made straight for a restaurant operated by the local fishery. The menu may have offered a *khoresh* or a *polo,* but we didn't look at it; we ordered skewered sturgeon, served lightly browned and hot from the coals. Sturgeon is not, in my opinion, a tender fish, yet it is tasty in its own rich way, something like swordfish but with a far stronger flavor at the skin. With the platters came fresh, mixed greens sprinkled with chopped hard-boiled eggs. Two cruets on the table contained olive oil and lemon juice, and our driver used both with a free hand, then smothered everything under a black blanket of pepper, but I enjoyed the simple crisp salad plain.

Sturgeon is Iran's most valuable catch but overfishing, the pollution of the waters by industrial plants and the deprecations of natural enemies that

Opposite: A rich and pungent Iranian stew called *dizi* leads a double life. A workingman's lunch when made with strips of mutton, it becomes a friends-for-dinner dish when the meat is shoulder of lamb as it is here. Other ingredients remain basically the same—chick-peas, tomato, onion and turmeric—though this stew acquires extra goodness with the addition of dried fava beans. Accompanying the dish is a plebian but versatile drink called *dugh,* made with tart, refreshing yoghurt.

Continued on page 164

In the picture above, carpet weavers and their children set a crowded table between lofty looms for their midday dinner: a meat and vegetable stew called *gormeh sabzi (see Recipe Index),* rice and fresh vegetables, watermelon and wheat bread. At right, a group of rug washers, having set out their rugs to dry *(background)* enjoy a midday meal of the spicy mutton stew called *dizi (see Recipe Index).*

At High Noon Rug Weavers and Washers Eat Well, Indoors or Out

Iranian carpet weavers and washers, heirs to one of the world's great traditions of decorative art, work long days that often begin at sunup. At midday, they interrupt their work for hearty meals that may include meat with peas, beans or typically enormous servings of Iranian rice. The intricate designs and bright colors of their craft surround them even at mealtimes. Home weavers, who often squeeze two or more huge vertical looms into their small mud-brick houses, may dine in the same room in which they weave their carpets. The rug washers shown on the opposite page, who work at a natural spring near Tehran called Cheshmeh Ali, are never out of sight of their products. By noon they have cleaned a number of old rugs and washed new ones to rinse away excess dye. With the rugs laid out to dry in patches of color on a sunny hillside, some workers eat while others join bathers to swim and sun—all watched over by stone bas-reliefs of an early shah and his court carved in the rocks in the background.

feed upon young fish, have depleted the Caspian, and a vigorous program of restocking is under way. Iran has begun the artificial breeding of 25,000,000 sturgeon a year, to be released in the fresh-water streams in which they are normally born. Tads weigh about one tenth of an ounce; the youngest and smallest are almost invisible until a sharp knock on the white basins in which they are kept sends them scampering. But they must not be coddled while they grow larger, lest an acquired laziness leave them less clever at foraging on their own and outwitting predators. After two or three months, they are released into one of the rivers that empty into the Caspian Sea. Gradually as they continue growing, they move toward and finally enter the Caspian. A few larger ones are kept in open-air tanks for the study of their life cycle; thanks to the easy living of the tanks, these fish may grow to seven inches long in a single year and double that length at the age of four. They may grow even more quickly in the Caspian, but many die or are eaten before they reach maturity. Yet the fish that do survive in the Caspian may grow to amazing size. The biggest specimen ever taken in Iranian nets weighed well over a ton and was estimated to have lived more than a century.

This grand old lady gave up almost 400 pounds of caviar. Her younger and less productive sisters average about a tenth of this yield, and their smaller cousins, the common sturgeon and the sevruga, still less. Each year, Iran harvests 200 tons or more of the pearly caviar—not the less expensive red variety (which comes from salmon, usually from salmon taken in the Pacific Northwest), but the costly gray-black grains, and on rare, unpredictable occasions, a blond variety. This is hailed as "golden" caviar and set aside for the Shah and his court. The rest is absorbed by both domestic and foreign buyers, more than 190,000 pounds of it going annually to the United States.

We dutifully looked into the fishery's freezing lockers, where sturgeon and other Caspian fish were stacked like tall piles of fire logs, and out at the docks, where a glistening fresh catch lay, the females already deprived of their roe. Then came the treat we had looked forward to—a taste of fresh Iranian caviar. In a large room where workers sorted and packed the eggs, we dug into our helpings—and I realized at once that I had never really *had* caviar back home. Exports to the United States are treated with sea salt alone. In Iran, on the other hand, borax as well as salt is used, and the two act together to preserve and to bring out the flavor. (All caviar is salted in some degree—in its natural state it tastes simply like plain raw fish—and the best is the kind called "malossol," the Russian term for "little salt.")

That night we spent on the Caspian "riviera" where Iranians come in summer to relax on the beach. Here members of the royal family have several villas. Greenery grows luxuriant—orange and lemon trees and climbing vines were in bloom—and our hotel tried hard to rival a *luxe* establishment of Nice or Cannes. It made for a serene, comfortable stay; our return to Tehran the next day, on the higher route through the mountains, was neither serene nor entirely comfortable but considerably more interesting.

The journey began placidly enough. We drove past flooded rice paddies reflecting the sky. Farmers in coolie hats were leaving thatch-roofed houses for the fields. Tea plantations spread trim, round bushes along the flat coast and up the hillsides. Not far from where we were, a graceful monument rises over the tomb of the diplomat Kashef-us-Saltaneh, who introduced the cul-

An elegant diner in Isfahan's Shah Abbas Hotel seems to lift her glass in salute to the principal figure in the mural facing her. The mural shows Shah Abbas himself, a Persian ruler who lived in Isfahan, being served fruits and wine. The present-day diners enjoy Iran's greatest dish, *chelo kebab,* made of rice and marinated, broiled meat. The rice is customarily topped with a raw egg yolk *(above),* which in this case was separated from the egg white and returned to the shell before the dish was served.

tivation of the tea plant into Iran at the beginning of the 20th Century.

Then we turned south, following the valley of the Chalus, a turbulent, brown mountain stream. Just past the first line of hills, the road entered country where bears and leopards are still a menace. Soon the steep-sided mountains loomed up and the road became an aimless, twisting thread, apparently leading nowhere. At one point rocks hung menacingly over our heads in distorted checkerboard formations.

We climbed, twisted and climbed again until the evergreens were all below us. Fog settled in, then snow. A goatherd appeared and pushed his flock against the mountain wall to let us pass while his shaggy dog barked furiously at the car. At last we came to the end of the twisting climb: a one-way tunnel over 1,300 yards long. An attendant made us wait for oncoming cars, but finally we drove on into the unlighted, narrow passage, guided by reflectors placed a few feet apart. Icicles hung from the roof, and toward the end water fell in splashes over the car. Then we emerged into sunshine and flowers again along the downward road to Tehran.

Tehran lies on an arid plateau 4,000 feet high but it is a lovely city for strolling. One morning we hurried through a light breakfast in our hotel—a breakfast made memorable by fresh pomegranate juice, ruby red and full of flavor—and went out into the tree-lined streets. Beside the curbs are flowing runnels that once carried part of the city's water supply; this water is now provided by river dams, and the curb-side rivulets have been reassigned the gracious task of nourishing the trees.

At midday we came on a group of workmen sitting in the leafy shade hav-

Two Beluga sturgeon are trundled through an Iranian fishery on the Caspian Sea after being stripped of their roe, which becomes costly caviar. Some 95 per cent of the world's caviar now comes from the Caspian, bounded by Russia and Iran. The United States was a major producer until this century, when pollution and overfishing doomed the nation's caviar industry.

ing lunch. Most of them were spooning up a version of one of Iran's many soup-stews, generically called *abgusht;* this one, called *dizi (Recipe Index),* was a muttony stew of strips of boiled meat served with boiled chick-peas and broth. The food looked nourishing, but it was the way it was eaten that held us spellbound. Each man had a bowl and a narrow-necked jug of *dizi,* both made of aluminum, and in addition, a pestle. With a methodical thump-thump he pounded his stew into a kind of meaty gruel in his bowl.

For our own lunch we chose a restaurant that offered an elaborate menu printed in Persian, which uses the flowing curves of Arabic script. We had memorized the names of the dishes we wanted to try, and ordering was no problem. Later, when the time came to pay the check, I simply dealt out Iranian paper money until the waiter gave me the signal to stop. He had an honest face, but even if I overpaid a little the food was worth the price.

Borani chogondar, a simple combination of yoghurt and cold boiled beets, was perked up with mint. Following that rice had to come. Not knowing how to say, "Just a little rice, please," we asked for two kinds of *khoresh* and waited, certain that in the end we would be sized up as picky eaters. The first dish, *gormeh sabzi (Recipe Index),* was cubes of tender lamb stewed fragrantly with greens—spinach, leeks, dill, mint and parsley—and the small, aromatic white beans of Iran. The second was an even more splendid stew called *fesenjan,* which consists of duck or chicken simmered with walnuts and pomegranate juice and scented with cardamom. Both had the tartness of citrus juice or peel, but it was subtly curbed just short of the point of astringency. With such fare, who needed rice?

Good as Iranian restaurant meals are, they cannot match the best served in private homes. There you find a comfortable blend of Western customs with distinctive native cuisine. In one home we visited, two or three servant girls kept out of sight, but a butler moved about impeccably admitting guests and serving Scotch and water on a tray. All the dishes were Iranian, even the soup, which was served in the living room. It was a cup of *ash sak,* a rich broth with tiny balls of ground lamb and a bright lacing of yoghurt, the whole made even richer in flavor by the spinach, split peas, parsley and dill. *Ash sak* is only one of some 20 different Iranian soups, all of them nourishing and savory but several unusual in their combinations of ingredients—one contains meatballs and pomegranate seeds.

For dinner a buffet had been set up. Rice was on hand, of course, but for once in Iran I was permitted to take only as much as I could finish; it was *reshte polo,* cooked with raisins and berries and counter-flavored with onion. The lamb, a little sweeter than the American kind, linked up excellently with the taste of the rice. It had been browned with onions, then cooked in a little water, according to Middle Eastern practice, roasting and steaming at the same time. The trick is to let the meat absorb the liquid, becoming completely tender without losing flavor. A pleasant accent was provided by the *dolmeh*—in this case, vine leaves stuffed with soft and lemony rice.

Over cordials in the living room, the evening reverted to its cosmopolitan beginning. The hours went by sociably until 11 o'clock sharp. Then, as if some Persian witching hour had struck, everyone thanked our hosts and went home. It was a fitting close to an exploration of what I consider the most imaginative and sophisticated cuisine of the Middle East.

CHAPTER VII RECIPES

Kababe Morgh

BROILED SKEWERED CHICKEN

To serve 4

1 cup finely grated onion
½ cup fresh lemon juice
2 teaspoons salt
2 two-pound chickens, each cut into 8 serving pieces
4 tablespoons melted butter
⅛ teaspoon ground saffron (or ⅛ teaspoon saffron threads pulverized with a mortar and pestle or the back of a spoon) dissolved in 1 tablespoon warm water

In a stainless-steel, enameled or glass bowl combine the onion, lemon juice and salt, stirring until they are thoroughly blended. Add the chicken and turn the pieces about with a spoon to coat them well. Marinate at room temperature for at least 2 hours or in the refrigerator for 4 hours, turning the pieces over occasionally.

Light a layer of coals in a charcoal broiler and let them burn until a white ash appears on the surface or preheat the stove broiler to its highest point.

Remove the chicken from the marinade and string the pieces tightly on 4 long skewers, pressing them together firmly. If you are broiling the chicken in an oven, suspend the skewers side by side across the length of a large roasting pan deep enough to allow about 1 inch of space under the meat.

Stir the melted butter and dissolved saffron into the marinade and brush the chicken evenly on all sides with 2 or 3 tablespoons of the mixture. Broil about 3 inches from the heat for 10 to 15 minutes turning the skewers occasionally and basting the chicken frequently with the remaining marinade. The chicken is done if the juices that trickle out are yellow rather than pink when a thigh is pierced with the point of a small, sharp knife.

Serve at once. *Kababe morgh* is traditionally accompanied by *chelo (below)* and may be garnished, if you like, with tiny, whole cherry tomatoes.

Chelo

STEAMED RICE

To serve 4 to 6

2 cups imported Iranian rice, or substitute other uncooked long-grain white rice
Salt
7 cups water
4 tablespoons butter, melted, plus 4 individual pats of butter
4 raw egg yolks
Freshly ground black pepper
Dried *sumak,* a slightly sour Persian spice, from the berry of a non-poisonous variety of sumac (optional)

If you are using Iranian rice, start at least 6 hours ahead. Spread it on a clean surface and pick out and discard any dark or discolored grains. Then wash it in a fine sieve or colander set under warm running water until the draining water runs clear. Finally place the rice in a large bowl or pot, add ¼ cup of salt and enough cold water to cover it by about 1 inch and soak overnight, or for at least 6 hours. If you are using other long-grain rice, wash it in the same way, but soak it in the salt water for about 2 hours.

In a heavy 3- to 4-quart saucepan equipped with a tightly fitting lid, bring 6 cups of fresh water to a boil over high heat. Drain the rice thoroughly and pour it into the boiling water in a slow, thin stream so the water does not stop boiling. Stir once or twice, then boil briskly, uncovered, for 5 minutes. Drain thoroughly in a sieve.

Pour 1 cup of fresh water and the melted butter into the saucepan and pour in the parboiled rice, mounding it slightly in the middle of the pan. Cover the pan tightly with a strip of aluminum foil and set the lid in place. Simmer the rice over moderate heat for 15 to 20 minutes, or until the grains are tender and have absorbed all the liquid in the pan.

Serve at once. Traditionally, when served with skewered broiled meat or chicken, the rice is served mounded into individual portions with a well in the center of each. A pat of butter is placed on top, a raw egg yolk is dropped in, and the top is sprinkled with salt, a few grindings of pepper and, if desired, a little dried *sumak.*

A setting of Oriental opulence befits the most princely *kebab* of all—*chelo kebab.* The dish consists of broiled meat and rice made rich with raw egg yolks and butter. This *chelo kebab* uses crisp pieces of chicken that were marinated in lemon juice, onion and salt before broiling.

To serve 4

1 cup chick-peas (garbanzos), preferably the small imported Italian chick-peas
1 cup dried broad beans (favas), or substitute other small dried beans
2 pounds lean boneless lamb shoulder, cut into 2-inch cubes
1 pound lamb bones, sawed, not chopped, into 1-inch-long pieces
2 medium-sized onions, peeled and quartered
1 quart water
1 tablespoon salt
Freshly ground black pepper
1 medium-sized fresh, ripe tomato, peeled, seeded and finely chopped *(see garides me saltsa, page 61)* or 1/3 cup chopped, drained, canned tomatoes
2 tablespoons fresh lemon juice
1/2 teaspoon turmeric
1/4 cup finely chopped onions

Dizi

BAKED LAMB, CHICK-PEA AND BEAN CASSEROLE

Starting a day ahead, wash the chick-peas in a sieve under cold running water, then place them in a large bowl or pan and add enough water to cover them by 2 inches. Soak at room temperature for at least 12 hours. Drain the peas in a sieve or colander.

In a heavy 2- to 3-quart saucepan, bring 1 quart of water to a boil over high heat. Drop in the beans and boil briskly for 2 minutes. Turn off the heat and let the beans soak for 1 hour. Drain and set the beans aside.

Spread out the lamb and lamb bones on the bottom of a heavy 3- to 4-quart casserole, arrange the onion quarters on top, and cover them with the chick-peas and the beans. Add 1 quart of fresh water, the salt and a few grindings of pepper. Bring to a boil over high heat, meanwhile skimming off the scum and foam as they rise to the surface. Reduce the heat to low, cover tightly and simmer for 1 hour. Stir in the tomato, lemon juice, and turmeric and simmer tightly covered for about 1½ hours longer, or until the chick-peas and beans are tender but still intact. (Check the casserole from time to time and add more water when necessary; the ingredients should be covered with liquid throughout the cooking period.) Taste for seasoning.

To serve, discard the bones, and transfer the meat to a plate. Strain the broth into a tureen, place the beans in a bowl and, with the back of a spoon, mash them to a purée. Stir in the chopped onions, then spread the purée on a deep heated platter and scatter meat over it. Traditionally, the broth is served first, followed by the beans and meat as a separate course.

To serve 4

1/4 cup olive oil
2 medium-sized onions, peeled and cut into 1/4-inch-thick slices
1/2 teaspoon turmeric
3½ cups shelled walnuts (about 1 pound), pulverized in a blender or with a nut grinder or mortar and pestle, plus 1 tablespoon coarsely chopped walnuts (optional)
4 cups water
2 teaspoons salt
Freshly ground black pepper
A 4½- to 5-pound duck, cut into quarters and trimmed of all exposed fat
1/4 cup bottled pomegranate syrup
1/3 cup fresh lemon juice
1/4 cup sugar

Fesenjan

BRAISED DUCK WITH WALNUT AND POMEGRANATE SAUCE

In a heavy 12- to 14-inch skillet, heat the olive oil over moderate heat. Add the onions and turmeric and, stirring frequently, cook for 8 to 10 minutes, or until the onions are richly browned. With a slotted spoon, transfer them to a heavy 5- to 6-quart casserole and set the skillet aside. Add the pulverized walnuts, water, salt and a few grindings of pepper to the onions in the casserole and stir until thoroughly blended. Bring to a boil over high heat, reduce the heat to low and simmer partially covered for 20 minutes.

Meanwhile, return the skillet to the stove, heat it until a light haze forms above it and add the duck to the oil remaining in the pan, adding more oil if necessary. Brown the duck lightly, turning it with tongs or a spoon and regulating the heat so that it colors evenly on all sides without burning.

Transfer the duck to the simmering walnut mixture, turning the pieces about with a spoon to coat them evenly. Bring to a boil, reduce the heat to low, cover tightly and simmer for 1½ hours, or until the duck is almost tender and shows little resistance when pierced with the point of a small, sharp knife.

With a large spoon, skim as much fat as possible from the surface of the walnut sauce. Combine the pomegranate syrup, lemon juice and sugar. Add them to the sauce. Simmer for 30 minutes longer and taste for seasoning.

To serve, arrange the duck attractively on a deep heated platter and moisten it with a cup or so of the sauce. Sprinkle it, if you like, with the coarsely chopped walnuts. Pour the rest of the sauce into a bowl or sauceboat and serve it separately. *Fesenjan* is traditionally accompanied by *chelo (Recipe Index).*

Chopped walnuts and a sweet-sour sauce are served over braised duck to make a piquant Persian dish called *fesenjan*.

Coucou Sabzi

THICK HERB, VEGETABLE AND EGG PANCAKE

To serve 4

- 1½ cups finely chopped parsley, preferably flat-leaf parsley
- ¼ cup finely chopped scallions
- ¼ cup finely chopped leeks
- ¼ cup finely chopped romaine lettuce
- ¼ cup finely cut fresh dill, or 2 tablespoons dried dill weed
- ¼ cup finely cut fresh mint, or 2 tablespoons crumbled dried mint
- 1 teaspoon oregano
- ¼ teaspoon turmeric
- 1 teaspoon salt
- ½ teaspoon freshly ground black pepper
- 6 eggs
- 2 tablespoons plus ⅓ cup olive oil

Combine the parsley, scallions, leeks, lettuce, dill, mint, oregano, turmeric, salt and pepper in a deep bowl. Add the eggs and 2 tablespoons of the oil and beat vigorously with a fork to combine them. Taste for seasoning.

In a heavy 10-inch skillet, heat the remaining ⅓ cup of oil over moderate heat until a light haze forms above it. Pour in the herb and egg mixture, spread it out evenly with a spatula. Cover and cook over low heat for 8 to 10 minutes until the edges are fairly firm but the center is still moist. Run a knife around the circumference of the pan to free the pancake, then cut it into 4 pie-shaped wedges. Cook uncovered for 1 or 2 minutes more, shaking the pan back and forth gently.

When the center of the pancake is firm but still slightly moist, cover the skillet with a flat plate and, grasping the plate and skillet firmly together, invert them and turn the pancake out on the plate. Then carefully slide the pancake back into the pan. Cover again and cook for 4 to 5 minutes more to brown the underside. Slide out of the pan to a serving plate and serve hot or cold.

Shireen Polo

STEAMED RICE WITH CHICKEN, NUTS, ORANGE PEEL AND CARROTS

To serve 4 to 6

- The peel of 2 oranges, cut into strips 1 inch long and ⅛ inch wide
- 8 tablespoons (1 quarter-pound stick) butter
- 3 medium-sized carrots, cut into strips about 1 inch long and ⅛ inch wide
- 1 cup slivered blanched almonds
- 2 cups sugar
- 1 teaspoon ground saffron (or 1 teaspoon saffron threads, pulverized with a mortar and pestle or with the back of a spoon), dissolved in 1 tablespoon warm water
- ¼ cup plus 2 tablespoons finely chopped unsalted pistachios
- 2 cups imported Iranian rice or other uncooked long-grain rice, soaked and drained *(see chelo, page 167)*
- ¼ cup olive oil
- A 2½- to 3-pound chicken, cut into 8 serving pieces
- 1 teaspoon salt
- 5 cups water
- 1 large onion, quartered
- 4 tablespoons melted butter combined with 1 tablespoon water

Blanch the orange peel by dropping it into a small pan of cold water, bringing it to a boil, then draining it immediately and running cold water over it.

In a heavy 10- to 12-inch skillet, melt the butter over moderate heat. When the foam subsides, add the carrots and, stirring frequently, cook for 10 minutes, or until they are soft but not brown. Add the orange peel, almonds, sugar and saffron, and reduce the heat to low. Stir constantly until the sugar dissolves, then cover tightly and simmer for 30 minutes. Stir in the ¼ cup of pistachios and cook for 2 or 3 minutes longer. Set aside.

Meanwhile, bring 6 cups of water to a boil in a heavy 3- to 4-quart casserole with a tightly fitting lid. Pour in the rice in a slow, thin stream. Stir once or twice, boil briskly for 5 minutes, then drain in a sieve.

In a heavy 12-inch skillet, heat the olive oil until a light haze forms above it. Pat the chicken dry with paper towels and brown it in the oil, a few pieces at a time, turning it with tongs and regulating the heat so that they color richly and evenly without burning. As they brown, transfer the pieces to a plate. Pour off and discard the fat remaining in the skillet and replace the chicken in the pan. Sprinkle the pieces with the salt and scatter the onion quarters on top. Pour in the 5 cups of water, bring to a boil over high heat, cover and simmer over low heat for 30 minutes, or until the chicken is tender.

While the chicken is simmering, pour the melted butter and water mixture into the casserole and spread half of the rice evenly over it. Add 2 cups of the carrot mixture, smooth it to the edges, cover with the remaining rice and spread the rest of the carrot mixture on top. Cover tightly and steam for 20 minutes, or until the rice is tender.

To serve, remove the bones from the chicken breasts and thighs. Spread half the rice on a heated platter and arrange the chicken over it. Mound the rest of the rice on top and sprinkle it with the remaining pistachios.

Before jewel-like Persian miniatures, two kinds of *polo*—one consisting of sweetened rice with chicken *(left),* the other of herbed rice with lamb—await serving.

Paludah

FRESH MELON AND PEACH COMPOTE

To serve 4 to 6

- 1 medium-sized Persian melon (about 4 pounds), or substitute 2 small cantaloupes
- ½ teaspoon salt
- 2 medium-sized fresh, ripe but firm peaches
- ½ cup sugar
- 3 tablespoons fresh lemon juice
- 2 tablespoons rose water
- Finely crushed or shaved ice (optional)

Cut the melon in half and remove and discard the seeds and stringy pulp in the center. With a melon baller or small spoon, scoop out as many melon balls as possible. Place the balls in a deep bowl, pour any juice from the melon shells over them and discard the shells. Toss the balls with the salt.

Peel the peaches, split them in half lengthwise and cut them into ½-inch-thick slices. Add the peaches, sugar, lemon juice and rose water to the melon and toss them about gently with a spoon to combine them well. Cover tightly and refrigerate for at least 2 hours, or until thoroughly chilled.

To serve, spoon the peaches and melon balls into individual compotes or dessert bowls. Top each portion, if you like, with crushed or shaved ice.

Sharbate Beh

QUINCE SHERBET DRINK

To make about 3 cups of syrup

- 2 medium-sized fresh quinces (about 1 pound)
- 3½ cups cold water
- 2 tablespoons plus ½ cup fresh lemon juice
- 2½ cups sugar

With a small, sharp knife remove the skins from the quinces. Slice each fruit lengthwise into quarters and cut out the seeds and cores. Combine 2 cups of the water and 2 tablespoons of the lemon juice in a bowl and, using the fine side of a stand-up hand grater, grate the quinces into the lemon-water mixture to prevent their discoloring. Drain the grated quince in a fine sieve, then wrap it in a double thickness of cheesecloth and squeeze vigorously over a bowl to wring out as much juice as possible before discarding the pulp.

In a 2- to 3-quart enameled or stainless-steel saucepan, bring the remaining 1½ cups of water and the sugar to a boil over moderate heat, stirring until the sugar dissolves. Increase the heat to high and cook briskly, uncovered and undisturbed, for 5 minutes, or until the syrup reaches a temperature of 220° on a candy thermometer. Add the quince juice and the remaining ½ cup of lemon juice and, stirring frequently, simmer over low heat for 5 minutes more. Pour the syrup into a bowl and cool to room temperature.

For each serving, pour ½ cup of the syrup into a tumbler or highball glass. Stir in ½ cup of cold water, then fill the glass with crushed or shaved ice.

Sharbate Rivas

RHUBARB SHERBET DRINK

To make 3 cups of syrup

- 1 pound fresh rhubarb, trimmed, washed and cut into 1-inch pieces
- 1½ to 2½ cups water
- 2½ cups sugar

Combine the rhubarb and 1 cup of the water in a 2- to 3-quart enameled or stainless-steel saucepan. Bring to a boil over high heat, reduce the heat to low, cover and simmer for 20 minutes. When the rhubarb is soft, pour the entire contents of the pan into a fine sieve set over a deep bowl and, with the back of a spoon, press out all the juice before discarding the pulp.

Measure the juice, add enough water to make 2 cups and return it to the pan. Add the sugar and bring to a boil over moderate heat, stirring until the sugar dissolves. Increase the heat to high and boil briskly, uncovered and undisturbed, for 5 minutes, or until the syrup reaches a temperature of 220° on a candy thermometer. Cool the syrup to room temperature.

For each serving pour ½ cup of the syrup into a tumbler. Stir in ½ cup of cold water, then fill the glass with crushed or shaved ice.

On an Iranian tray *(opposite)*, peach-and-melon compotes are flanked by quince *(left)* and rhubarb sherbets. A diner may add syrup or rose water from silver vessels and nibble puffed chick-peas or sunflower seeds.

VAT

VIII

From the Land of the Pharaohs

At Giza, in Egypt, the pyramids of three pharaohs compose the background for an international group of restaurant diners. The guests, who include an American couple and Egyptian and foreign students, are having a dessert course of apples and pomegranates. Beyond the pyramids that dominate their view lies one of the suburbs of Cairo.

An air of timeless mystery pervades Egypt and its capital, Cairo, the largest city in the Arab world. From the outskirts of the city the pyramids of Giza loom in the distance; Cairo's museums remind the visitor that he is in a land whose recorded history is measured in millennia rather than centuries. The sense of the past is not, of course, *all*-pervasive. One does not feel it so much on the busy boulevards of the modern areas. And it is not that the ancient heart of the city is drowsing or dead; to the visitor, Cairo's four million inhabitants seem to swarm the streets in tidal masses all day long. There is unrestrained shouting, and drivers horn-blast their way through the pedestrians. Yet in the midst of this bustle the traveler's mind is haunted by a sense of Egypt's roots stretching back over the millennia.

This presence of the past came to my wife and me most strongly at the Museum of Agriculture, in Cairo's Dukki district. Here, in a quiet hall, are displayed the actual foods and spices as well as the farming, hunting and fishing implements of Egypt's distant history. There are grains of barley from the tomb of Tutankhamen, who reigned in the 14th Century B.C., and some withered flowers that were buried with Ramses II about a century later. Looking at linen fabrics, one realizes that the Egyptians knew how to weave exquisitely when the peoples of Western Europe still wore animal skins. Ropes and hawsers, some as much as three inches thick, were fashioned then, as they are now, from date-palm fibers or papyrus stalks.

At the Museum of Agriculture the ubiquitous flat, round Arab bread shows up in antique prototype; other breads take diverse shapes, down to gay, small loaves decorated with human forms—feast cakes for children of a bygone civilization. Some of the first leavened bread in history was made in Egypt—though how the ancient bakers discovered it will probably remain a mystery for all time. Their basic loaf was made of wheat or barley flour, but all sorts of variations were devised to please the upper classes—mashed dates were mixed into the dough, for example, and honeyed cakes made in the shapes of bulls or geese. Every nobleman had slaves and servants to grind the grain and cultivate his walled-in garden of grapevines, fruit trees, herbs and such vegetables as okra, onions and leeks.

We know a good deal about the cuisine of ancient Egypt. The nobleman's usual breakfast was based on bread—and also on beer, a brew whose flavor and potency can only be imagined because it was fermented from such diverse ingredients as barley, wheat, dates and spiced bread. Wine, too, was made, and fine vintages were drunk from gold or silver goblets. Mushrooms were reserved for the Pharaoh himself, but boiled cabbage was a favorite with all his court, especially before a feast, because it was believed to promote sobriety. For lordly three-day banquets, a whole ox might be roasted on a spit and served by topless dancer-waitresses. Yet many details of such feasts, and of the people's everyday food, are lost in the mists of time.

There is no mystery about how people eat in Cairo today—they eat hugely. At dinner one day, a Cairo friend announced quite seriously that more food must be consumed per capita in Egypt than in any other nation. (He was wrong, of course, but there was no need to dampen his enthusiasm.) We were seated, I remember, at a low, round brass table, my wife and I on a divan and our friend on an ottoman. And even before our dinner began, as though to enforce his point, the friend remarked that a man must have two or three filling disks of Arab bread at each meal.

After some conventional hors d'oeuvre we were served a really exceptional soup made with *milookhiyya (Recipe Index),* an exotic green vegetable similar to spinach in its appearance and to okra in its properties. The leaves release a viscous liquid as they cook, so that strands trail off the diner's spoon as he lifts it. For this unusual soup, the *milookhiyya* had been chopped fine and boiled in chicken stock, with a little cumin and a great deal of garlic. Any stock would do, said our friend, but his own preference was the broth from young Egyptian rabbit, raised commercially and slaughtered at the tender age of four months. He rolled his eyes at the thought.

There followed a plate of unspiced *gambari*—prawns from the Red Sea—broiled with their tails left on as convenient handles, and so fresh that they were almost sweet to the taste. Then we were introduced to a substantial dish, the classic Egyptian *feta,* a favorite holiday treat. It is built up in layers, beginning with bread at the bottom of the bowl, rice over that, and almost any kind of meat on top, all moistened with broth. As in the *milookhiyya* soup, the garlic was not spared.

Dessert seemed superfluous, but we were in Egypt, and so went on to eat two kinds. The simpler one, *mihallabiyya (Recipe Index),* was a thickened rice pudding, not especially sweet but fragrant with rose water. The other was a regal confection named *esh es seraya,* or "bread of the palace." The lower part consisted of bread soaked in sugar syrup (honey and butter are sometimes used) and baked to a cakelike texture; its top was an astounding crown of pure, unsweetened cream—*ishta*—thick enough to be picked up with a fork.

Ishta is made from rich milk, which is set out to separate until the stiff coagulate on top can be stripped off in rolls. Unfortunately for the United States, homogenized milk will not yield *ishta,* which depends upon a separate component of rich cream in the milk.

Over dinner we discussed Egyptian eating habits with our friend. The men of his country, he told us, rarely go out to dinner with their wives. A wife stays at home, spending long hours each day in the kitchen. She does not necessarily spend them alone. Under Muslim law, a man may have as many as four wives at once—though by custom the second must be approved by the first. Even when he restricts himself to one wife, he will usually try to lighten her tasks by hiring a "cook"—actually, a kitchen maid who stands by to peel vegetables and clean up while the mistress of the house prepares all the food, tasting and nibbling as she goes, and acquiring the rounded contours Egyptian men admire.

We met few "modern" women in Egypt, though they do exist—university graduates, writers, artists, technicians and even high government officials. Among them are the faculty members of the Higher Institute of Home Economics, in the Boulac district of Cairo, where some 750 students are trained to be professional home economists. The four-year curriculum offers courses in Arabic, English and French, textiles and sewing, food chemistry, hygiene and nutrition. A canteen provides direct experience in food preparation; apartments are maintained and lived in by the students. Both Western and

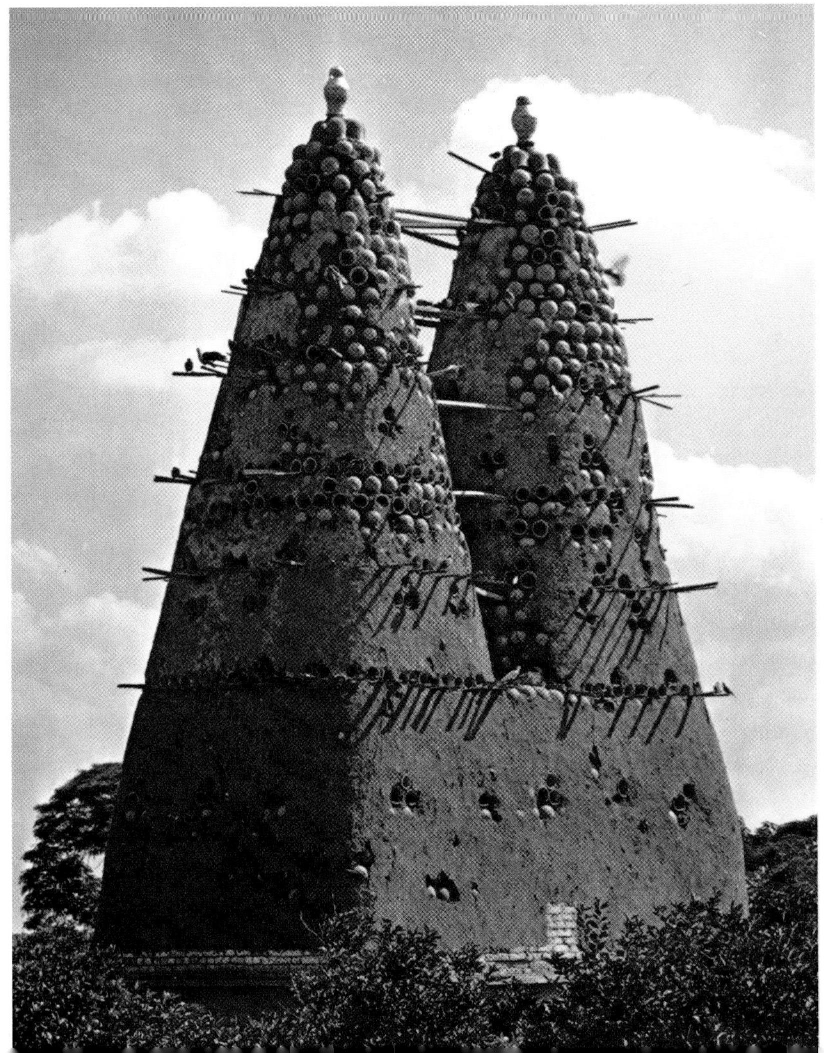

Pigeons, one of the delicacies of the Egyptian cuisine, are often raised in twin-spired, 40-foot-high dovecotes like this one near Tanta, northwest of Cairo. Adult birds enter and leave the mud-and-brick cote through the open ends of clay pipes, hatching their eggs in nests behind the clay plugs that dot the wall. The tender fledglings are best to eat, Egyptian chefs believe, when six weeks old, at the age they would just begin to fly.

A Cairo dispenser of *fool,* the Egyptian street dish of boiled and seasoned beans, uses a long-handled spoon to reach the bottom of the pot set into his counter. Customers bring their own containers and may take their food home to share with others. The boy in the foreground will have his *fool* at home, reheated in the pot in which he carries it.

Egyptian cooking are taught, and there is a course in experimental foods. At the end, a Bachelor of Science degree awaits the graduate, along with a job in a restaurant, a hospital or the Ministry of Health.

On a visit to the institute, we were received in a large, airy office by two staff officials, both gracious women who had studied in the United States. Coffee was served, and the Egyptian ladies sipped theirs by hooking a pinkie under the saucer of the demitasse and raising the whole assembly to their lips—a feat of delicate balance I did not attempt. In the conversation that followed, our hostesses expressed concern over their nation's bread-heavy diet, especially among the poor farmers called fellaheen. In an attempt to improve this fare, students make field trips to the villages and live with fellaheen families for weeks at a time. Each member of a family and every ounce of food he eats are weighed, a record is kept, and eventually recommendations are made for balanced meals—fewer starches and glasses of heavily sugared tea, more milk and cheese.

At the end of our visit we were shown into a large, clean kitchen where a baking class was in session. The students were beating flour, eggs and sugar together for cookies, and their instructor demonstrated how to squeeze the mixture from a pastry tube into fluted dollops on a buttered pan. The girls were attentive, yet shyly aware that they had visitors. Just before we left, I asked if any boys were enrolled at the institute. I can still hear the laughter that ensued. Obviously, to the minds of these well-brought-up Egyptian girls, my question *had* to be a joke.

Egypt imports wheat to keep up with the voracious national appetite for

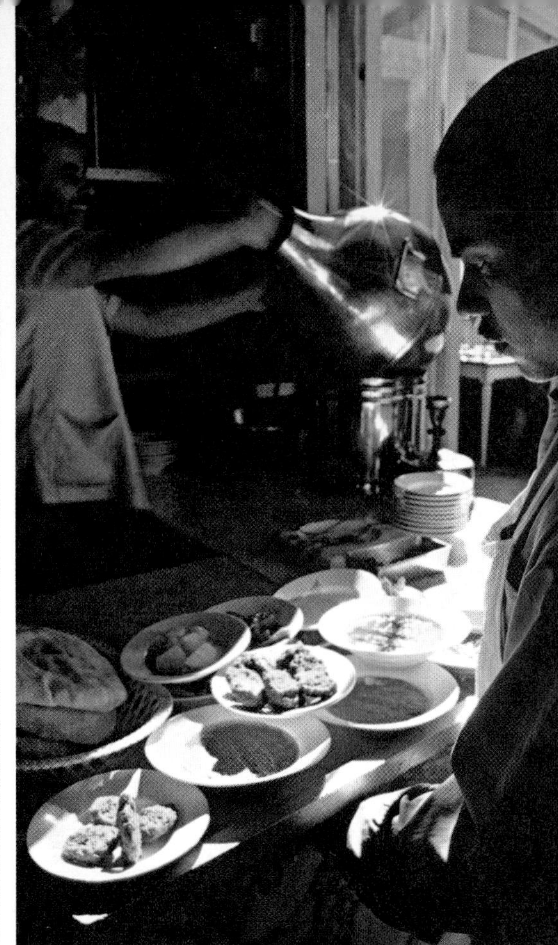

In a Cairo *fool* shop, an attendant stirs the boiling beans *(above left)* in a traditionally shaped pot. *Fool* and a deep-fried bean dish called *tamiya* are popular because they are cheap —Egyptians call them "the poor man's meat"—but even the best restaurants serve them. The waiter collecting dishes of *fool (above)* has two orders of *tamiya* on his tray.

bread, but it exports fruits, vegetables and surplus rice, using part of the profits to improve agricultural methods and achieve greater crop yields for a steadily growing population. Part of this expanding food supply will come from newly created farmland. Until recently 97 per cent of Egypt's land was too dry to be tilled. The difference between arable and arid land can be seen dramatically along the irrigation canals that draw off the waters of the Nile. There is no tapering-off area between green earth and bleak desert; the change comes as sharp as a saber slash wherever the river's moisture ends.

But now much more life-giving water will be available since the government has harnessed the Nile near Aswan, 500 miles upstream from Cairo, in the stupendous achievement called the High Dam. As a result over a million acres will be brought under cultivation and the yield of Egypt's farmlands is expected to increase by as much as a third. Hundreds of thousands of acres, long under cultivation but yielding only a single annual crop after the Nile's yearly flood, are producing three cereal harvests under irrigation.

Our room in Cairo overlooked the historic river, and we enjoyed sitting on our balcony at cocktail time, watching the fast water buses and the slow feluccas with their old-fashioned lateen sails canted on stubby masts. In that setting old tales seemed terribly real: and I could almost see the ancient ceremonies that paid respect to these vital waters. Every year, for example, a Bride of the Nile, a lovely virgin, was chosen to be thrown into the river as a ritual sacrifice to assure good crops in the year ahead. The practice came to an abrupt end one year when a Caliph decided to spare the virgin. The Nile flooded on schedule, no famine occurred, the harvest proved bountiful. Gradually, the custom grew of substituting a life-sized doll for the virgin, and dolls have fooled the river god up to the present time—though the token ceremony may die out now that his caprices are controlled by the dam. I remember looking down at the river from our balcony and thinking that its waters will never again be tawny with silt. At that moment, in fact, they glimmered with an odd pastel sheen in the approaching twilight. I asked my wife to describe the river's color.

"Nile green," she said—and she was right.

One day, knowing that a typically huge Egyptian dinner lay ahead of us, we nibbled our way through lunch, sampling some of the Cairo street foods sold in small, open-front restaurants, each with its own specialty. The plan was sensible enough, but every portion served to us was a hearty one, designed to make a full meal in itself, and I must have offended the street restaurateurs by the quantities I did not finish.

Our first target was *fool midammis (Recipe Index)*, a nourishing bean dish that appears on Egyptian breakfast tables nearly every morning. The beans, a small, dried domestic variety, darken to a purplish shade when cooked. *Fool* is based upon a slow baking (or a gentle simmer on top of the stove) that takes almost all day. The dressing for the dish is appropriately simple: rich olive oil and plenty of lemon juice. We were offered a side dish of hard-boiled eggs, which are sometimes cooked to mealiness right in the bean pot.

In another street restaurant we tried tangy deep-fried patties of *tamiya*, made of fava beans mashed and seasoned with garlic, onions, green coriander, parsley and cayenne. (We now serve *tamiya* at home as hot hors d'oeuvre, adding a pinch of bicarbonate of soda to keep the patties moist and light.) Then out into the crowds again for a final nibble, *kushari*. The dish is a mélange of spaghetti, rice and lentils; as the chef spoons it into the bowl he sprinkles flakes of fried onion on top and adds a bit of hot tomato sauce. The counters of a *kushari* stand bear bottles containing two kinds of sauce, one of vinegar with cloves of garlic floating in it, the other based on hot red peppers. Either sauce turns a bland dish into a fiery treat.

It would have been pleasant to buy a roasted sweet potato from a street vendor, but more eating was unthinkable. Instead, we walked off some of our newly acquired calories and found ourselves at a spice bazaar. Just outside it we dodged little carts pulled by donkeys, their harness bells tinkling cheerfully in the dusty air. The bazaar itself was a cosmic blend of smells—cumin, caraway seeds, saffron, camphor, sandalwood, myrrh, ambergris. Opened burlap bags revealed colorful stores of powdered henna, used by women to dye their hair red and as a cosmetic for the hands. There were nameless twisted dried roots, brewed by rules laid down in ancient pharmacopoeias into tonics for newly delivered mothers. Shopkeepers invited us in to see their merchandise, and the noise of haggling filled the air.

Our walk eventually took us back to the hotel for a siesta, a midday break made almost mandatory in Cairo by the hot, cloudless days. After dark, with appetites again at the ready, we kept a dinner date at the home of a professional chef. There were four in our party, and the table was set for four, with no place for the chef's wife or anyone else. The host sat with us as we ate, chatting about his creations and beaming whenever we exclaimed over them.

Well might he beam; I still beam too when I recollect the buttery richness of the foods he served. His first platter was mounded with a *mehshi*—stuffed vegetables, among them zucchini and narrow eggplants, skillfully cored without tearing the skins and filled with rice-dill and rice-lamb mixtures that encompassed a whole spectrum of flavors. I helped myself to one of each vegetable and was chided hospitably: "An Egyptian could eat all these himself."

But I was saving room for the next course, a thick stew of tender lamb and baby okra. This is a common dish in the Middle East, but at this meal it met uncommon standards of appearance and taste. Sliced carrots had been set at the bottom of the cooking pot, which also served as a mold; when the stew was unmolded for serving, the carrots gleamed at the top like golden medallions. The okra had been parboiled, sautéed in butter, and arranged in radial spokes, with the stem ends outward; the meat, already browned with onions, filled the spaces between the spokes. The secret of such a stew, the chef said, lies in one word, *daspika,* a long, slow simmer in the last stage of cooking that permits all the ingredients to bloom and interact. We scooped up our stew with bread, like practiced Arabs.

The meal ended with a glamorous dessert: *couscous (Recipe Index),* the cereal dish of North Africa, popular all the way westward to the Atlantic Ocean. It is the national dish of Morocco, where it is cooked unsweetened, with lamb, beef or chicken (or all three) and a variety of vegetables and spices. To make the sweet Egyptian version properly, one starts by sprinkling flour with water, a few drops at a time, and rubbing the moistened mixture between the palms to form tiny grainlike shapes. Steaming follows, kneading with a fork to get rid of lumps, and still more steaming until the pellets swell.

Nowadays *couscous* can be bought by the package, or granules of semolina may take its place, but our host had used the traditional manual method. He delivered to our table a sweet hillock rich with melted butter and brightened with patches of red currants on brown coconut shreds. "Finish this," he said, "and I will bring out another platter." The second serving was unnecessary, though the chef, tempted by his own creation, finally forgot his Arab manners and took some for himself.

Couscous is eaten only rarely in Egypt, but pigeons are a common item of diet. We tried them, along with an even more remarkable dish, at a modern resort restaurant a pleasant automobile drive from Cairo. To get there, we sped along a four-lane divided highway running northward to the Mediterranean, with the Nile delta stretching on either side, green and flat. The industry and agriculture of today and yesterday played leapfrog before our eyes: a suburban factory with tall stacks gave off black smoke; men and women worked side by side in the fields, breaking ground with crude mattocks; an up-to-date television assembly plant loomed to one side; a boy washed a sloe-eyed buffalo in a canal; a new housing project sprawled in box after identical box along the road; women walked by, some with tattooed faces half covered by veils; steel towers carrying high-tension lines strode across the land.

The day was hot, and it was relaxing to sit at last in the breeze-swept upper level of the restaurant. Around us were flowering gardens, and at one side of the grounds stood three tall, conical structures—the dovecotes that supply the kitchen. The pigeon population, the proprietor told us, numbers about 500, and the birds multiply fast enough to meet the heaviest demand.

The pigeons allotted to us were stuffed with *fireek*—our old friend *burghul* from Lebanon, or its next of kin—and baked in individual earthenware casseroles until even the bones offered little resistance. If the dominant flavor of the dish seemed somewhat bland, that was probably the natural result of the emphatic appetizer that preceded the pigeons—and made our excursion headily worthwhile. Its name is *fetir mishaltet,* and it comes in three parts, a bread and two dips. All are extraordinary. The dough used for the bread is mixed thoroughly with butter and separated into balls. With buttered hands, the cook tosses each ball into the air higher and higher, until it spreads to a diameter of two feet, becoming thinner all the time. The technique resembles that of whirling the dough for a pizza pie, but the end product is only a little thicker than *filo* pastry. A stack of 10 such leaves, baked very lightly so they do not become flaky, constitutes a serving. The accessory dips were alternatives of sweet or super-savory—"black honey," or blackstrap, derived from sugar cane; and *mish,* a gray, salty peasant cheese, the strongest I have ever tasted. It is made by pouring ordinary milk-cheese into a crock with milk and salt, adding a starter from the previous batch of *mish*—and giving the micro-organisms a full year to accomplish their work.

Our stay in Egypt was all but ended. At the Cairo airport, on another sweltering day, we waited for our plane. We could clearly see the vents of the air-conditioning apparatus, but for some reason no one threw the switch to turn it on. I sought relief from a beer, and munched good Egyptian peanuts, red-skinned and gamey. And we waited, baffled and stifling.

Looking around me, I noticed two men in an inconspicuous corner, kneeling on little rugs and touching their foreheads to the floor, their lips moving as they whispered the prescribed prayers to Allah. The sight was one more reminder of the depth of faith commanded by Islam, a piety we had observed repeatedly. In the month of Ramadan, when Muhammad experienced the revelation of the Koran, Muslims may not eat or drink while there is daylight in the sky, though they may dine all night, as permitted by the Koran, "until the white thread shows clearly to you from the black thread at the dawn." The timing of Ramadan varies, for in the lunar Muslim calendar the months change through the seasons in 33-year cycles; fasting becomes a great hardship to farmers when Ramadan falls in summer, but they still observe the rule. Understandably, the end of the month calls for nationwide feasting.

Charity is another Muslim commandment; the more one gives to the needy, the more merit one acquires in Heaven. During a four-day religious observance known as the Great Feast or the Feast of Sacrifice, those who have the means distribute money among their servants. In Egyptian villages traditionalists slaughter livestock—sheep, goats, buffalo or camel. The ritual killing may be performed in a front yard by the head of the household or by a hired butcher, and some of the food is given to the poor.

This feeling must underlie a second pious vignette I saw at the airport. A woman seated near me reached into her purse and gave a coin to the floor-sweeper as he passed her. I could see no reason for the gift except the Muslim characteristic of charity. Such sights did something to take our minds off the heat until we were airborne at last, but Muriel still wondered about that air conditioning. "Why on earth didn't they turn it on?" she asked.

"The mysterious Middle East," I explained.

Like little girls the world over, four-year-old Ayyam Wassef spends much of her time in the kitchen watching the grownups cook. In the picture above, she peers into a wire-mesh sieve through which her grandmother is pressing *couscous* dough into tiny pellets of pasta. The dough itself is made by a slow process in which *couscous* wheat meal and salted water are rubbed together by hand until all the grains of meal are evenly moistened.

Egypt's Versatile Couscous: A Main Dish and a Sweet

Across the breadth of North Africa, *couscous* is a staple food. Typically, it consists of finely ground wheat meal (usually semolina) combined with salted water in a kind of pasta, usually topped with meat sauce as a main dish. Egyptian cooks, however, often sprinkle the pasta with confectioners' sugar and nuts and serve their *couscous* as a sweet. In Egypt, *couscous* is sold in a ready-to-cook form, but many households, like that of the Wassefs *(shown above and on the following pages)*, prefer to prepare their own. Whether ready-made or homemade, the pasta is steamed in a colander set over boiling water before it comes to the table.

For the main dish of a formal dinner, *couscous (center, above)* is served by the Wassefs in much the way an Italian family would serve spaghetti: as a delicately flavored base for a seasoned sauce. The bowl of steamed *couscous* shown here is topped with generous pieces of lamb and chicken simmered together in a brown gravy enriched by onions, fresh coriander leaves and mastic. (Mastic, an aromatic gum exuded by trees on the Greek island of Chios, looks like small, irregularly shaped white pebbles and tastes rather like licorice.) Egyptian families, like those of many other Middle Eastern countries, make little distinction between the separate courses of a meal; even on this formal occasion the Wassefs served the appetizers and soup right along with the meat and poultry dishes. Besides the *couscous,* their dinner includes *(left to right) milookhiyya* soup made from a dried native herb, slices of white cheese *(gibna),* stuffed and braised pigeons *(hamam mahshi),* baked molded rice with chicken *(biram ruzz),* and separate bowls of black and spiced olives. (The soup and main dishes are listed in the Recipe Index.)

In its role as a sweet, *couscous* resembles a porridge or hot cereal and is served sprinkled with sugar. Ayyam Wassef spoons it up happily for dessert. As a special treat, sweet *couscous* is also sometimes topped with a scattering of peanuts—the only nut grown widely in Egypt.

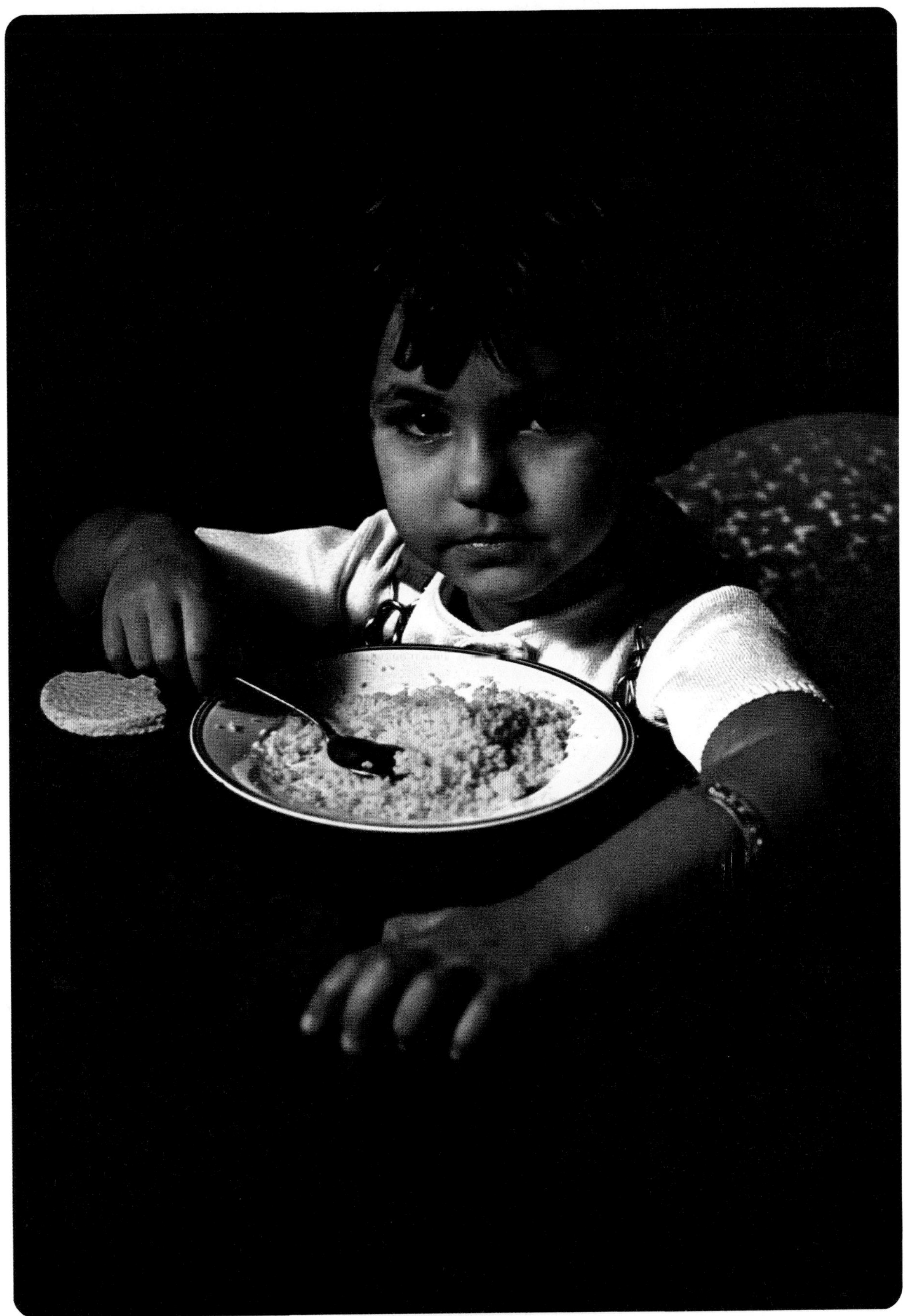

CHAPTER VIII RECIPES

Biram Ruzz

MOLDED BAKED RICE WITH CHICKEN

To serve 6 to 8

- 4 tablespoons softened butter, plus 2 tablespoons butter, cut into 1/4-inch pieces
- 3 cups uncooked medium- or long-grain white rice
- A 2- to 2½-pound chicken cut into 6 to 8 serving pieces
- Salt
- Freshly ground black pepper
- 1½ cups milk
- 1 cup heavy cream
- 4 cups chicken stock, fresh or canned

NOTE: In Egypt, as in much of the Middle East, rice is eaten in enormous quantity. This mold, therefore, is mainly composed of rice (about 9 cups when cooked), and the chicken is more or less a flavorful accompaniment for the rice.

Preheat the oven to 400°. Using a pastry brush, heavily coat the bottom and sides of a round, deep 3-quart casserole or baking dish with the 4 tablespoons of softened butter.

Spread 1½ cups of the rice evenly in the dish, arrange the pieces of chicken skin side up on top and sprinkle them liberally with salt and pepper. In a small saucepan, bring the milk, cream and 2 cups of the stock to a boil over high heat and pour over the chicken. Spread the rest of the rice on top and dot evenly with the 2 tablespoons of the cut-up butter.

Bake uncovered on the lowest shelf of the oven for 15 minutes. Meanwhile, bring the remaining 2 cups of stock to a simmer in a small saucepan and keep it barely simmering over low heat. Pour 1 cup of the simmering stock into the casserole and bake for 15 minutes longer. Pour in the remaining stock and transfer the casserole to the upper third of the oven. Continue baking for another 30 minutes, then remove the casserole from the oven, cover tightly with a lid or foil and let it rest at room temperature for about 20 minutes.

To unmold and serve, run a sharp knife around the inside edges of the casserole to loosen the *biram ruzz* and let it rest for 10 minutes longer. Place a heated serving platter upside down over the top, and, grasping the casserole and platter together firmly, quickly invert them. The *biram ruzz* should slide out easily. Serve at once.

Hamam Mahshi

BRAISED PIGEONS WITH CRUSHED WHEAT STUFFING

To serve 4

- 8 tablespoons butter (1 quarter-pound stick)
- ½ cup finely chopped onions
- The pigeon hearts, gizzards and livers, finely chopped
- 2½ cups *fireek* (coarsely crushed green wheat grains)
- 2 teaspoons finely cut fresh mint or 1 teaspoon dried mint, crumbled
- 1½ teaspoons salt
- Freshly ground black pepper
- 4 one-pound oven-ready pigeons, or substitute 4 one-pound doves, young partridge, baby pheasant, quail, woodcock or grouse
- 1½ cups cold water
- 2½ cups chicken stock, fresh or canned
- Parsley sprigs

Over moderate heat melt 4 tablespoons of the butter in a heavy 10- to 12-inch skillet. When the foam begins to subside, add the onions and the pigeon giblets and, stirring frequently, cook for 8 to 10 minutes, or until the onions are soft and light brown. Add the *fireek,* mint, 1 teaspoon of the salt and a few grindings of pepper and stir for 2 or 3 minutes until the grains are coated with butter. Set aside. Preheat the oven to 350°.

Pat the pigeons thoroughly dry inside and out with paper towels and sprinkle their cavities with the remaining salt and a few grindings of pepper. Then stuff 5 tablespoons of the *fireek* mixture into the breast cavity and 1 tablespoon into the neck cavity of each pigeon. Set the remaining *fireek* aside. Fasten the neck skin to the back of each bird with a skewer and close the breast openings by lacing them with skewers or sewing them with heavy white thread. Truss the birds by tying their legs together and brush the skins with the remaining 4 tablespoons of butter.

Place the pigeons, breast side up, in a heavy 4- to 5-quart casserole and pour in the water. Bring to a boil on top of the stove, cover tightly and

Egypt's golden crusted *biram ruzz (at left)* is a creamy rice and chicken casserole, unmolded here on a contemporary blue-glass plate which in turn rests upon a copper tray of traditional design. The statuette in the background is an iron reproduction of an ancient sphinx.

Overleaf: Plump young pigeons, stuffed with crushed wheat and mint and roasted until fork-tender, are the highlight of many an Egyptian feast. In this version, an extra measure of the stuffing is simmered with stock and presented in a separate bowl. The Egyptian cookbook at the right is turned to a recipe for stuffed pigeons (called *hamam mahshi* in Arabic) and held open by a blue *ankh*—a crosslike symbol of life dating to the days of Pharaohs.

braise in the middle of the oven for 45 minutes. Baste the pigeons with the liquid in the casserole, and continue braising for 1 hour longer. To test for doneness, pierce the thigh of a bird with the point of a small, sharp knife. If the juices that run out are slightly pink, cook for another 5 to 10 minutes.

A half hour or so before the pigeons are done, bring the chicken stock to a boil in a 2- to 3-quart saucepan over high heat. Stirring constantly, add the reserved *fireek* mixture and bring to a boil again. Reduce the heat to low, cover tightly, and simmer for 30 minutes, or until the grains are tender and have absorbed all the liquid.

To serve, arrange the pigeons on a heated platter and remove the trussing strings and skewers. Moisten the pigeons with the liquid remaining in the casserole, and garnish the platter with parsley. Fluff the *fireek* with a fork and serve it separately in a heated bowl.

Baked *bamia,* ringed with lemon, is studded with the ends of the okra placed spokelike between its ground beef layers.

Bamia

BAKED MOLDED OKRA AND BEEF

To serve 4

1½ pounds fresh okra
4 tablespoons butter plus 1 tablespoon softened butter
½ cup finely chopped onions
1 pound ground lean beef, preferably chuck
1 teaspoon finely chopped garlic
6 tablespoons canned tomato purée
1½ to 2 cups beef stock, fresh or canned
1 teaspoon salt
Freshly ground black pepper
Lemon wedges

Wash the fresh okra under cold running water, and with a small, sharp knife, scrape the skin lightly to remove any surface fuzz. Cut ⅛ inch off the stem at the narrow end of each pod.

In a heavy 10- to 12-inch skillet, melt 2 tablespoons of butter over moderate heat. When the foam subsides, add the okra and, stirring frequently, cook for about 5 minutes until it stops "roping," or producing thin white threads. With a slotted spoon, transfer the okra to paper towels to drain.

Pour off the fat remaining in the skillet, add 2 more tablespoons of butter and melt it over moderate heat. Drop in the onions and cook for 8 to 10 minutes, or until they are soft and lightly browned. Add the meat, mashing it with the back of the spoon to break up any lumps, and cook until all traces of pink disappear. Stir in the garlic, tomato purée, 1 cup of the stock, the salt and a few grindings of pepper. Cook briskly uncovered until most of the liquid in the pan has evaporated and the mixture is thick enough to hold its shape almost solidly in the spoon. Remove from the heat.

Preheat the oven to 325°. With a pastry brush coat the bottom and sides of a circular baking dish 7 or 8 inches in diameter and about 3 inches deep with the tablespoon of softened butter. Spoon half the meat mixture into the casserole, smoothing and spreading it to the edges with a spatula. Arrange the okra over the meat, placing the pieces closely together side by side in a spokelike pattern with the cut ends facing out. Spread the remaining meat mixture evenly over the okra, masking it completely, and sprinkle over it ½ cup of the stock.

Bring to a boil over moderate heat, cover tightly with a lid or foil and bake in the middle of the oven for about 1 hour. (Check the casserole occasionally, and if the top seems dry pour in up to ½ cup more stock, a few tablespoons at a time.) Cool the *bamia* uncovered for 5 minutes, then unmold it in the following fashion: Run a long, sharp knife around the inside edges of the casserole, place a heated serving plate upside down over the top and, grasping the casserole and plate together firmly, invert them. The *bamia* should slide out easily. Serve garnished with lemon wedges.

Milookhiyya

EGYPTIAN GREEN HERB SOUP

To serve 4 to 6

1 quart chicken stock, fresh or canned
1 cup dried *milookhiyya* (spinachlike Egyptian herb), picked clean and finely crumbled
1 tablespoon tomato paste
1 teaspoon salt
Freshly ground black pepper
2 teaspoons finely chopped garlic
2 teaspoons ground coriander *(cilantro)*
2 tablespoons butter

In a heavy 3- to 4-quart saucepan, bring the stock to a boil over high heat. Stir in the *milookhiyya,* tomato paste, salt and a few grindings of pepper and reduce the heat to low. Stirring occasionally, simmer for about 20 minutes, or until the *milookhiyya* has dissolved and the soup is thick and smooth.

With a mortar and pestle or the back of a spoon, mash the garlic and coriander to a smooth paste. In a small skillet, melt the butter over moderate heat. When the foam has almost subsided, add the garlic and coriander and, stirring constantly, cook for a minute or two until the garlic is lightly browned. Add the entire contents of the skillet to the soup and, stirring constantly, simmer for 2 or 3 minutes more.

Taste for seasoning and serve at once from a heated tureen. In Egypt, *milookhiyya* is often accompanied by hot cooked rice and sliced boiled chicken or game birds, presented separately on individual plates.

Mihallabiyya

COLD RICE-FLOUR DESSERT

To serve 6

½ cup rice flour, or substitute ½ cup cornstarch
4 cups cold milk
6 tablespoons sugar
1 teaspoon vanilla extract
1 teaspoon ground cinnamon
2 tablespoons dried currants
2 tablespoons shelled, unsalted pistachios, finely chopped

Dissolve the rice flour (or cornstarch) in 1 cup of the milk. In a 2- to 3-quart saucepan combine the remaining 3 cups of milk and the sugar and bring to a boil over high heat, stirring until the sugar dissolves. Reduce the heat to low, add the dissolved rice flour or cornstarch and, stirring constantly, simmer for about 10 minutes, or until the mixture is thick enough to coat the spoon heavily. Stir in the vanilla, then pour the *mihallabiyya* into a large shallow, heatproof platter or small individual dessert bowls. Sprinkle with cinnamon and scatter the currants and chopped pistachio nuts decoratively on top. Refrigerate for at least 2 hours, or until thoroughly chilled.

Kammooniyya

BAKED FISH WITH TOMATOES AND RICE

To serve 4

FISH

2 tablespoons plus ¼ cup vegetable oil
2 large onions peeled and sliced ¼ inch thick
3 medium-sized garlic cloves, peeled and cut crosswise into paper-thin slices
1 teaspoon ground cumin
1 cup finely chopped celery
½ cup canned tomato purée
1 cup water
1½ teaspoons salt
Freshly ground black pepper
4 skinned porgy fillets, each about ½ pound, or substitute other firm white fish fillets
1 medium-sized tomato, sliced ¼ inch thick

RICE

¼ cup vegetable oil
½ cup finely chopped onions
2 cups uncooked medium- or long-grain white rice
3 cups cold water
1 teaspoon salt
Freshly ground black pepper

Preheat the oven to 350°. With a pastry brush spread 1 tablespoon of the oil on the bottom and sides of a shallow baking-serving dish just large enough to hold the fillets side by side in one layer.

In a heavy 10- to 12-inch skillet, heat ¼ cup of oil over moderate heat until a light haze forms above it. Add the sliced onions, garlic and cumin and, stirring frequently, cook for 7 or 8 minutes, or until the onions are soft and golden brown. Be careful not to let the garlic burn. With a slotted spoon, transfer the onion mixture to a plate. Add the celery to the oil remaining in the skillet and stir it for about 5 minutes until it is soft but not colored. Return the onions to the pan and stir in the tomato purée, water, ½ teaspoon of the salt, and a few grindings of pepper. Stirring constantly, cook briskly until most of the liquid in the pan has evaporated and the mixture is thick enough to hold its shape almost solidly in the spoon. Remove the pan from the heat.

Wash the fish fillets under cold running water and pat them completely dry with paper towels. Sprinkle them with the remaining teaspoon of salt and arrange them side by side in the baking dish. Pour the sauce over the fish, smoothing and spreading it to the edges of the dish with a spatula. Arrange the tomato slices on top of the fillets and sprinkle them with the remaining tablespoon of oil. Cover the dish tightly with a lid or foil. Bake in the middle of the oven for 20 minutes, remove the cover and bake for 15 minutes longer, or until the sauce has begun to bubble and the tomatoes are lightly browned.

Meanwhile, prepare the rice in the following fashion. In a heavy 3-to 4-quart saucepan, heat the ¼ cup of oil over moderate heat until a light haze forms above it. Add the chopped onions and, stirring frequently, cook for about 10 minutes, or until they are deeply browned. Pour in the rice and stir for 2 or 3 minutes until the grains are well coated with oil. Add the water, 1 teaspoon of salt, and a few grindings of pepper, and return to a boil, still stirring. Cover the pan and reduce the heat to its lowest point. Simmer for 20 minutes, or until the rice has absorbed all the liquid. Remove the pan from the heat and let the rice rest covered for 5 minutes before serving.

Serve the fish directly from the baking dish. Fluff the rice with a fork, and serve it separately from a heated bowl.

Fool Midammis

BROAD BEAN SALAD

To serve 4

1 cup dried *fool misri* (small fava or broad beans)
1 tablespoon *ads majroosh* (dried red lentils), or substitute other dried lentils
¼ cup olive oil
1 tablespoon fresh lemon juice
½ teaspoon salt
1 tablespoon finely chopped parsley, preferably flat-leaf parsley
8 pitted black olives, preferably the Mediterranean type

Wash the beans and lentils in a sieve or colander set under cold running water until the water runs clear. Then drain thoroughly.

In a heavy 3- to 4-quart saucepan, bring 1 quart of water to a boil over high heat. Add the beans and lentils, reduce the heat to low and partially cover the pan. Simmer for 3 to 4 hours, or until the beans are tender and show no resistance when pressed gently between your fingers. Check from time to time to make sure that the beans are moist. If they seem dry, add a few tablespoons of boiling water. When they are done, there should be almost no liquid left in the pan. Transfer the entire contents of the pan to a bowl and cool to room temperature.

With a whisk or fork, beat the oil, lemon juice and salt together in a deep bowl. Add the beans and lentils and, mashing them gently with a fork, stir until they absorb most of the dressing.

To serve, spread the bean mixture on a platter or individual plates, sprinkle the top with parsley, and garnish with olives.

Basboosa

SWEET SEMOLINA CAKE WITH LEMON SYRUP

To make an 8-by-12-inch flat cake

SYRUP
1½ cups water
1 cup sugar
2 tablespoons fresh lemon juice
¼ teaspoon bottled rose water

CAKE
12 tablespoons melted and cooled unsalted butter
3 cups yellow semolina
3 cups sugar
½ to ¾ cup cold water
20 whole blanched almonds, split in half lengthwise

First prepare the syrup in the following fashion: Combine 1½ cups of water, 1 cup of sugar and the lemon juice in a small saucepan. Stirring constantly, cook over moderate heat until the sugar dissolves. Increase the heat to high and cook briskly, uncovered and undisturbed, for 5 minutes (timing it from the moment the syrup boils), or until the syrup reaches a temperature of 220° on a candy thermometer. Remove the pan from the heat, stir in the rose water and set the syrup aside to cool.

Meanwhile bake the cake. Preheat the oven to 350°. With a pastry brush, coat the bottom and sides of an 8-by-12-inch baking pan with 1 tablespoon of the melted butter.

In a deep mixing bowl, stir the semolina and 3 cups of sugar together until thoroughly combined. Stirring constantly, pour in up to ¾ cup of water, a few tablespoons at a time, using only enough to moisten all the semolina. When the mixture becomes too resistant to stir, work in the water with your hands. Then add 8 tablespoons (½ cup) of the melted butter, a tablespoon or so at a time, and beat vigorously with a large spoon until it is completely absorbed.

Pour the batter into the baking pan, and with a metal spatula or the back of a spoon, spread it evenly into the corners of the pan. Then with a sharp knife and a ruler, score the surface into diamonds by making parallel lines about 2 inches apart and ½ inch deep, then crossing them diagonally to form diamond shapes. Gently press an almond half in the center of each diamond. Brush the cake with 3 tablespoons of melted butter and bake in the middle of the oven for 1 hour, or until the cake is firm to the touch and the top is delicately browned.

Remove the cake from the oven and immediately sprinkle the syrup over the top, a tablespoon or two at a time. Use only as much of the syrup as the cake will absorb readily; it should be soft but not soggy. Let the cake cool to room temperature before serving it.

Glossary

ADS MAJROOSH (Arabic): Dried red split lentils.

ANGINARA (Greek): Artichoke.

ARAB BREAD (*khoubz araby,* Arabic; *pita,* Greek): Round flat pancakelike loaves of slightly leavened bread. Each loaf puffs in the middle, then deflates to leave a pocket inside that can be used for such fillings as meat, cheese or vegetables.

ARAK (Arabic): Potent anise-flavored apéritif. In Syria and Lebanon it is made from grapes; in Egypt and Iraq it is often made from dates. *See also, mastiha, ouzo, raki.*

AVGOLEMONO (Greek): Egg-and lemon-sauce served with fowl, fish, and vegetables, and also used to flavor soups.

AYRAN (Turkish): A drink consisting of lightly salted yoghurt and water.

BAKLAVA (Greek; Turkish); *baklawa,* Arabic): Sweet pastry, made from layers of *filo* with nut and spice filling and steeped in syrup.

BAMIYA (Arabic): Okra.

BATEMJAN (Persian): Eggplant.

BÖREK (Turkish; *bourekia,* Greek): Fried or baked dish consisting of layers of *filo* filled with cheese or seasoned meat; a sweet version contains a filling of nuts, cinnamon and syrup.

BULGUR: Burghul.

BURGHUL (Arabic): Cereal made from whole grains of wheat. It is processed by boiling the grain, drying it, removing some of the outside bran particles, and cracking the kernel. It may be of fine, medium or full grain size; the color varies from light to dark brown depending on the type of wheat from which it is made.

CHALLAH (Israel): Braided white bread.

CHELO (Persian): Steamed or boiled rice.

CHICK-PEAS (*hummus,* Arabic): Round dried peas, usually pale tan or dark brown in color, and about 1/4 to 1/2 inch in diameter. Also known by the Spanish name of *garbanzo.*

COUCOU (Persian): Beaten eggs cooked with vegetables, meat or herbs to make a kind of thick pancake.

COUSCOUS: Tiny pastalike pellets usually made with semolina and salted water. Also, the finished cooked dish of steamed *couscous,* with sauce or flavoring.

DOLMA (Turkish; also spelled *dolmeh*): Literally, any stuffed food; more specifically, the term denotes a savory filling wrapped in vine leaves, cabbage leaves, hollowed out vegetables or other wrapper.

DUGH (Persian): A drink consisting of lightly salted yoghurt whey and water.

FELAFEL (Arabic): Deep-fried balls of chick-peas and crushed wheat.

FENUGREEK: Very small red-brown seeds with a pleasant bitter flavor and a currylike aroma.

FETA (Greek): Firm white "pickled" cheese with a somewhat sour flavor, made from sheep's or goat's milk.

FILO (Greek; also spelled *phyllo*): Tissue-thin sheets of pastry, which can be purchased fresh or frozen.

FIREEK (Arabic): Green wheat grain, roasted and cracked.

FOOL (Arabic; also spelled *foul*): *Fava* or broad beans. *Fool misri* are small Egyptian *fava* beans.

HALVA (also spelled *halwa, helve*): Sweet made with semolina, rice flour or farina and flavored with nuts, fruits, chocolate, spices or flower petals.

HUMMUS (Arabic): Chick-peas. Also, *hummus bi tahina,* a dip made from highly seasoned puréed chick-peas.

JEZVE (Turkish; *kafeibriki,* Greek): Special vessel for brewing coffee, with a long handle, narrow neck and wide mouth.

KAFES (Greek; *kahve,* Turkish): Pulverized, not ground, roasted coffee beans. The coffee may be purchased ready to use or pulverized at home in a special grinder.

KASSERI (Greek): Firm pale yellow cheese, usually made from sheep's milk.

KAYMAK (Turkish): Dessert topping made by cooking cream or milk over low heat until it is reduced to about one-sixth its original volume and is as thick as softened cream cheese. During the cooking process, the *kaymak* is aerated by being spooned up above the pan and poured back into it.

KEFALOTIRI (Greek): Hard, pale yellow grating-type cheese, similar to Parmesan, made from goat's or sheep's milk.

KHORESH (Persian): Stew or stewlike sauce served, typically, with *chelo.*

KIBBI (Arabic): Mixture of ground meat and *burghul.*

KÖFTE (Turkish): Fried balls of ground mutton.

KOKORETSI (Greek; *kokoreç,* Turkish): Innards of young lambs wrapped in intestines and grilled on a spit.

KOOFTEH (Persian): Mixture of ground meat with rice and seasonings.

LABAN (Arabic): Yoghurtlike product.

MANSAF (Arabic): Bedouin feast of lamb and rice.

MASGOOF (Arabic): Literally means grilled. In Iraq it is used to describe fish grilled over aromatic wood.

MAST (Persian): Yoghurt.

MASTIC: Licorice-flavored resin from the mastic tree, found on the island of Chios. It is used as a chewing gum and also as a flavoring in cooking and in the production of *mastiha.* It is sold in pellet and syrup form.

MASTIHA (Greek): Potent brandy-based apéritif, flavored with the gummy resin of the mastic tree.

MATZOH (Israel): Flat, crisp unleavened bread.

MAVRODAPHNE (Greek): Heavy, sweet red dessert wine.

MAZZA (Arabic; *meze, mezedakia,* Greek): Food eaten as a snack, first course, or accompaniment to a drink.

MILOOKHIYYA (Arabic; also called Spanish okra): Edible green leaf of a plant of the hibiscus family. It is related to okra and exudes a similar viscous liquid, but the flavor more closely resembles that of spinach or sorrel.

MIZITHRA (Greek): Soft, white, fresh pot-type cheese with a mild flavor, made from the whey which is a byproduct of *feta* cheese.

NOKHODCHI (Persian): Puffed chick-peas, eaten like peanuts or ground into flour for a special type of cookie.

ORZO (Greek; also called *minestra*): Tiny oval pasta, somewhat resembling grains of rice.

OUZO (Greek): Potent anise-flavored apéritif made from grain.

PANIR (Persian): Hard, white cheese usually made from goat's milk.

POLO (Persian): Rice cooked or served with fruit, vegetables, fowl or meats.

PSARI (Greek): Fish.

RAKI (Turkish): Potent anise-flavored apéritif made from potatoes, plums, molasses, wine or grain.

RETSINA (Greek): Distinctive white wine with a piny, resinous flavor. Rosé *retsina* is called *kokkineli.*

RICE FLOUR: Finely ground rice. When made from regular-milled or polished grains, the flour is white; when made from brown rice, which has the outer bran still intact, it is creamy in color.

ROSE SYRUP: Sugar syrup flavored with rose water. Other Middle Eastern syrups are flavored with tamarind, pomegranate, wild cherry, anise and mint.

ROSE WATER: Liquid flavoring distilled from fresh rose petals.

SACCOULA (Greek): Drained

yoghurt with the consistency of softened cream cheese. To make it, unflavored yoghurt is dropped into a fine mesh sieve and set over a bowl, then refrigerated for at least four hours or until all the liquid has drained from the yoghurt.

SAMNEH (Arabic): Clarified cow's or sheep's butter with a distinctive, almost rancid flavor.

SEMOLINA: Finely granulated meal made from the branless inner kernels of durum wheat grains. It is amber yellow, clear and translucent, and so finely ground as to resemble flour. Because of its high gluten content, semolina is widely used in the manufacture of pasta products, including the Greek *orzo* and the North African *couscous*.

SKORDALIA (Greek): Sauce or dip made from garlic, oil and potato or bread.

SUMAK(*somagh,* Persian): Edible berries of a special variety of sumac tree. The berries are red, with a sharp, somewhat sour flavor.

TAHINA (Arabic): Thick paste made from crushed sesame seeds. It has the consistency of fresh peanut butter and a pleasant nutlike flavor.

TARAMA (Greek): Small, light-orange carp roe preserved with salt, and sometimes oil.

TARATOOR (Arabic): Sauce made from *tahina,* lemon and garlic.

TULUM (Turkish): Firm white "pickled" cheese with a sharp flavor made from sheep's or, occasionally, goat's milk.

TZATZIKI (Greek): Garlic-flavored yoghurt dip, often made with *saccoula*.

VINE LEAVES: Whole leaves picked fresh from grape vines and preserved in brine.

YAOURTI (Greek): Yoghurt.

ZHUG (Yemenite): Fiery combination of garlic, hot peppers, caraway seeds, cardamom and coriander pounded together, used as seasoning in soups and in such hot sauces as the Yemenites' *hilbeh* *(Recipe Index)*.

Mail-Order Sources

The following stores, grouped by region, accept mail orders for Middle Eastern foods. All carry canned and dried ingredients; a few will ship fresh ones. Some also stock Middle Eastern kitchen utensils. Because policies differ and managements change, check with the store nearest you to determine what it has in stock, the current prices, and how best to buy the items you are interested in. Some stores require a minimum amount on mail orders, ranging from $2.50 to $25.00.

East

Cardullo's Gourmet Shop
6 Brattle St.
Cambridge, Mass. 02138

George Malko
185 Atlantic Ave.
Brooklyn, N.Y. 11201

Sahadi Importing Co., Inc.
187 Atlantic Ave.
Brooklyn, N.Y. 11201

Kalustyan Orient Export Trading Corp.
123 Lexington Ave.
New York, N.Y. 10016

Kassos Brothers
570 9th Ave.
New York, N.Y. 10036

European Grocery Store
520 Court Pl.
Pittsburgh, Pa. 15219

Stamoolis Bros. Grocery
2020 Penn Ave.
Pittsburgh, Pa. 15222

Midwest

American Oriental Grocery
20736 Lahser Rd.
Southfield, Mich. 48075

Demmas Shish-Ke-Bab
5806 Hampton Ave.
St. Louis, Mo. 63109

Heidi's Around the World Food Shop
1149 S. Brentwood Blvd.
St. Louis, Mo. 63117

Italo-American Importing Co.
512 Franklin Ave.
St. Louis, Mo. 63101

South

Antone's Import Co.
P.O. Box 3352
(807 Taft and 8111 S. Main)
Houston, Tex. 77001

Barzizza Brothers, Inc.
351-353 S. Front St.
Memphis, Tenn. 38101

International Gift Corner
181 Union Ave.
Memphis, Tenn. 38101

Greek American Grocery Co.
2690 Coral Way
Miami, Fla. 33145

Progress Grocery Co.
915 Decatur
New Orleans, La. 70116

Central Grocery Co.
923 Decatur
New Orleans, La. 70116

West

Greek Importing Co.
2801 W. Pico Blvd.
Los Angeles, Calif. 90006

Europa Grocery Co.
321 S. Spring
Los Angeles, Calif. 90013

Mediterranean and Middle East Import Co.
223 Valencia St.
San Francisco, Calif. 94103

Haig's
441 Clement St.
San Francisco, Calif. 94118

Angelo Merlino & Sons
816 6th Ave. S.
Seattle, Wash. 98134

DeLaurenti's Italian Market
Stall 5, Lower Pike Place Market
Seattle, Wash. 98101

Canada

Main Importing Co., Inc.
1188 St. Lawrence
Montreal 126, Quebec

Sayfy's Groceteria
265 Jean Talon East
Montreal 327, Quebec

Recipe Index: English

NOTE: An R preceding a page refers to the Recipe Booklet. Size, weight and material are specified for pans in the recipes because they affect cooking results. A pan should be just large enough to hold its contents comfortably. Heavy pans heat slowly and cook food at a constant rate. Aluminum and cast iron conduct heat well but may discolor foods containing egg yolks, wine, vinegar or lemon. Enamelware is a fairly poor conductor of heat. Many recipes therefore recommend stainless steel or enameled cast iron, which do not have these faults.

First Courses

Soups

Breads

Sauces

Meat

Poultry

Fish

Vegetables

Rice and Cereals

Desserts and Drinks

Recipe Index: Middle Eastern

General Index

Numerals in italics indicate a photograph or drawing of the subject mentioned.

Credits and Acknowledgments

The sources for the illustrations which appear in this book are shown below.

Photographs by David Lees pages—13, 16, 17, 23, 30, 32, 33, 42, 49, 50, 51, 52, 53, 54, 55, 68, 71, 72, 74, 75, 76, 77, 78, 79, 80, 81, 92, 94, 96, 97, 99, 102, 103, 104, 105, 106, 107, 130, 134, 135, bottom 139, 140, 141, 142, 143, 145, 152, 155, 156, 157, 158, 159, 162, 163, 165, 176, 179, 180, 181, 185, 186, 187.
Photographs by Richard Jeffery—Cover; pages—9, 14, 19, 26, 27, 34, 37, 38, 41, 47, 58, 60, 63, 64, 67, 84, 87, 88, 90, 111, 113, 115, 116, 119, 146, 148, 150, 161, 168, 169, 171, 173, 175, 189, 190, 191, 192.
All other photographs pages 4—Top left Monica Suder bottom Monica Suder, Charles Phillips. 11—Map by Lothar Roth. 20—Joseph Nettis. 21—Richard Meek. 22—Drawings by Matt Greene. 24,25—René Burri from Magnum. 29—Louis Goldman from Rapho Guillumette. 90—Drawings by Matt Greene. 120—Richard Cleave. 123—Map by Lothar Roth. 125—Courtesy of The American Museum of Natural History. 126, 127—The New York Botanical Gardens. 129—Richard Cleave. 138—Ben Martin for TIME. 139—Top Ben Martin for TIME. 166—Tor Eigland from Black Star for TIME.

Five experts on various phases of the Middle Eastern cuisine contributed recipes used in this book and tested them in The Foods of the World kitchen. Faiza Abdel-Ghani, wife of a member of the U.A.R. delegation at the United Nations, has lived in New York for several years. Saber Khouri, a native of Syria, founded the Mecca Restaurant in New York and operated it for more than 40 years; he has catered banquets for many Middle Eastern dignitaries. Hände Sürmelioğlu was for five years deputy director of the Turkish Tourist and Information Service in New York. Heibatollah Tussi, an Iranian, has cooked at the American Officers' Club in Tehran, the Hotel Tehran Plaza and Iranian consulates both here and abroad. Molly Lyons BarDavid writes a column on food for the *Jerusalem Post* and is the author of several cookbooks.

The editors wish to thank the numerous individuals who gave generous assistance to members of the staff as well as to the author and photographer during their travels. Among them are: *in Greece,* Christos Constantinou; Drossoula Vassiliou Elliott; Maria Giustozzi, Hellenic Tours S.A.; His Honor Ianis Kublis, Mayor of Delphi; His Honor Isidoros Mandas, Mayor of Arachova; Spyros Marinatos, Director, Greek Archaeological Service; Panos Misirlis; Vassilis Morikis, Delphi Hotel; John D. Motz, Agricultural Attaché, American Embassy; Dimitrios Pouris, Director, Greek National Tourist Organization; Dr. and Mrs. Venos Vlondis; *in Turkey,* Bay Mahmut Baler; Davut R. Giresunlu, President, Turkish Republic Bank of Tourism; Ziya Hunerman, Regional Director, Ministry of Tourism and Information; Bay Aslan Sadikoglu; *in Lebanon,* Eve Akel; Mr. and Mrs. John Fistere; Marie Karam Khayat; George N. Rayess; Abu Said; *in Jordan,* Helen Keiser; *in Israel,* Izchak Niran Nikolai; Lilly Rivlin; Shalom Tenami; *in Iran,* Mr. and Mrs. Parviz Raein; *in Egypt,* Ahmed Abdullah, chef, Nile Hilton Hotel; Mrs. Habiba Wassef, M.D., Applied Nutrition Research Unit, National Research Center; Mrs. Bushra Abd El Wahab Zafer, Deputy Dean, and Mrs. Esmat El Sayid Roshdi, Higher Institute of Home Economics; *in New York City,* Mrs. Malka Ben-Yosef, Israel Consulate; Mr. Thomas Brewster, Glen Cove, Long Island, and Country Floors, Inc.; Dr. Ismet Giritli, Middle East Institute, Columbia University; Michael Hamarah, Consulate of the Hashimite Kingdom of Jordan; Yetta Kaufman; Miss Nahid Mahdavi and Miss Soudi Amiralai, Iranian Consulate; Esther Negren; Reverend Father Eugene N. Pappas, Greek Archdiocesan Cathedral of the Holy Trinity; Dr. Muhammad A. Rauf, Director, Islamic Center; Mrs. Kouros Satrap; Lilly Stuckey, Bernard L. Lewis, Inc.; Turkish Tourism and Information Office; Lee Weidner; Dr. Stephen G. Xydis, Hunter College; Greek Island, Ltd.; Holy Land Center, Inc.; Inch in the Yard; A. Morjikian Co., Inc.; Raphaelian Rug Co.; Dorothy Schlesinger, Antiques; John Soleimani, Importer; Unique Handicrafts Corp.; *in Washington, D.C.,* R. A. Seelig, United Fresh Fruit and Vegetable Association; *in Beltsville, Md.,* Dr. August E. Kehr and Dr. Raymon Webb, Agriculture Research Service, U.S. Department of Agriculture; *in San Juan, P.R.,* The Mélange.

Sources consulted in the production of this book include: *Greek Holiday* by Anne Anthony, Icaros, Athens; *The Israeli Cookbook* by Molly Lyons Bar-David, Crown; *Caravan, the Story of the Middle East* by Carleton S. Coon, Henry Holt; *Israeli Cookery* by Lilian Cornfeld, Avi Publishing Co.; *The Owl's Watchsong* by John A. Cuddon, Horizon Press; *Turkey: Old and New* by Selma Ekrem, Scribner; *The Art of Persian Cookery* by Forough Hekmat, Doubleday; *The Arabs, a Short History* by Philip K. Hitti, Henry Regnery; *Food from the Arab World* by Marie Karam Khayat and Margaret Clark Keatinge, Khayats, Beirut; *In a Persian Kitchen* by Mazda Maideh, Tuttle; *The Loom of History* by Herbert J. Muller, Harper and Row; *Turkish Cooking* by Ifran Orga, André Deutsch, London; *Rice, Spice and Bitter Oranges* by Lila Perl, World Publishing Co.; *The Greek Cookbook* by Sophia Skoura, Crown; *Turkish Recipes* by the Turkish Information Office of New York; *Cooks, Gluttons and Gourmets* by Betty Wason, Doubleday; *Iran: Past and Present* by Donald N. Wilbur, Princeton; and *The Art of Greek Cookery* by the Women of St. Paul's Greek Orthodox Church, Doubleday.

PRODUCTION STAFF FOR TIME INCORPORATED

John L. Hallenbeck (Vice President and Director of Production), Robert E. Foy and Caroline Ferri. Text photocomposed under the direction of Albert J. Dunn